Denver Union Cemetery

Denver
Lancaster County
Pennsylvania

By Kenneth D. McCrea, Ph. D.

Denver Union Cemetery

Denver, Lancaster County, Pennsylvania

by

Kenneth D. McCrea, Ph. D.

Published by:

**McCrea Research, Inc.
Stevens, PA**

International Standard Book Number:

ISBN-13: 978-1494796839
ISBN-10: 149479683X

Available from:

Amazon.com,
CreateSpace.com,
and other retail outlets.

CONTENTS

FORWARD

The purpose of this book is to make the genealogical information recorded on the gravestones in the Denver Union Cemetery available to those people who are not able to travel to the cemetery. In addition, I have attempted to collect additional information on many of the people buried in the Cemetery. Some of the additional information in this book came from secondary sources, such as the Internet, and as such may contain errors. Corrections may be sent to the author (within a reasonable time) at the following email address: Ken@GermanNames.com.

Inscriptions from the gravestones in the cemetery were copied in 1955 and they are in the possession of LancasterHistory.org [formerly the Lancaster County Historical Society]. Those copied inscriptions were found to contain errors and omissions, and are not entirely in the same order as the graves in the cemetery. They also do not include burials made after the date when they were copied.

When transcribing documents and newspaper articles for this book, I have retained the spelling, capitalization, word usage, and errors found in the originals. In many cases, capitalization was used differently than would be used today. In names of streets, the word "street" was rarely capitalized, as in "Main street." The same was true of county names, such as in "Lancaster county."

The spelling of surnames was also not consistent. In some of the obituaries presented here, the surname of the deceased is sometimes spelled in more than one way. Surname spelling on the gravestones is also variable. On Dietrich Gockley's gravestone his name is spelled "Gackli."

Hyphenated numbers in the index refer to grave numbers. Entries in the index starting with "R&N-" refer to grave numbers in the "Selected References and Notes" section of the book. Married women have been indexed under both their maiden names and their married names.

Women's maiden names are given within parentheses, and if a woman's maiden name is unknown, that is shown in empty parentheses "()." Additional married surnames are shown in square brackets "[]."

Kenneth D. McCrea, Ph. D.
Stevens, PA
December 2013

ACKNOWLEDGEMENTS

I wish to thank the following people who assisted me in the preparation of this book: Brenda Creasy and Milton Haldeman, who provided information from their genealogical databases. Cynthia Marquet of the Historical Society of the Cocalico Valley who assisted with the research, and David Martin, current caretaker of the Cemetery, for allowing me access to the burial permits in the possession of the Denver Mennonite Church. I also wish to thank Joanne Colon, Alice Hummer, and Cynthia Marquet for helping to proofread the book.

Panoramic View of the Old Section of Denver Union Cemetery.
The Denver Mennonite Church is the low white building on the right.

Panoramic View of the New Section of Denver Union Cemetery.

4

History of the Denver Union Cemetery

The Denver Union Cemetery started out as a small cemetery for the Gockley family, as well as for the Lutz and other families in the Denver area. It has been called various names, including the "Gockley Cemetery," the "Brick Church Cemetery," the "Denver Cemetery," the "Union Station Graveyard," the "Denver Mennonite Cemetery," and other less frequently used names.

The Cemetery was incorporated in the Lancaster County, Pennsylvania Court of Common Pleas:

Notice is hereby given that an application will be made on the 17 h day of October, A. D. 19(4, at 10 o'clock a. m., to the Court of Common Pleas of Lancaster County, Pennsylvania, by J. Frank Lutz, Isaac Rupp, George S. Ludwig. Henry R. Lutz and John G. Burkholder, under the Act of Assembly entitled, "An Act to provide for the incorporation and regulation of certain corporations," approved April 29, 1874, and the supplements thereto, for the charter of an intended corporation to be called The Union Cemetery Association of Denver, Lancaster County, Pennsylvania, the character and object of which are to purchase land and to locate and establish, regulate and control a cemetery or public burial ground near the Borough of Denver, in East Cocalico Township, Lancaster County, Pennsylvania, to lay out any lands purchased in suitable lots and sell the same for burial purposes, and to improve, embellish and ornament said cemetery, and to do such other acts as properly pertain to cemetery associations as provided by law. The proposed charter is now on file in the Prothonotary's Office at Lancaster, Pa.   A. F. SCHENCK,
    sept19-4t   Solicitor.

Notice of intent to incorporate as published in the *Lancaster Law Review* on September 19th, 26th, and October 3rd. The same notice was also published in the *Denver Press* on September 23rd, 30th, and October 7th and the *Lancaster Daily New Era* on September 19th, 26th, and October 3rd.

The Union Cemetery Association of Denver.

Be it known that the subscribers having associated themselves together for the purpose of establishing a Cemetery or public burial ground and being desirious (sic) becoming incorporated agreeably to the provisions of the Act of Assembly of the Commonwealth of Pennsylvania entitled "An Act to provide for the Incorporation and regulation of certain corporations" approved April 29th 1874 and its supplements do hereby declare set forth and certify that the following are the purposes objects articles and conditions of said Association for and upon which they desire to be incorporated. All of the subscribers are citizens of the State of Pennsylvania.

I. The name of the Corporation shall be "The Union Cemetery Association of Denver Lancaster County Pennsylvania.

II. The purposes for which this corporation is formed are to purchase land to locate and establish regulate and control a cemetery or public burial ground near the Borough of Denver in East Cocalico Township Lancaster County, Pennsylvania to lay out any lands purchased in suitable lots and sell the same for burial purposes and to improve embellish and ornament said Cemetery and to do such other acts as properly pertain to Cemetery Associations by law.

III. The location of the said corporation and the place wherein its business is to be transacted is in the village of Stevens East Cocalico Township Lancaster County Pennsylvania.

IV. The Corporation is to have perpetual existence.

V. The corporation has no capital stock. The membership thereof shall be composed of the subscribers and their associates and of such other persons as may from time to time be admitted to membership in such manner and upon such requirements as may be prescribed by the by-laws.

VI. The oversight and management of said corporation shall be vested in a Board of Trustees. The said Trustees shall be elected by the members of the corporation from among the adult members of the same and the term and time of the election of said trustees shall be fixed by the by-laws. The Trustees shall hold office until their successors are elected subject nevertheless to the power of a motion of any Trustee or Trustees from the said office by the said corporation for legal cause and upon such proper and legal notice and hearing as may be provided by the by-laws. The names and residences of those chosen for Trustees until an election is duly had under this charter are as follows viz. J. Frank Lutz, Stevens; Isaac Rupp, Stevens; George S. Ludwig, Stevens; Henry R. Lutz, Denver; and John G. Burkholder, Denver.

VII. Such other officers as the corporation shall see fit to create and elect by the by-laws shall be elected at such times and in such numbers and in manner by such persons for such terms and at such places at the by-laws shall prescribe and regulate and be subject to amotion as therein set forth.

VIII. This corporation shall have power to hold purchase and transfer such real estate and personal property as its purposes may require not exceeding the amount limited by law and all the property thereof shall be taken and held to enure subject to the control and disposition of the members of this corporation.

IX. The by-laws of this corporation and laws of the Commonwealth of Pennsylvania and the

Constitution of the United States they shall be altered and amended as provided for by the by-laws themselves and prescribe the powers and functions of the Trustees and other officers therein mentioned and those to be hereafter elected the times and places of their meetings and meetings of this corporation the number of members who shall constitute a quorum at the meetings of this corporation and of the officers thereof the qualifications of the members the manner of selecting officers and the powers and duties of such officers and all other concerns and the internal management of the corporation.

Witness our hands and seals this 16th day of September Anno Domini One Thousand Nine Hundred and Four.

(Signed) J. Frank Lutz, George S. Ludwig, Isaac Rupp, Henry R. Lutz, John G. Burkholder

Commonwealth of Pennsylvania County of Lancaster SS. Before me the subscriber a Notary Public in the State of Pennsylvania personally appeared J. Frank Lutz, Isaac Rupp, George S. Ludwig, Henry R. Lutz, and John G. Burkholder five of the subscribers to the foregoing certificate of incorporation and in due form of law acknowledge the same to be their act and deed. Witness my hand and official seal this 16th day of September A. D. 1904.

Irwin B. Lutz Notary Public, my commission expires 1/19/07

Lancaster County SS. Charter filed in the office of the Prothonotary of the Court of Common Pleas in and for said county this 19th day of September 1904. John B. Miller, Dep'y Prothonotary

In the Court of Common Pleas of Lancaster County Penna And now this seventeenth day of October 1904 the within Charter and Certificate of Incorporation having been presented to me A. B. Hassler Judge of said County accompanied by due proof of publication of notice of this application as required by the Act of Assembly and rule of this Court in such cases made and provided I certify that I have examined and perused the said Charter and have found the same to be in proper form and within the purposes named in the class specified in section second of the Act of Assembly of the Commonwealth of Pennsylvania entitled "An Act to provide for the incorporation and regulation of certain corporations" approved April 29th 1874 and the supplements thereto and the same appearing to be lawful and not injurious to the community. It is hereby ordered and decreed that the charter is approved and that upon the recording of the same and this order the subscribers thereto and their associates shall be a corporation for the purposes and upon the terms therein stated by the name style and title of the Union Cemetery Association of Denver Lancaster County Pennsylvania. Attest W. D. Stauffer for Proth'y [seal]

By the Court A. B. Hassler, Judge

B. S. McLane, Deputy Recorded

Recorded Oct. 31, 1904

Land Ownership of the Denver Union Cemetery

The land on which the cemetery is located was originally warranted to Jacob Haigy on 2 AUG 1736. The land was described a "one hundred & fifty acres of land situate upon Cocalico Creek, whereon he has been three years settled, and adjoining to Michael Bear."

The "return of survey" gives additional details of how the land came into the hands of the next owner:

"Pennsylvania, SS-

Whereas in pursuance of a Warrant from the Honorable the Proprietaries Dated the 2^d Day of August 1736 there was Surveyed to Jacob Haigy a tract of land situate in Cocalico Township in the County of Lancaster, but the said Jacob Haigy not complying with the Conditions of the said Warrant the same together with the Survey made in pursuance thereof are become void.

Now in pursuance of a Warrant dated the 22d Day of May 1751 requiring me to make return into the Surveyor's Office of the Land Surveyed as afores^d in order that the same may be granted and confirmed unto Christian Picksler (alias Bixler) I do hereby certify the Bounds and Limits of the said Land to be as follows Viz. Beginning at a post and from thence extending by other Land of the Said Christian Picksler South Twenty Degrees East Ninety four perches [a "perch" is 16.5 feet] to a marked Hickory, thence by Abraham Ream's Land South Eighty four degrees East Thirty three perches to a post, North thirty two degrees East fifty perches to a dead oak marked, South Eighty four Degrees East Twenty two perches to a dead oak marked, South thirty Degrees West Forty six perches to a marked white oak, & South Seventy one Degrees East Seventy seven perches to a marked Black oak, thence by Jacob Knup's Land North twenty seven Degrees East Two Hundred and Sixty six perches to a marked Hickory thence by vacant Land North West Ninety four perches to a marked Hickory, thence by vacant Land and Land of Michael Bear South Sixty two Degrees West Two hundred perches to the place of Beginning Containing One hundred and Sixty six Acres and the usual allowance of six acres Pc^t [percent] for Roads &c. Returned into the Secretary's Office the 22nd Day of May Anno Dom. 1751.

Nich^l Scull, Survey^r Genl"

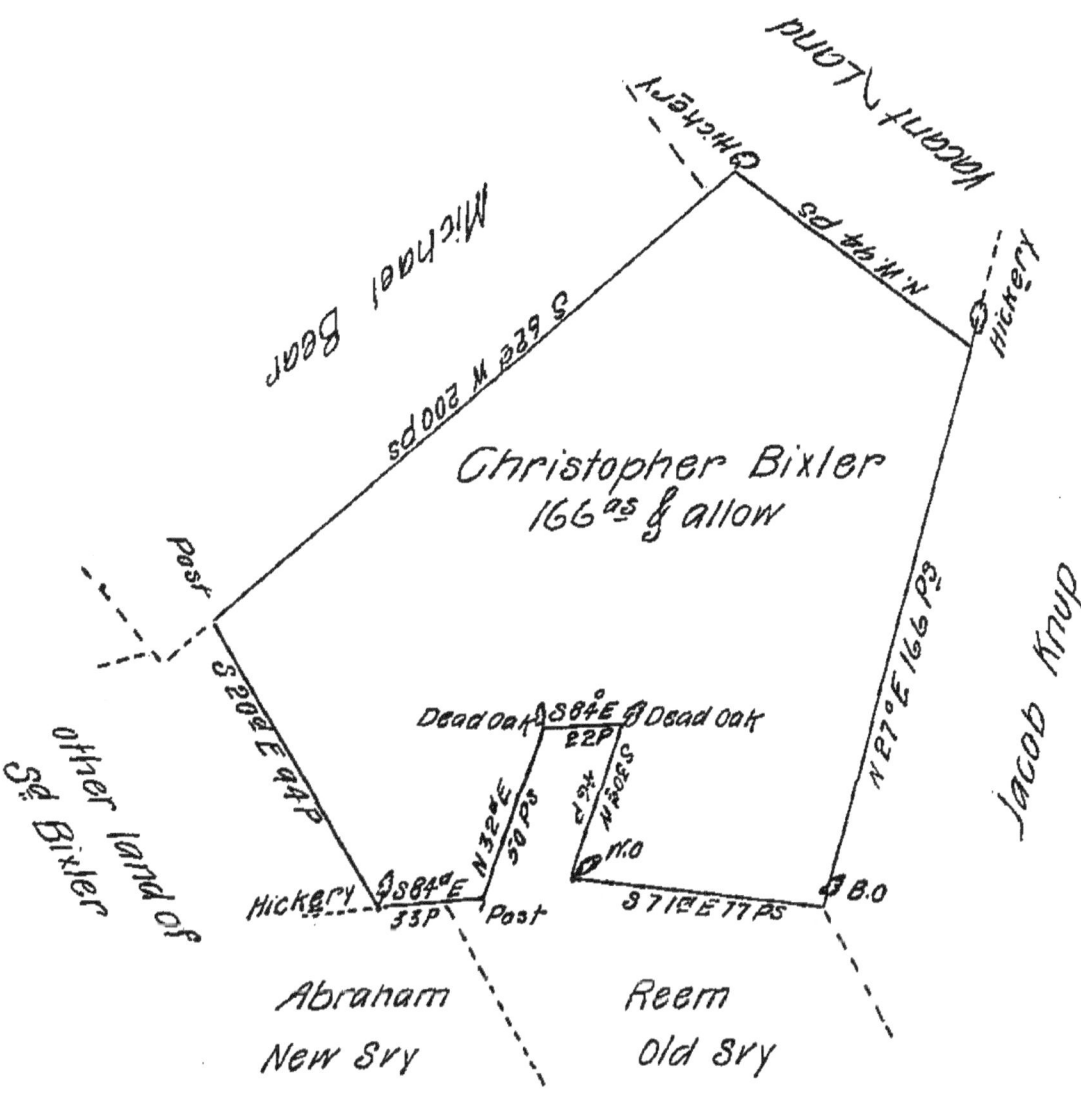

Christian Bixler's survey (under the name "Christopher Bixler") was recorded in Survey Book Volume C-155, Page 168.

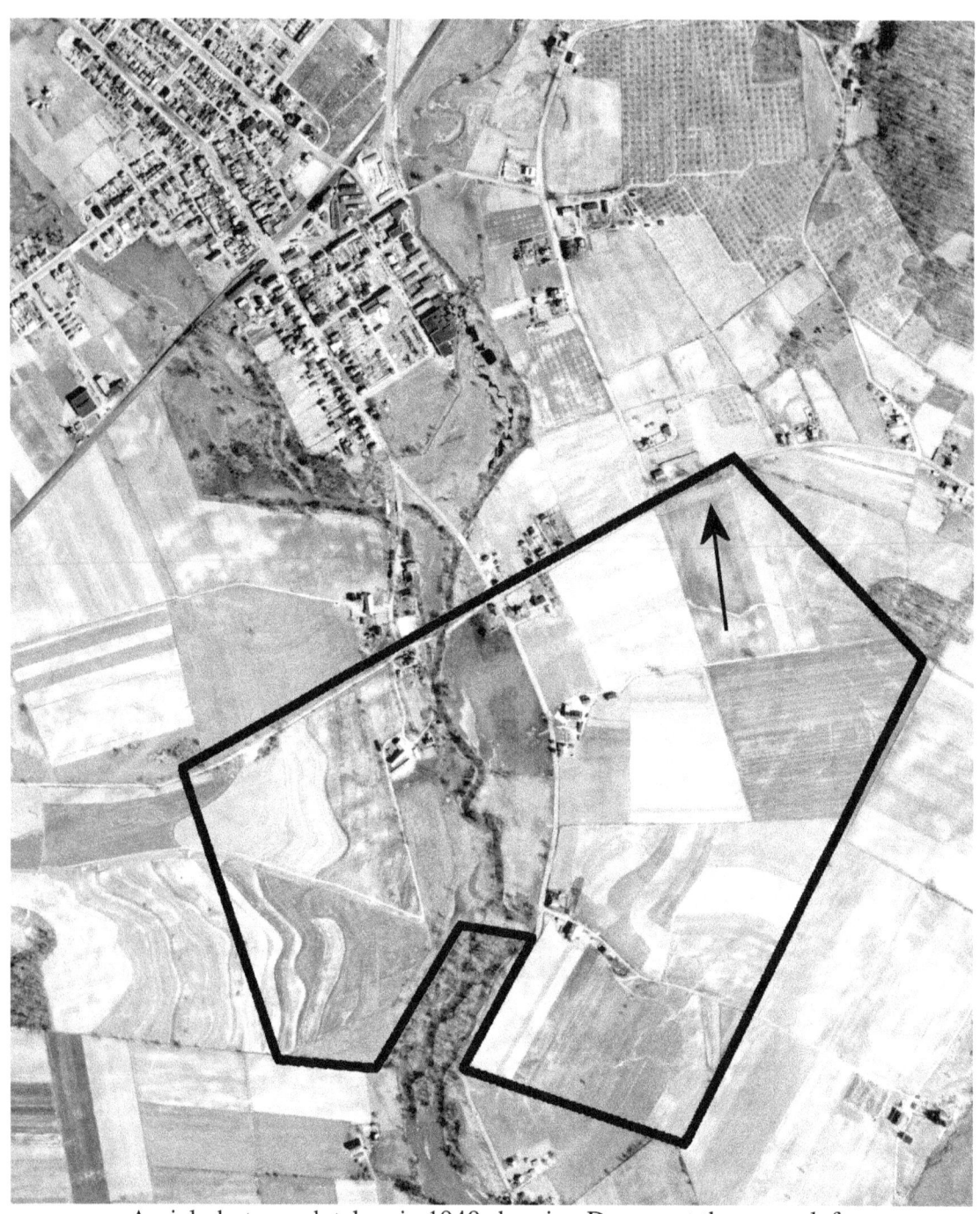

Aerial photograph taken in 1940 showing Denver at the upper left,
and the location of Christian Bixler's land.
The arrow shows the location of the Denver Union Cemetery.

The land was patented, along with two adjoining tracts, to Christian Bixler. The patent was recorded in Patent Book Volume A-16, page 636. Christian Bixler, Sr. conveyed the land to his three sons, Christian, Jr., Jacob and Abraham through his will written on 15 MAR 1758 and probated on 19 APR 1762 (Lancaster County, PA Will Y-2:25). Christian, Jr. and his wife Mary, who lived in Berks County, sold their interest in the property to Christian's two brothers, Jacob and Abraham on 12 MAR 1764 (Lancaster County Deed Book L, page 289). On 12 MAR

1764 Jacob and Abraham Bixler divided original land comprised of three parcels into two parts, with Abraham receiving the one that would contain the cemetery (Lancaster County Deed L-285). Abraham Bixler and his wife Ann conveyed the property to their son-in-law Dietrich Gockley on 29 JUN 1799 (Lancaster County Deed H-3:439).

Dietrich Gockley wrote his will on 5 SEP 1827, with a codicil dated 12 JUN 1828, (Lancaster County Will P-1:211, proved 30 JUN 1828) by which he conveyed the land containing the cemetery to his sons David and Jonas Gockley, as follows: "I give and bequeath unto my son David, the whole of the plantation on which I now live, except fifty acres of farming land, six acres of meadow ground, twelve acres of woodland to be measured off at Henry Bare's line, to begin at the bureing (sic) ground; and also twenty five acres of woodland, over the hill, at Voneidies [Von Nieda's] line, and also adjoining Peter Miller & Peter Winehold, which together would be ninety three acres; which said ninety three acres I give and bequeath unto my son Jonas, and my son David..."

The land jointly bequeathed to Jonas and David was partitioned between the two brothers on 10 JUN 1830 via Lancaster County, PA Deed O-7:40. David Gockley retained the portion of the property including the cemetery. David Gockley conveyed the land to Benjamin Brubaker on 10 APR 1869. This deed was not recorded, but it was referenced in the next deed, Benjamin Brubaker and wife Mary to the Trustees of Denver Union Cemetery (Lancaster County, PA Deed T-17:588, dated the 3rd. day of April A.D. 1905).

The current deed for the Cemetery property was written in 1928, and is transcribed in full here:

This Deed, Made this ninth day of June in the year nineteen hundred and twenty eight. Between H. R. Lutz, I. J. Rupp, Geo S. Ludwig, Edwin Snyder and J. Frank Lutz Trustees of The Denver Union Cemetery of East Cocalico Township, Lancaster County and State of Pennsylvania, of the first part; (hereinafter called Grantors) and The Trustees of the Union Station Grave-Yard, of the same place; (hereinafter called the Grantees).

Witnesseth, That in consideration of one ($1.00) Dollars, in hand paid, the receipt whereof is hereby acknowledged, the said Grantors do hereby grant and convey to the said Grantees their successors heirs and assigns, ALL those certain two tracts of land situated in East Cocalico Township, County of Lancaster and State aforesaid, Bounded and described by lines, courses and distances as follows to wit;

Tract No. 1, BEGINNING at a stake on the north side of a public road leading from Adamstown to Denver, thence in and along same and lands of J. T. Busser and Samuel Gockley South sixty four degrees and one quarter West eighteen perches to an iron pin; thence by the old grave and other lands of Benjamin Brubaker now Monroe Longnecker South seventeen degrees and three quarters East five perches and two tenths to an iron pin; thence by same North seventy two degrees and a quarter East eighteen perches and four tenths to an iron pin; and by the same North seventeen degrees and three quarters West seven perches and one tenths to an iron pin of the south side of said road; thence across the same North thirty seven degrees and three quarters West one perch and four tenths to the place of Beginning, Containing One Hundred and Twenty two Perches, Strict measure.

It being the same tract of land which Benjamin [Brubaker] and wife [Mary] by their [deed] dated the 3rd. day of April A.D. 1905, did grant and confirm The Trustees of Denver Union Cemetery, their successors or assigns forever, And recorded at Lancaster in the recorders office in deed-book T. No. 17, page 588 &c. will appear. [Sale price: $95.31]

Tract No. 2, BEGINNING at a stake at the road leading from Denver to Adamstown, thence by the said Denver Union Cemetery South twenty one degrees and one half East one hundred and five feet to a stake, thence by the same South seventy two degrees and a quarter West twenty nine feet to a stake; thence by the said Union Station Grave yard North twenty one degrees and one half West one hundred and five feet to a stake at the above said public road; thence along said public road North seventy degrees East twenty nine feet to the place of Beginning, Containing Eleven and one sixth Perches of land, more or less.

Being the same tract of land which the Trustees of Union Station Graveyard by their deed dated the 23rd. day of May A.D. 1914, did grant and confirm unto the Trustees of Denver Union Cemetery Association their successors or assigns forever, As in and by the said recited indenture duly executed and recorded at Lancaster in deed book R. Vol. 25, page 284 &c. will more fully and at large appear.

And the said Grantors do hereby covenant and agree to and with the said Grantees that they the Grantors their successors executors and administrators, SHALL and WILL WARRANT and forever DEFEND the herein above described premises, with the hereditaments and appurtenances, unto the said Grantees their successors and assigns, against the said Grantors and against every other person lawfully claiming or who shall hereafter claim the same or any part thereof.

In Witness Whereof, said Grantors have hereunto set their hands and seals the day and year first above written.

> (signed)
> H. R. Lutz
> I. J. Rupp
> Geo. S. Ludwig
> Edwin Snyder
> J. Frank Lutz

Sealed and Delivered in the presence of us:
> James J. Coldren
> J. R. Shirk

State of Pennsylvania
County of Lancaster, SS.

On this 9th day of June A. D. 1928, before me the subscriber a Justice of the Peace in and for said County came the above named H. R. Lutz, I. J. Rupp, Geo. S. Ludwig, Edwin Snyder and J. Frank Lutz and acknowledged the foregoing Deed to be their act and deed and desired the same to be recorded as such. Witness my hand and official seal the day and year aforesaid.

> (signed) J. R. Shirk

Recorded in Lancaster County Pennsylvania Deed Book K, Volume 45, Page 586 on 28 December 1956.

The previous deed for the much smaller Tract #2 referenced in the deed above, R-25:284, the Trustees of Union Station Graveyard to the Trustees of Denver Union Cemetery Association (written 23 May 1914) references the previous deed (including an agreement to build the stone wall around the Cemetery), which is transcribed here in full. Note: no formal incorporation was found for the "Union Station Graveyard."

Lancaster County, Pennsylvania Deed Z-11:45-46
Benjamin Brubaker and Daniel Kline et al.

Article of Agreement indented made concluded and agreed upon, the first day of September A. D. 1877. Between Benjamin Brubaker of the township of East Cocalico County of Lancaster and State of Pennsylvania of the one part Daniel Kline and John Lutz, architects builders and repair men of the Meeting House and stone wall to be put up at the Gockley's Grave Yard situate in East Cocalico township Lancaster County or the occupiers and possessors of the Gockley's Grave Yard and Meeting House that is to be erected hereafter of the second part. Witnesseth that the first party for the consideration hereinafter mentioned doth for himself his heirs executors and administrators covenant promise grant and agree to and with the second party by these presents that he the said first party shall and will on or before the first day of April A. D. 1878 at the proper costs and charges of both parties by such deeds of conveyances as he or they or their Counsel learned in the law shall advise well and sufficiently grant convey and assure unto the second party in fee simple clear of all incumbrance all that certain small tract of land along the line of land of Samuel Gockley North east from the Gockley's Grave Yard about two hundred feet to a certain point agreed already by both parties, broad at both ends about twenty five feet, containing about one fourth of an acre of land in East Cocalico Township Lancaster County Pa. and in case the holders and occupiers wishes to enlarge said Grave Yard the party of the first part binds himself his heirs executors, administrators and assigns to sell them a quantity of land not exceeding one acre, adjoining said Grave Yard and as such a place of said Grave Yard that it will make the least damage to the farm of the first party, in consideration whereof the party of the second part is to pay the party of the first part so much per acre as other land will sell in the vicinity of said Grave Yard the second party also agrees to pay to the party of the first part the sum of one dollar for the first mentioned fourth acre of land on the delivery of the deed. In witness whereof the parties to these presents have hereunto set their hands and scals the day and year above first written.
> (signed) Benjamin Brubaker, Daniel Kline, John Lutz

Witness present:
J. G. Garman David Gockley
Lancaster County, SS: Personally appeared before me a Justice of the Peace in and for said County David Gockley who being duly affirmed according to law does depose and say I seen Daniel Kline, now dead, sign and put his name to the above Indenture of Agreement dated September 1st 1877. Affirmed and subscribed before me this 17th of March 1883.
> David Gockley

[Daniel Kline died on 15 JAN 1883]

J. G. Garman, J. P.

Lancaster County, SS.

On the 17 of March 1883 before me a Justice of the Peace in for said County personally appeared the within named Benjamin Brubaker and John Lutz and in due form of law acknowledged the within named Indenture of Agreement to be their and each of their act and deed and desired that the same might be recorded as such according to law. Witness my hand and seal the day and year aforesaid. J. G. Garman, J. P.

Recorded March 22, 1883.

A 1909 article mentions improvements made to the Cemetery:

Reading Eagle, 9 JUN 1909, page 10.

Lancaster County, Denver

Improvements to Cemetery

The Denver Union Cemetery Association has made some decided improvements to its grounds adjoining the brick meeting house near town. Additional ground has been added to the property and every block has been dug up and seeded with special lawn grass.

Notes on the Photography of the Gravestones

Many of the early gravestones are significantly weathered and difficult to read. Many of the photographs in this book have been significantly adjusted by increasing the contrast and adjusting the "brightness" to enhance the readability of the inscriptions. For some of the graves, this process can create a strange appearance of the stone in the photo, but it was necessary to be able to read the inscription in the printed image.

Under direct lighting many of the stones are unreadable and look almost blank. Utilizing natural lighting from a very shallow angle (2-5 degrees from the direction of the face of the stone) creates shadows within the letters, enhancing the inscription. An example of the difference shallow-angle side lighting is shown in the pair of photographs below.

In one case, Sarah, wife of David Petticoffer, the inscription for her is located on the north side of the monument where direct sunlight probably never shines. The photograph of the inscription for her was taken using a large mirror to direct sunlight onto the stone from a shallow angle. This greatly enhances readability as can be seen in the photographs below (shown without any contrast enhancement of the original image).

Diffuse lighting (north facing).　　　Shallow-angle side lighting using a mirror.

Known Unmarked Burials

The following obituaries reference burials which were or may have been in the Denver Union Cemetery for which there are currently no readable gravestones. There are a number of graves in the cemetery marked with only initials, and it is possible that some of those are for these burials. They are presented here in date order.

Samuel Sweigart, Sr.

Ephrata Review, 7 AUG 1896, page 3
Fell Over Into A Gutter And Died
Samuel Sweigart, of this Borough, Meets His End in This Manner
Samuel Sweigart, a resident of North State street, this borough, a man in the seventy-first year of his age, met his death in a violent manner, on Saturday night last. Between seven and eight o'clock on Sunday morning, Christian Fassnacht, while driving along the road leading from this place to Reading, some distance northeast of the borough limits, noticed a man lying in a deep gutter by the wayside. Suspecting that the man was dead, Mr. Fassnacht called Jacob Stober, who was near by driving cattle to pasture. Together they made an examination of the body, found that life was extinct, and recognized the form to be that of Samuel Sweigart, who has since April 1st last, resided near the extreme end of North State street. The place where his body was found is about one-fourth of a mile beyond the borough limits and three-fourth of a mile from the

business centre of the town, it being along the slope at the Bitzer farm.

Mr. Fasnacht came to Ephrata, and notified Deputy Coroner Gemperling, of Lancaster, who happened to be visiting here and the latter with his examining physician, Dr. I. N. Lightner, went to the place, for the purpose of holding an inquest. The following jury was empanelled: E. E. Royer, Chas. K. Mohler, Henry Shirker, Phares M. Waltman, D. F. Britigam and B. F. Lewis.

The doctor made an examination and found an abrasion of the skin on the right cheek and a slight contused wound of the right temple. He, Sweigart, evidently got too near the edge of the gutter, fell over into it face downward, and being unable to rise, was suffocated to death. The inquest was begun at about 9:30 o'clock and the testimony of John Martin, wife and daughter, who reside on the Bitzer farm was first heard. They testified to having seen Swigart sitting along the roadside at the orchard fence, as late as 10 or 11 o'clock Saturday night. He was in an intoxicated condition and was talking to himself. At the latter hour they retired.

The body was then removed to the home of the deceased, and the inquest continued, the following witnesses being heard: Winfield Beck, of Hahnstown, James Kiehl, of this place, C. Fasnacht, Jacob Stober, and Harry Kilhafner, of near town. Mr. Beck testified that he had called at the Sweigrt home on Saturday evening and after taking a drink, Swigart and he walked out the road to near the place where the former was found next morning, and spent several hours together, after which he, Beck, stated that he went home.

Mr. Kiehl testified to having seen Sweigart on that evening in an intoxicated condition.

Messrs. Fasnacht and Stober testified to having found the body as stated above.

From the testimony given and from the examination of the physician, the jury returned a verdict that the deceased had come to his death from suffocation, while lying in a stunned and helpless condition occasioned by a fall, while in a state of intoxication.

Mr. Swigart was a first class mechanic, his trade being that of a stone mason, though he had worked at the trade very little in the past ten years. He was born in East Cocalico township. besides his aged wife he is survived by the following children: Mrs. Samuel Ludwig, Brunnerville; Mrs. Abraham Turner, Reamstown; John, August and Frank, residing at home; Samuel Swigart, of Denver; Mrs. Henry Lutz, Millway; Wellington and Martin, living in Ohio; Monroe, residing at Lincoln, and Mrs. Albert Shoups of Hahnstown.

The funeral took place on Wednesday morning from the residence of the deceased, on North State state (sic). Interment was made in the Denver cemetery.

Franklin Sweigart

Ephrata Review, 13 APR 1900, page 2
Killed on the Railroad
Franklin Sweigart's Life Crushed Out by the Cars
A Few Minutes After Leaving His Home he was Run Down by a Train and Killed

This community was terribly startled and shocked on Saturday evening last by the announcement that Franklin Sweigart, a well-known stone mason of this borough, had come to his death by being run down by the passenger train due here at 6:45 o'clock. It frequently happens that on Saturday this train is late. This was the case on Saturday evening, and young Sweigart who is about twenty-two years of age, believing that the train had gone by, left the home of his mother, Mrs. Samuel Sweigart, at 534 North State street, soon after 8 o'clock to come in to the business centre of the town. That was the last seen of him alive. As he had so frequently done, he started to walk in on the railroad track, and having been doing some drinking during the day and early evening, he was in a merry mood and started singing and playing a mouth organ he had with him. Apparently he did not seem to realize his danger, and doubtless was so absorbed with his music that he did not hear the approach of the train.

The unfortunate young man was struck at the whistle post just this side of what is known as the white bridge at the Walnut street crossing, and was pushed or rolled along the track a distance of about 120 paces, to the milk station building, where his body was left, so terribly mangled as to be almost unrecognizable, the train passing over the body. The train did not stop until it reached the railroad station, and the engineer was not aware that his train had crushed out the life of a man. In fact it is stated that he knew nothing of the occurrence until he had reached the Lancaster Junction on the return trip on Sunday morning, when he found a vest on the pilot of the engine. The train was one hour and a quarter late on reaching the railroad station, arriving here at 8:15 o'clock.

At about 9 o'clock, John Shrantz, who is employed as a watchman for the railroad company at the red bridge over the Cocalico creek, near Fahnestock's mill, was on his way to his home on Washington avenue, this borough, his duties being over. He also walked in on the railroad, and while doing so he stumbled over the body which he did not at first recognize. He informed Charles Moyer who resides at the corner of Duke and Chestnut streets, about half a square away from the milk station.

The men gathered up as much of the remains as they could find and placing them on several boards brought them to the Chestnut street crossing where between 10 and 11 o'clock an inquest was held, Deputy Coroner P. K. Royer, having been notified in the mean time. The young man's mother and brothers had also been informed. Undertaker E. B. Wolf, of Denver, was also notified of the tragic death by telephone.

On getting to the scene, Deputy Coroner P. K. Royer selected as a jury, Messrs. A. M. Achey, C. G. Ammon, John W. VonNeida, F. B. Hassler, Martin S. Gross and I. B. Good. Dr. John F. Mentzer served as examining physician. The man was recognized to be Frank Sweigart by his neck, he having a wry neck. Some letters and photographs were also found in his clothing which was strewed along the track. Every vestige of clothing, except one shoe had been stripped from the body in the contact with the wheels. The body was terribly mutilated. The rear part of the skull was cut off, and the brains were scattered along the railroad track. One leg was cut off at the ankle and the other leg was smashed. The trunk of the body was badly cut, gashes several inches deep being found therein. Both arms were broken, but the shoulders were not injured. The verdict of the jury after examination by the physician was that the deceased had come to his death by being run over by the train at 8:15 p. m. while under the influence of liquor.

Undertaker E. B. Wolf, of Denver, took charge of the remains, at about midnight, having come on from Denver for that purpose, and prepared them for burial.

The victim of the dreadful accident was unmarried; he was a stonemason by trade and was known as a good workman. His father was found dead some years ago on the road leading to Mohler's meeting house. He was kind to his mother, who is greatly distressed by his sad and untimely end. Besides his mother, he leaves several brothers and sisters as follows: Augustus and John, at home; Samuel, at Denver; Martin, of Iowa; Kate, wife of Henry Lutz, of Akron; Walter, of Aurora, Portage county, Ohio; Eliza, wife of Samuel Ludwig, of Clay, and Monroe.

The funeral took place on Wednesday morning at 9:30 o'clock from the home of the mother of the deceased, 534 North State street. Services were held in the Brick meeting house, Denver, and interment was made in the adjoining cemetery, Rev. S. Schweitzer, and Elder Israel Wenger officiated.

Samuel Sweigart, Jr.

Lititz Record, 22 NOV 1901, page 8
Fatal Railroad Accident at Denver

Samuel Sweigart, a stone mason, who resided in Ephrata township, between Ephrata and Stevens, was injured on the Reading and Columbia railroad at Denver on Saturday night and died a few hours later in the Reading hospital. Sweigart was walking on the tracks and it was said that he was slightly intoxicated. He had not walked a long distance when a freight train, which was going towards Reading, struck him and knocked him down. The wheels then passed over him, cutting off both legs and one of his hands. Immediately after the accident the injured man was placed aboard the train and taken to the Reading Hospital. The accident occurred at 7.30 o'clock and at 11 o'clock the man succumbed to his injuries. Mr. Sweigart had a brother who was killed by the cars in Ephrata some time ago. He was a married man and is survived by his wife and several children.

John Sweigart

Philadelphia Inquirer, 11 JAN 1911.
Special to the Inquirer.

Lancaster, PA. Jan. 10. -- John SWEIGART, of Ephrata, aged 32, died today in a hospital in this city, from wounds received by being struck by a trolley car. The accident occurred while he was seated on the tracks. His father, Samuel SWEIGART, was killed by a fall on a trolley road near Reading. John's brothers, Samuel Jr., and Frank, while lying on the tracks of the Reading Railroad, near Denver, were struck and killed by a freight train. A disposition to sit or lie on railroad tracks seems to have possessed the entire family.

Ephrata Review, 13 JAN 1911, page 2
Obituary
Death of John Sweigart

During Sunday night John Sweigart, of near this borough, died at the General Hospital, Lancaster, as the result of injuries sustained by being struck by a trolley car on November 16, 1910, just south of this borough, where Sweigart sat on a rail. There is a curve there and the car struck Sweigart before he was seen. Deceased was fifty-two years old and he was well known in this vicinity.

The remains were brought to this borough by Funeral Conductor L. Y. Eitnier, who was placed in charge of the funeral arrangements, and prepared for the burial.

The deceased is survived by his mother, and the following brothers and sisters: Augustus, residing on the Jonas Nolt farm, near Old Bethany church, Ephrata township; Monroe, of Elizabethtown; Martin, of Lititz; Mrs. Albert Shupp, of near Reamstown, and Mrs. Samuel Ludwig, residing near Oregon. The mother resides with her son, Augustus Sweigart. The funeral was held Thursday afternoon from the home of Augustus Sweigart, brother of the deceased, with interment in the Denver cemetery.

Mary Beckey

Reading Eagle, 19 JAN 1937, page 20

Mrs. Mary F. Beckey

Fritztown. Jan. 19. - Mary F. (Schuler), widow of Davilla Beckey, died at the home of her son-in-law and daughter, Mr. and Mrs. Matthias Dotterer, here, aged 81 years. Her husband died 32 years ago. There survive five children, Charles, Allentown; Katie, wife of Matthias Dotterer, with whom she resided; William, Shillington, and Clara, wife of Raymond Miller, and Elizabeth, wife of Allen Swoyer, Reading. She was a member of the Reformed Church.

Funeral Friday at 1:30 p. m. from the home, the Rev. D. J. Wetzel officiating. Interment in Denver Cemetery, in charge of Funeral Directors F. F. Seidel, Inc.

Early photograph of the Frankhouser graves (circa 1907-1911). From the
Withers Monument Works collection at the Reamstown Historical Society and Museum.

Photograph from 2013 showing that the two small gravestones to the left are absent.

19

Aerial photograph of the Cemetery showing grave numbering pattern.
Rows were numbered 1 to 47 starting at the east end of the Cemetery.
Grave numbers within each row start at the south end of each row.
This numbering was done only for the purposes of this book.

Grave: 1-2 Name: Susana (Bitzer) Johns Born: 15 DEC 1836 Died: 22 NOV 1919 Parents: John B. & Elizabeth (Royer) Bitzer Spouse: Christian R. Johns Notes:	Grave: 1-4 Name: Eastman Hermes Born: 7 MAY 1880 Died: 27 APR 1881 Parents: Henry F. & Anna E. (Kline) Hermes Spouse: unmarried Notes: Eastman's mother was a daughter of Abraham E. Kline, who was a brother of Daniel Kline (1818-1883).

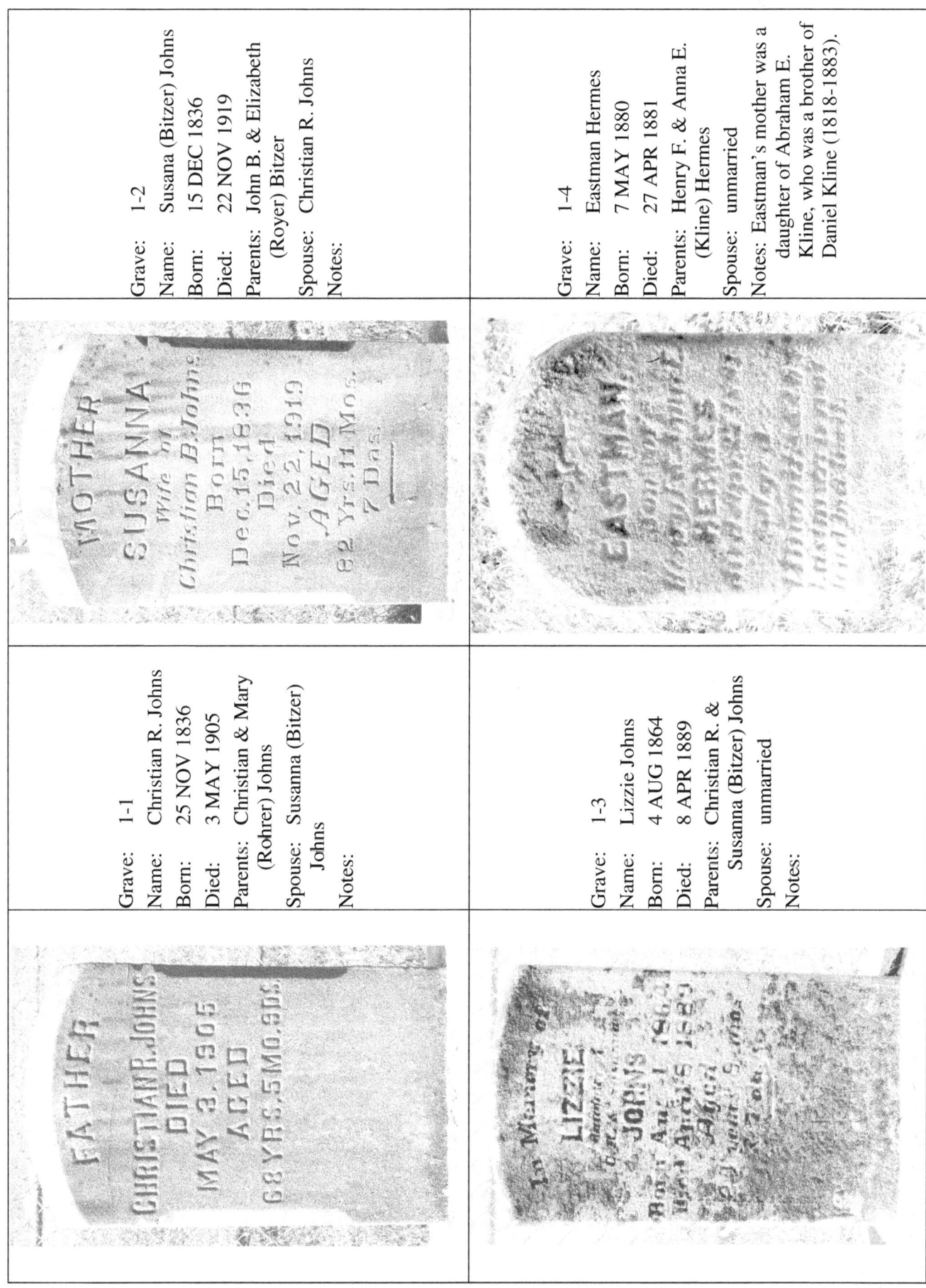

Grave: 1-1 Name: Christian R. Johns Born: 25 NOV 1836 Died: 3 MAY 1905 Parents: Christian & Mary (Rohrer) Johns Spouse: Susanna (Bitzer) Johns Notes:	Grave: 1-3 Name: Lizzie Johns Born: 4 AUG 1864 Died: 8 APR 1889 Parents: Christian R. & Susanna (Bitzer) Johns Spouse: unmarried Notes:

Grave: 1-6
Name: Emmaline (Renninger) Ludwig
Born: 3 NOV 1856
Died: 18 JUL 1928
Parents: William & Susanna (Messner) Renninger
Spouse: George S. Ludwig
Notes:

Grave: 2-1 2-2
Name: Daniel Z. Givler Anna G. (Brubaker) Givler
Born: FEB 1866 27 OCT 1864
Died: 3 FEB 1945 22 JAN 1918
Parents: Samuel & Catharine (Zell) Givler Benjamin M. & Nancy B. (Gockley) Brubaker
Notes: Married on 31 DEC 1892 at Denver, PA.

Grave: 1-5
Name: George S. Ludwig
Born: 16 AUG 1852
Died: 28 NOV 1928
Parents: William & Lydia (Sollenberger) Ludwig
Spouse: Emma (Renninger) Ludwig
Notes:

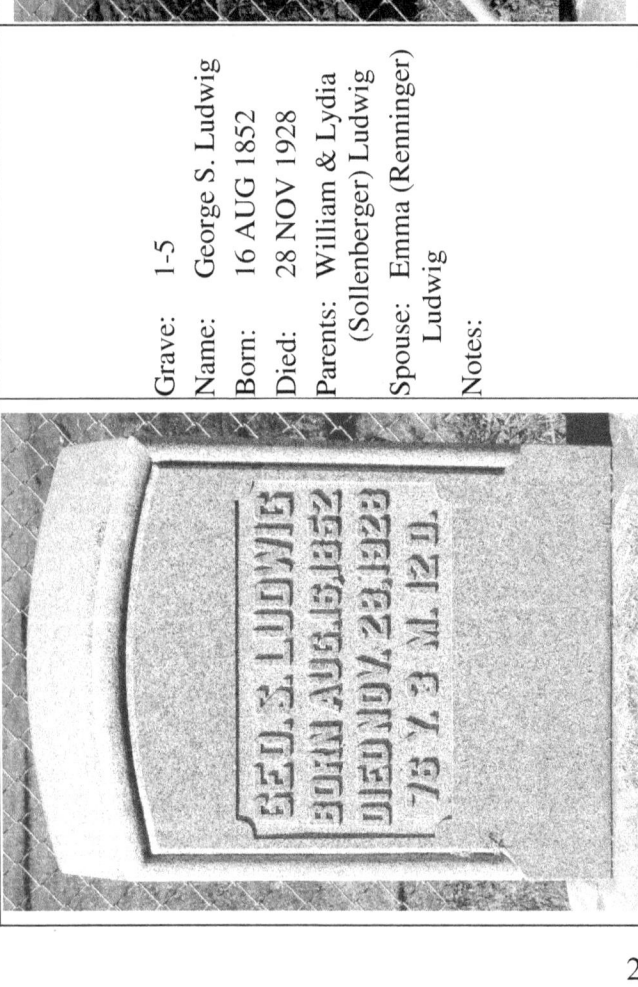

Grave: 1-7
Name: Milton Ludwig
Born: 4 SEP 1884
Died: 13 AUG 1888
Parents: George S. & Emmaline (Renninger) Ludwig
Spouse: unmarried
Notes:

Grave: 2-6	Grave: 2-8
Name: Annie B. Gockley	Name: Susanna (Gockley) Royer
Born: 21 DEC 1848	Born: 25 NOV 1833
Died: 10 APR 1928	Died: 6 JAN 1852
Parents: Samuel & Elizabeth (Bates) Gockley	Parents: David & Susanna (Bear) Gockley
Spouse: unmarried	Spouse: Reuben R. Royer
Notes:	Notes:

Grave:	2-3	
Name:	infant son Givler	
Born:	5 FEB 1895	
Died:	5 FEB 1895	
	2-4	Katie B. Givler
	21 DEC 1893	
	1898	
	2-5	Benjamin B. Givler
	14 MAR 1897	
	1898	
Parents:	Daniel Z. & Anna (Brubaker) Givler	
Spouse:	unmarried	
Notes:		

Grave: 2-7
Name: Jonas Gockley
Born: 26 JUL 1807
Died: 9 NOV 1881
Parents: Dietrich & Barbara (Bixler) Gockley
Spouse: J. Catharine (Weaver) [Price] Gockley
Notes: Catharine was the widow of John Price. She married Jonas on 27 APR 1854. She died on 12 SEP 1883 and is buried in Charles Evans Cemetery in Reading, PA.

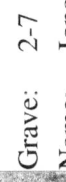

Grave: 2-10
Name: David Gockley
Born: 2 DEC 1804
Died: 17 FEB 1886
Parents: Dietrich & Barbara (Bixler) Gockley
Spouse: Susanna (Bear) Gockley
Notes:

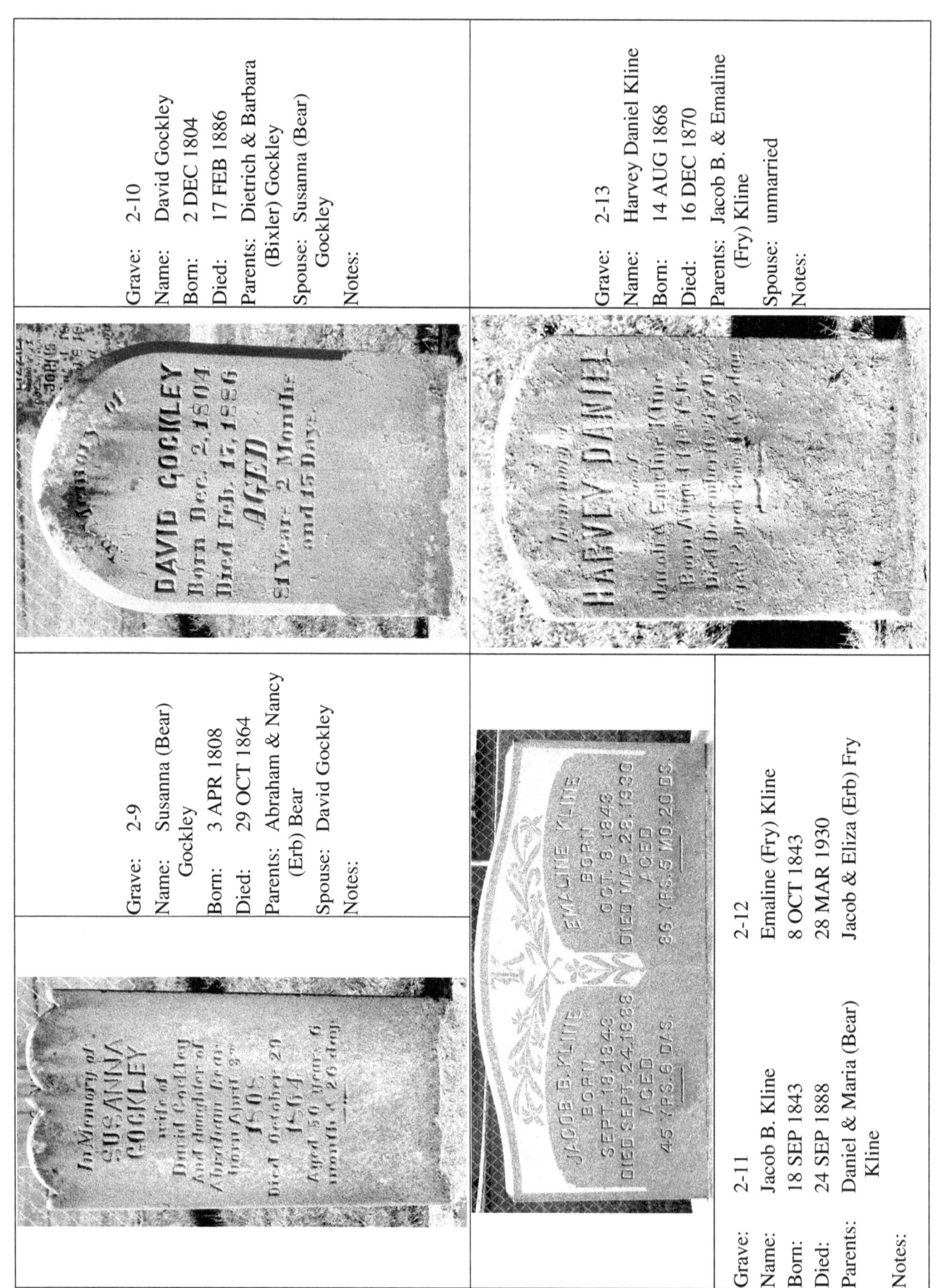

Grave: 2-13
Name: Harvey Daniel Kline
Born: 14 AUG 1868
Died: 16 DEC 1870
Parents: Jacob B. & Emaline (Fry) Kline
Spouse: unmarried
Notes:

Grave: 2-9
Name: Susanna (Bear) Gockley
Born: 3 APR 1808
Died: 29 OCT 1864
Parents: Abraham & Nancy (Erb) Bear
Spouse: David Gockley
Notes:

Grave: 2-11
Name: Jacob B. Kline
Born: 18 SEP 1843
Died: 24 SEP 1888
Parents: Daniel & Maria (Bear) Kline
Notes:

Grave: 2-12
Name: Emaline (Fry) Kline
Born: 8 OCT 1843
Died: 28 MAR 1930
Parents: Jacob & Eliza (Erb) Fry

Grave: 2-15 Name: Daniel Kline Born: 25 MAR 1855 Died: 2 JUL 1855 Parents: Daniel & Maria (Bear) Kline Spouse: unmarried Notes:	Grave: 2-17 Name: Maria (Bear) Kline Born: 31 MAY 1816 Died: 31 AUG 1881 Parents: Abraham & Nancy (Erb) Bear Spouse: Daniel Kline Notes:

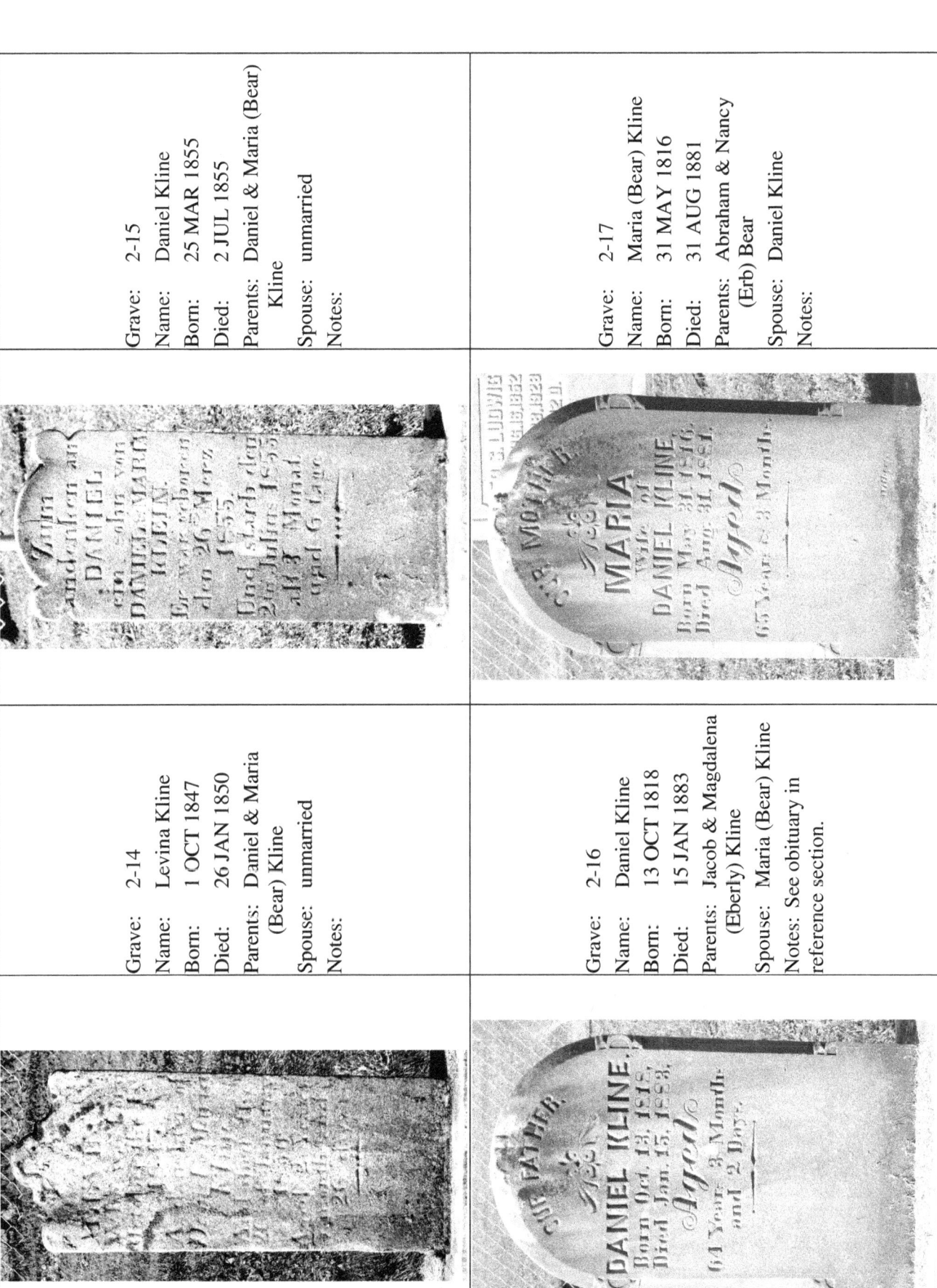

Grave: 2-14 Name: Levina Kline Born: 1 OCT 1847 Died: 26 JAN 1850 Parents: Daniel & Maria (Bear) Kline Spouse: unmarried Notes:	Grave: 2-16 Name: Daniel Kline Born: 13 OCT 1818 Died: 15 JAN 1883 Parents: Jacob & Magdalena (Eberly) Kline Spouse: Maria (Bear) Kline Notes: See obituary in reference section.

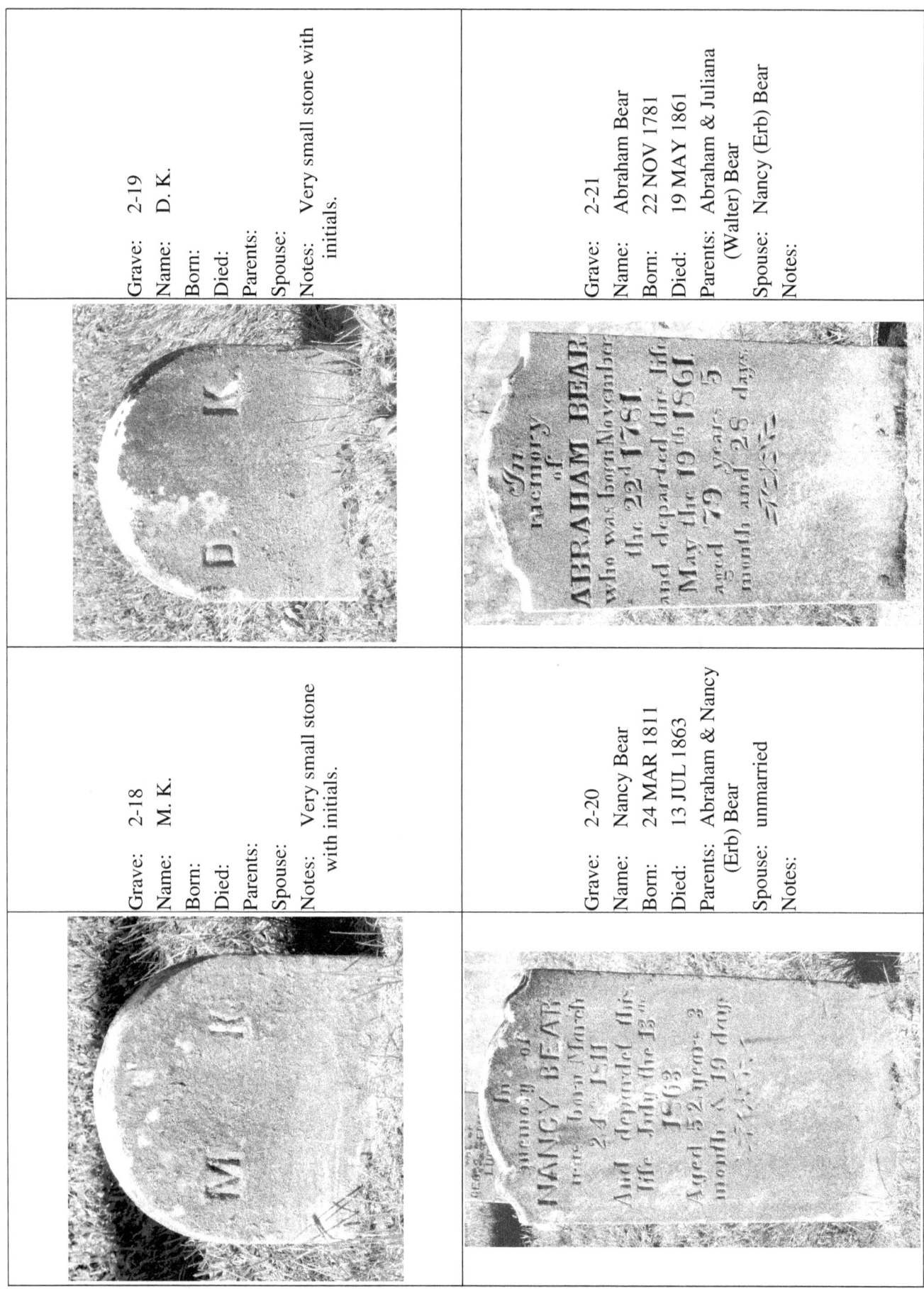

Grave: 2-19
Name: D. K.
Born:
Died:
Parents:
Spouse:
Notes: Very small stone with initials.

Grave: 2-21
Name: Abraham Bear
Born: 22 NOV 1781
Died: 19 MAY 1861
Parents: Abraham & Juliana (Walter) Bear
Spouse: Nancy (Erb) Bear
Notes:

Grave: 2-18
Name: M. K.
Born:
Died:
Parents:
Spouse:
Notes: Very small stone with initials.

Grave: 2-20
Name: Nancy Bear
Born: 24 MAR 1811
Died: 13 JUL 1863
Parents: Abraham & Nancy (Erb) Bear
Spouse: unmarried
Notes:

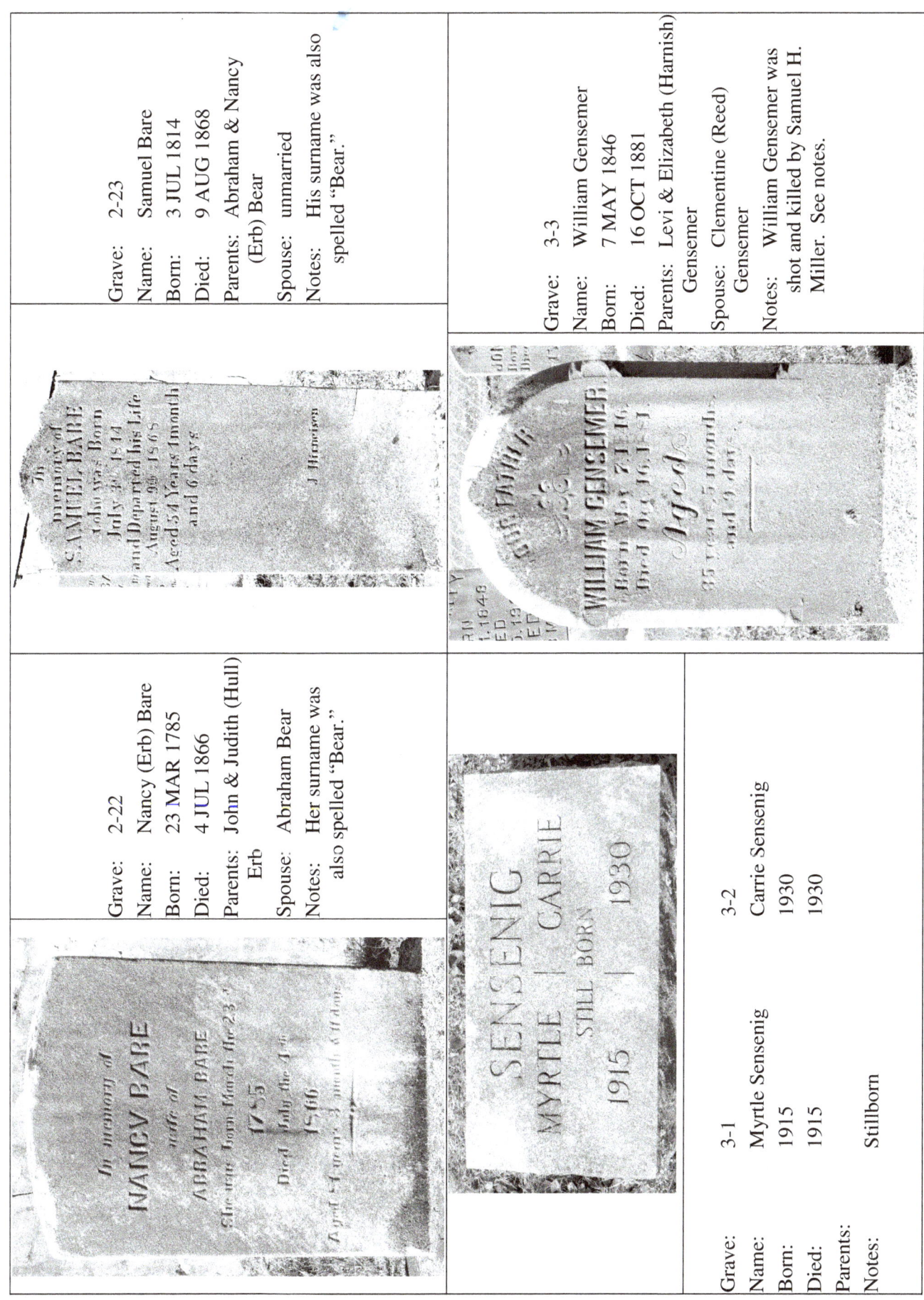

Grave: 2-23
Name: Samuel Bare
Born: 3 JUL 1814
Died: 9 AUG 1868
Parents: Abraham & Nancy (Erb) Bear
Spouse: unmarried
Notes: His surname was also spelled "Bear."

Grave: 3-3
Name: William Gensemer
Born: 7 MAY 1846
Died: 16 OCT 1881
Parents: Levi & Elizabeth (Harnish) Gensemer
Spouse: Clementine (Reed) Gensemer
Notes: William Gensemer was shot and killed by Samuel H. Miller. See notes.

Grave: 2-22
Name: Nancy (Erb) Bare
Born: 23 MAR 1785
Died: 4 JUL 1866
Parents: John & Judith (Hull) Erb
Spouse: Abraham Bear
Notes: Her surname was also spelled "Bear."

Grave: 3-1
Name: Myrtle Sensenig
Born: 1915
Died: 1915
Parents:
Notes: Stillborn

3-2
Carrie Sensenig
1930
1930

Grave: 3-5 **Name:** Eliza Ann (Kilhefner) Dissinger [Shimp] **Born:** 14 NOV 1838 **Died:** 15 MAR 1917 **Parents:** Henry & Sarah (Stayer) Kilhefner **Spouse:** (1) Isaac S. Dissinger, (2) Henry F. Shimp **Notes:** Buried under the surname of her first husband.	**Grave:** 3-7 **Name:** A. G. **Born:** **Died:** **Parents:** **Spouse:** **Notes:** Very small stone with initials.
Grave: 3-4 **Name:** Isaac S. Dissinger **Born:** 5 SEP 1839 **Died:** 28 FEB 1879 **Parents:** Samuel N. & Mary (Storck) Dissinger **Spouse:** Eliza Ann (Kilhefner) Dissinger **Notes:** Served as a 1st Lieutenant in Co. I, 107th PA Infantry during the Civil War. He was wounded in battle.	**Grave:** 3-6 **Name:** L. M. S. **Born:** **Died:** **Parents:** **Spouse:** **Notes:** Very small stone with initials.

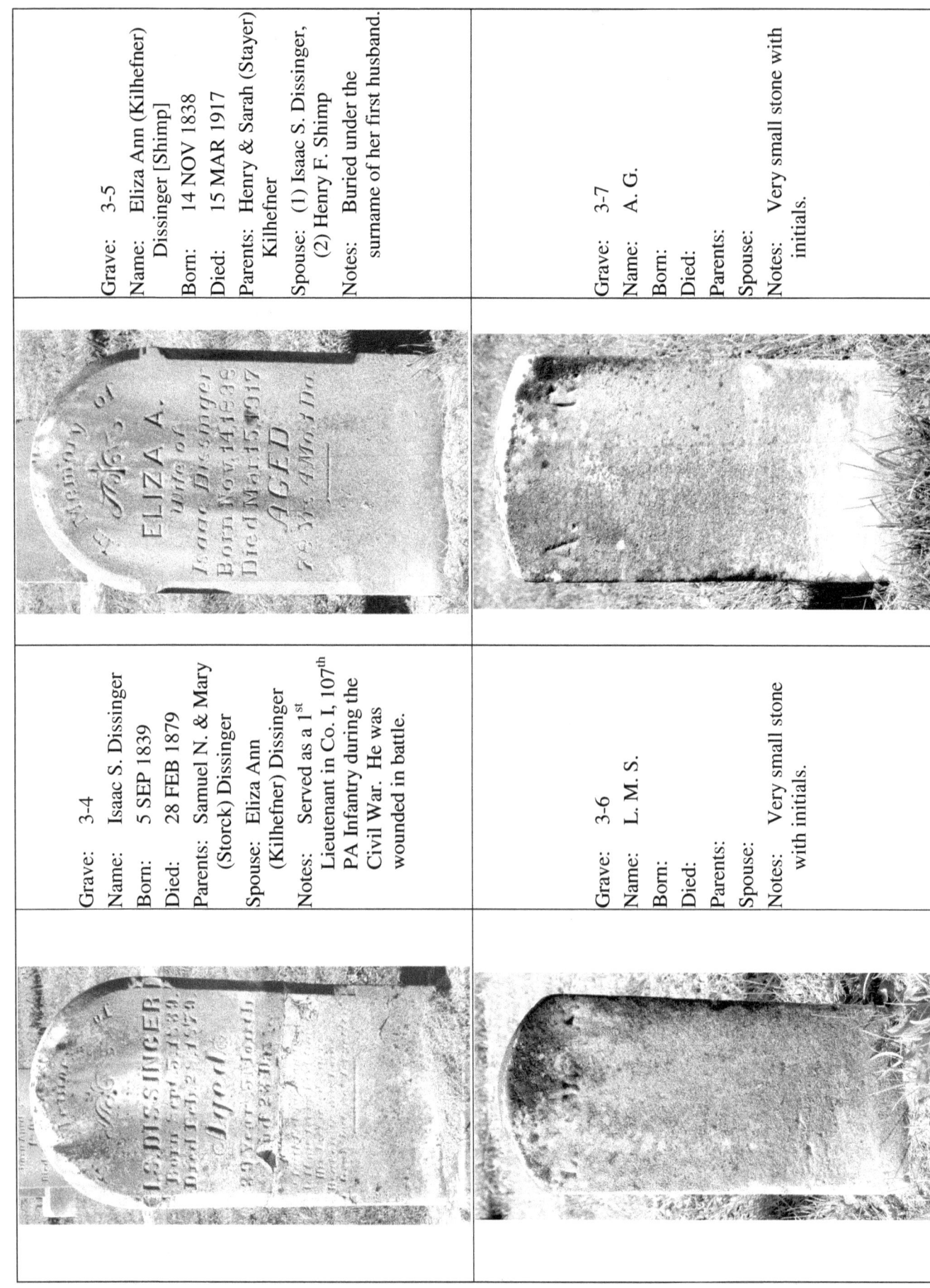

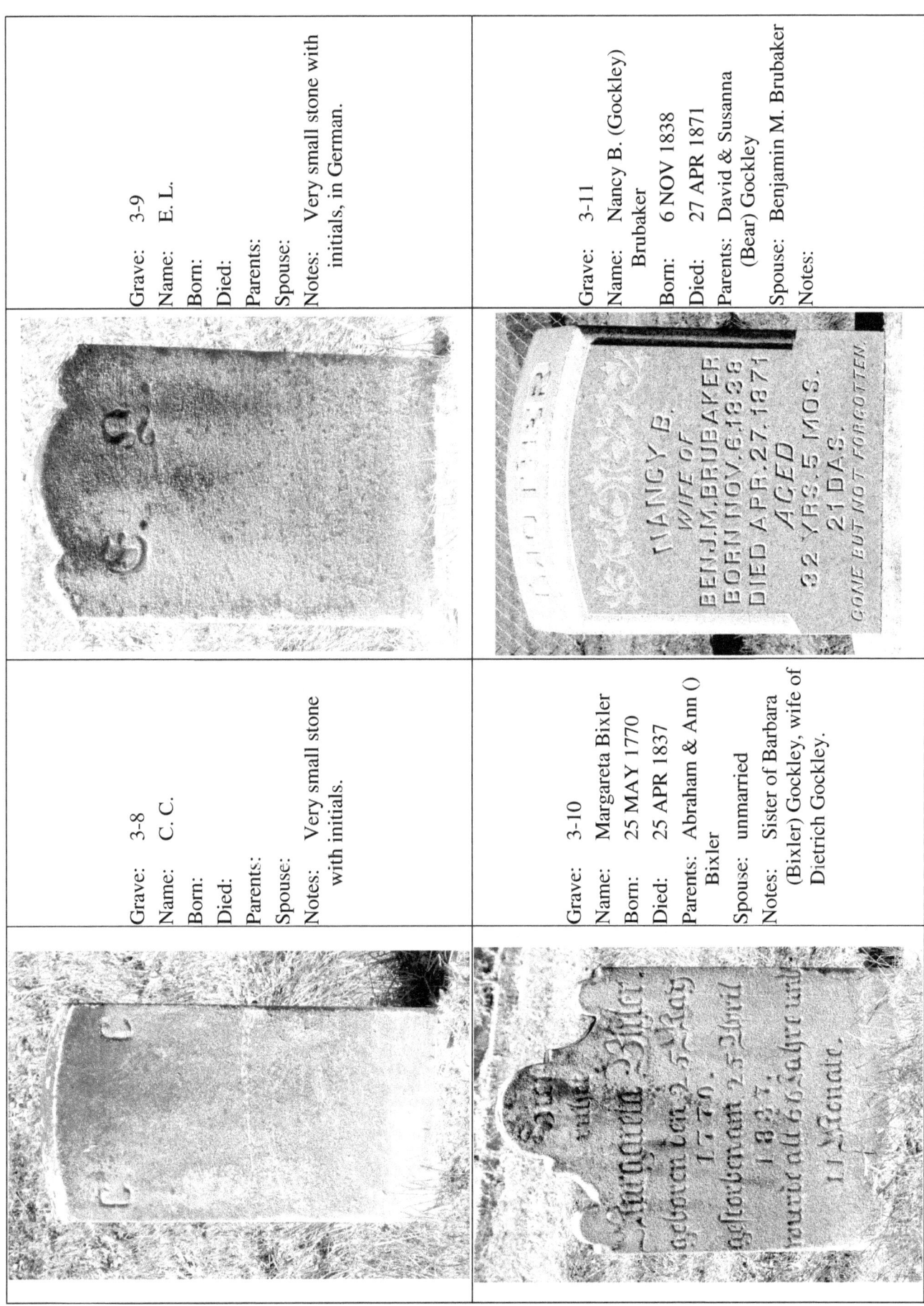

Grave: 3-8
Name: C. C.
Born:
Died:
Parents:
Spouse:
Notes: Very small stone with initials.

Grave: 3-9
Name: E. L.
Born:
Died:
Parents:
Spouse:
Notes: Very small stone with initials, in German.

Grave: 3-10
Name: Margareta Bixler
Born: 25 MAY 1770
Died: 25 APR 1837
Parents: Abraham & Ann () Bixler
Spouse: unmarried
Notes: Sister of Barbara (Bixler) Gockley, wife of Dietrich Gockley.

Grave: 3-11
Name: Nancy B. (Gockley) Brubaker
Born: 6 NOV 1838
Died: 27 APR 1871
Parents: David & Susanna (Bear) Gockley
Spouse: Benjamin M. Brubaker
Notes:

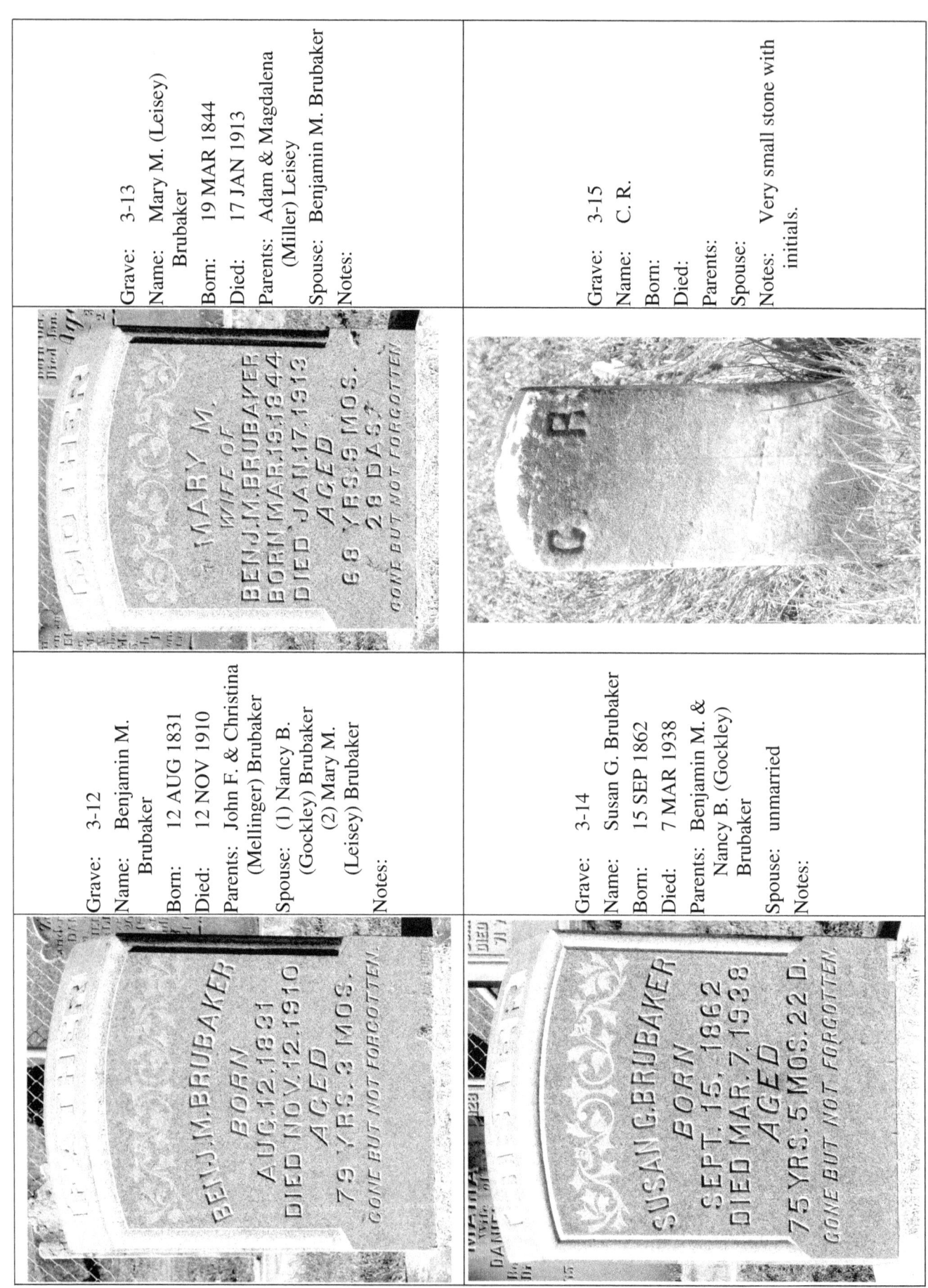

Grave: 3-13
Name: Mary M. (Leisey) Brubaker
Born: 19 MAR 1844
Died: 17 JAN 1913
Parents: Adam & Magdalena (Miller) Leisey
Spouse: Benjamin M. Brubaker
Notes:

Grave: 3-15
Name: C. R.
Born:
Died:
Parents:
Spouse:
Notes: Very small stone with initials.

Grave: 3-12
Name: Benjamin M. Brubaker
Born: 12 AUG 1831
Died: 12 NOV 1910
Parents: John F. & Christina (Mellinger) Brubaker
Spouse: (1) Nancy B. (Gockley) Brubaker
(2) Mary M. (Leisey) Brubaker
Notes:

Grave: 3-14
Name: Susan G. Brubaker
Born: 15 SEP 1862
Died: 7 MAR 1938
Parents: Benjamin M. & Nancy B. (Gockley) Brubaker
Spouse: unmarried
Notes:

30

Grave: 3-17 Name: George Shimp Born: 29 SEP 1801 Died: 22 JAN 1871 Parents: Andrew & Elizabeth (Mueller) Shimp Spouse: Susanna (Eberly) Shimp Notes:	Grave: 3-19 Name: Susanna (Shimp) Shober Born: 23 FEB 1847 Died: 17 MAR 1882 Parents: George & Susanna (Eberly) Shimp Spouse: Reuben E. Shober Notes:

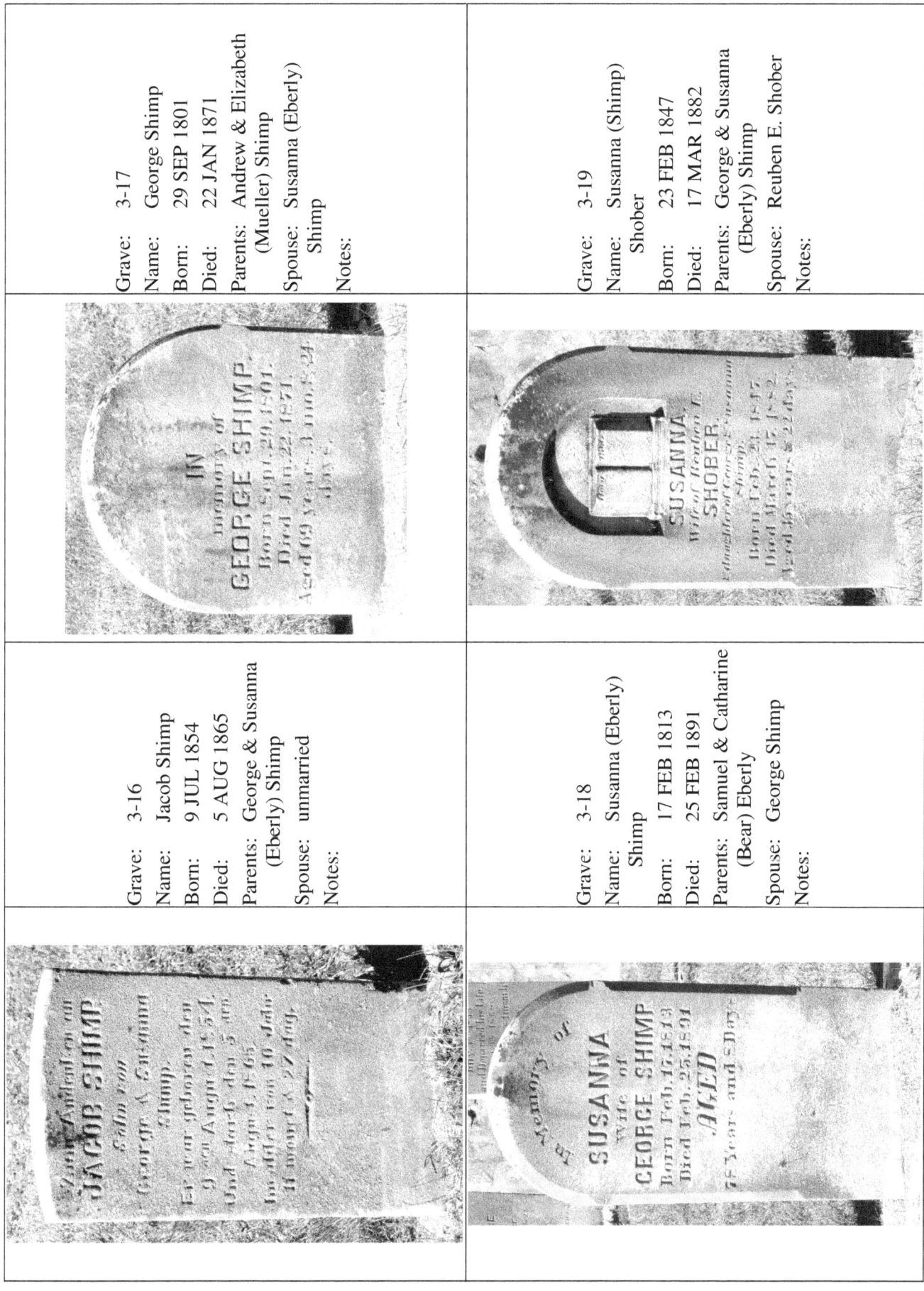

Grave: 3-16 Name: Jacob Shimp Born: 9 JUL 1854 Died: 5 AUG 1865 Parents: George & Susanna (Eberly) Shimp Spouse: unmarried Notes:	Grave: 3-18 Name: Susanna (Eberly) Shimp Born: 17 FEB 1813 Died: 25 FEB 1891 Parents: Samuel & Catharine (Bear) Eberly Spouse: George Shimp Notes:

SCHWEAR

RICHARD 1912 — 1961

EMMA 1911 —

Grave:	4-4
Name:	Emma Miller (Steinmetz) Schwear
Born:	21 APR 1911
Died:	20 APR 1981
Parents:	John F. & Lizzie (Miller) Steinmetz

Grave:	4-6
Name:	Eliza Ann (Fasnacht) White
Born:	1 JAN 1843
Died:	23 MAY 1905
Parents:	Fasnacht
Spouse:	Peter M. White
Notes:	

Grave:	4-3
Name:	Richard Samuel Schwear, Sr.
Born:	12 AUG 1912
Died:	18 SEP 1961
Parents:	Samuel & Mary (Stohler) Schwear
Notes:	

SMITH

RALPH M. APR 2 1911 JULY 3 1984

FRANCES P. FEB 2 1928 APR 27 2003

	4-2
	Frances P. (Peters) Smith
	2 FEB 1928
	27 APR 2003
	Milo & Virginia () Peters

Grave:	4-1
Name:	Ralph N. Smith
Born:	2 APR 1911
Died:	3 JUL 1984
Parents:	Jacob & Sallie (Moyer) Smith
Notes:	

Grave:	4-5
Name:	Peter M. White
Born:	13 SEP 1835
Died:	26 DEC 1921
Parents:	John & Rachel (Mosser) Weit/White
Spouse:	Eliza Ann (Fasnacht) White
Notes:	Peter was baptized at Muddy Creek Lutheran Church on 15 MAY 1836.

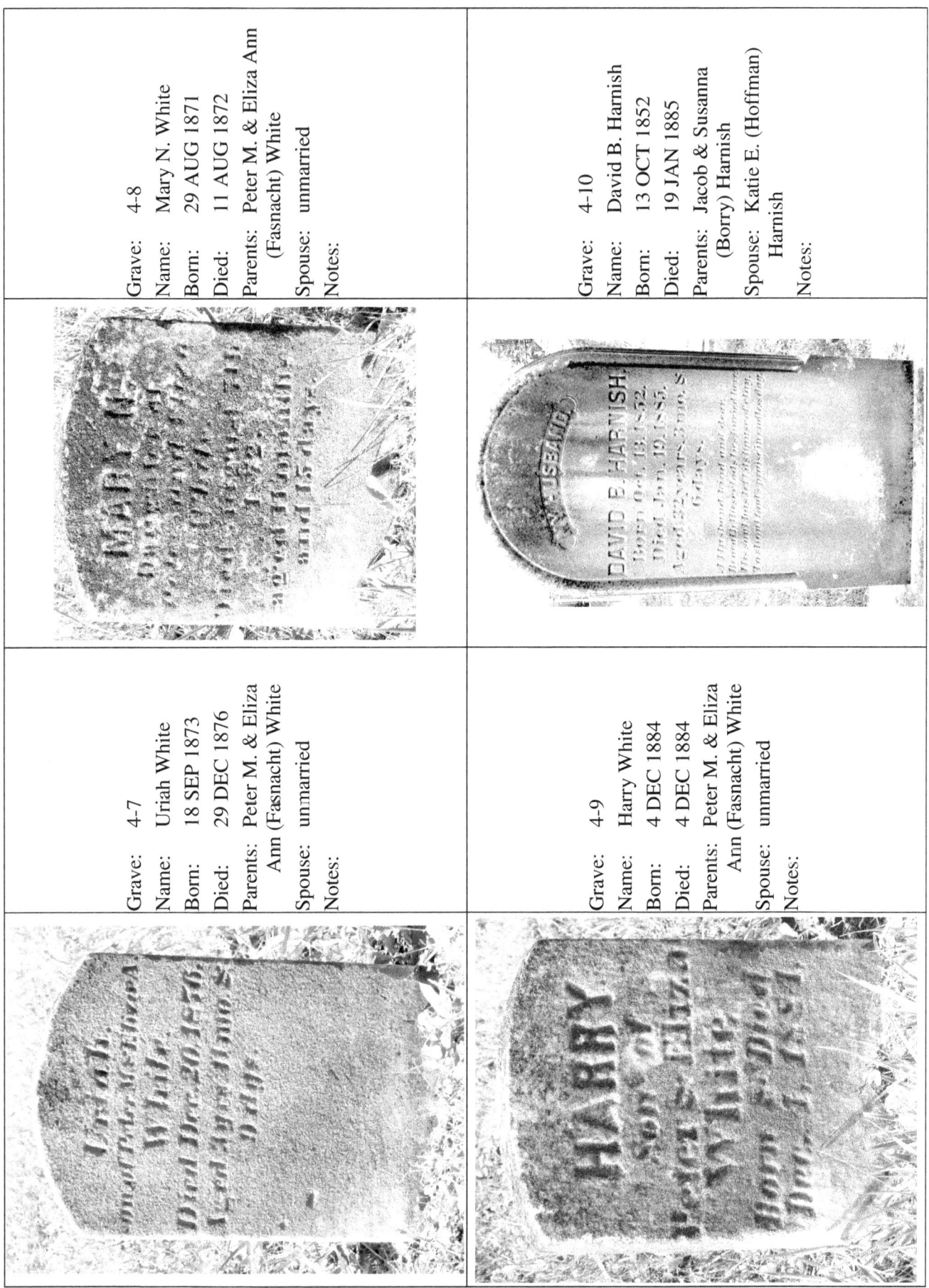

Grave: 4-8
Name: Mary N. White
Born: 29 AUG 1871
Died: 11 AUG 1872
Parents: Peter M. & Eliza Ann (Fasnacht) White
Spouse: unmarried
Notes:

Grave: 4-10
Name: David B. Harnish
Born: 13 OCT 1852
Died: 19 JAN 1885
Parents: Jacob & Susanna (Borry) Harnish
Spouse: Katie E. (Hoffman) Harnish
Notes:

Grave: 4-7
Name: Uriah White
Born: 18 SEP 1873
Died: 29 DEC 1876
Parents: Peter M. & Eliza Ann (Fasnacht) White
Spouse: unmarried
Notes:

Grave: 4-9
Name: Harry White
Born: 4 DEC 1884
Died: 4 DEC 1884
Parents: Peter M. & Eliza Ann (Fasnacht) White
Spouse: unmarried
Notes:

Grave: 4-12
Name: I. T.
Born:
Died:
Parents:
Spouse:
Notes: Very small stone with
initials.

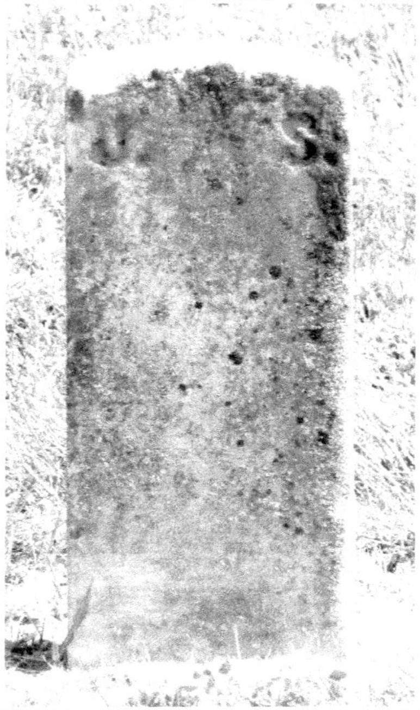

Grave: 4-14
Name: J. S.
Born:
Died:
Parents:
Spouse:
Notes:

Grave: 4-11
Name: Howard H. Harnish
Born: 30 SEP 1882
Died: 3 OCT 1882
Parents: David B. & Katie E.
(Hoffman) Harnish
Spouse: unmarried
Notes:

Grave: 4-13
Name: A. L.
Born:
Died:
Parents:
Spouse:
Notes:

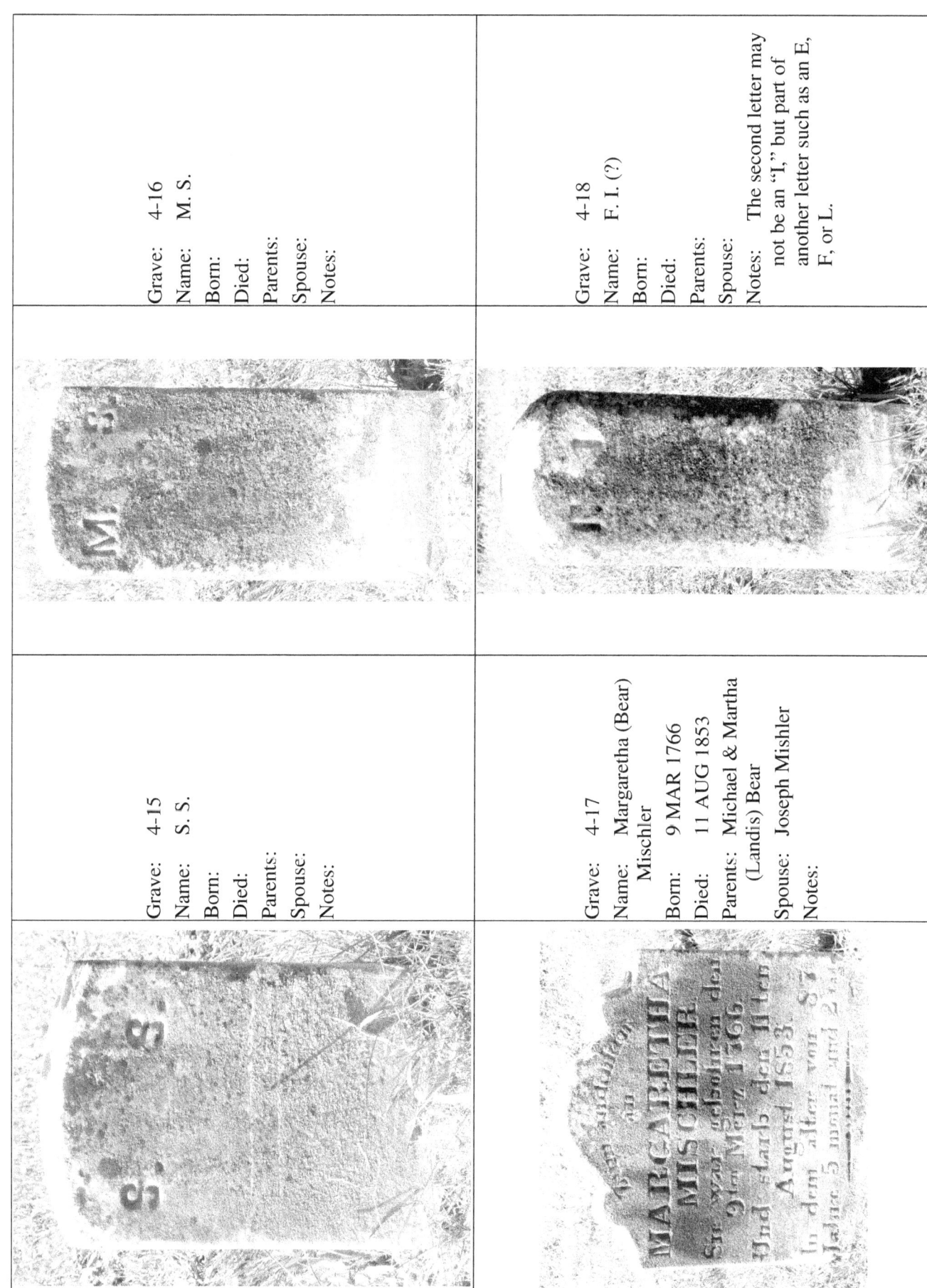

Grave: 4-16
Name: M. S.
Born:
Died:
Parents:
Spouse:
Notes:

Grave: 4-18
Name: F. I. (?)
Born:
Died:
Parents:
Spouse:
Notes: The second letter may not be an "I," but part of another letter such as an E, F, or L.

Grave: 4-15
Name: S. S.
Born:
Died:
Parents:
Spouse:
Notes:

Grave: 4-17
Name: Margaretha (Bear) Mischler
Born: 9 MAR 1766
Died: 11 AUG 1853
Parents: Michael & Martha (Landis) Bear
Spouse: Joseph Mishler
Notes:

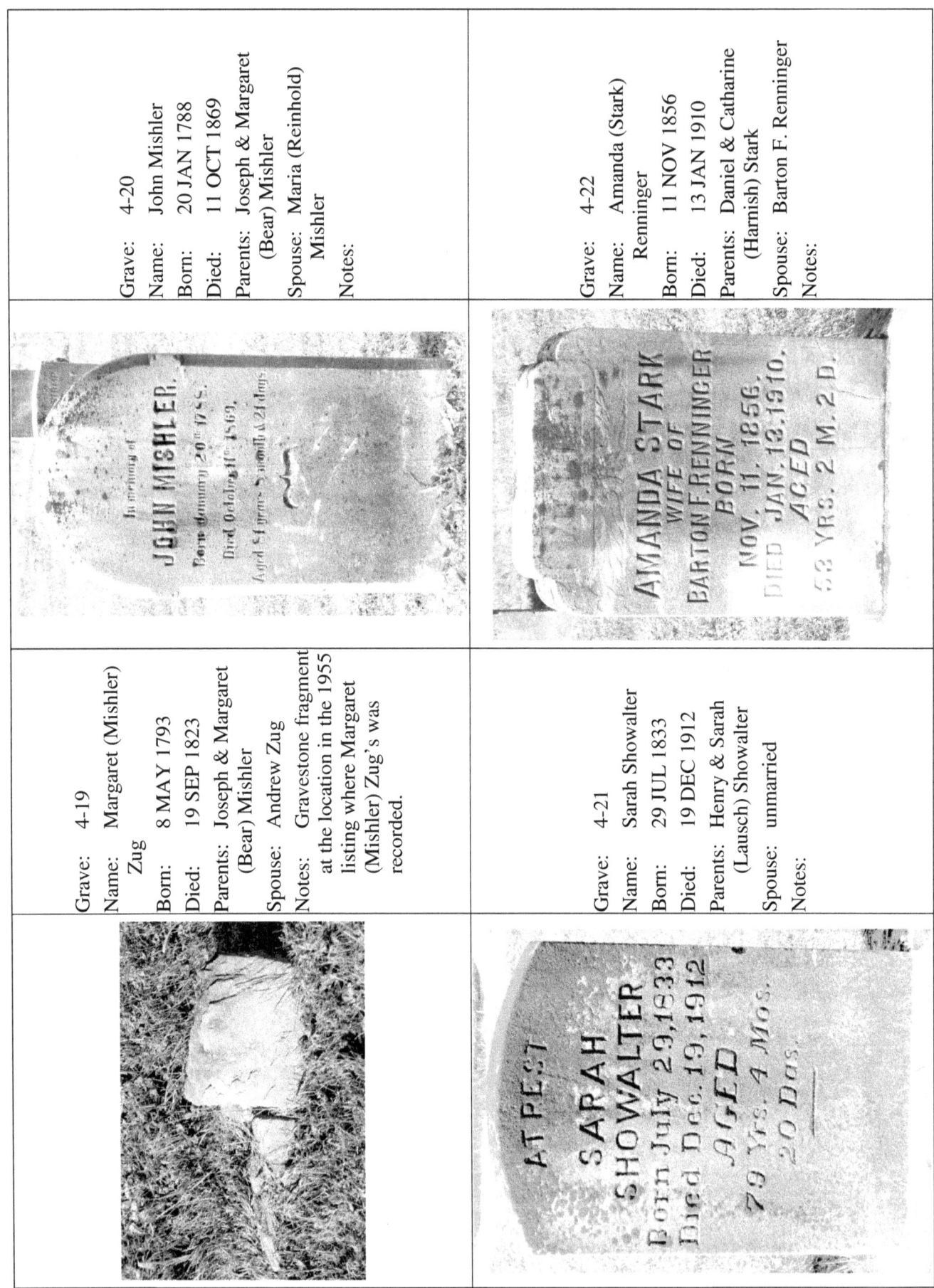

Grave: 4-20	**Grave:** 4-22
Name: John Mishler	**Name:** Amanda (Stark) Renninger
Born: 20 JAN 1788	**Born:** 11 NOV 1856
Died: 11 OCT 1869	**Died:** 13 JAN 1910
Parents: Joseph & Margaret (Bear) Mishler	**Parents:** Daniel & Catharine (Harnish) Stark
Spouse: Maria (Reinhold) Mishler	**Spouse:** Barton F. Renninger
Notes:	**Notes:**
Grave: 4-19	**Grave:** 4-21
Name: Margaret (Mishler) Zug	**Name:** Sarah Showalter
Born: 8 MAY 1793	**Born:** 29 JUL 1833
Died: 19 SEP 1823	**Died:** 19 DEC 1912
Parents: Joseph & Margaret (Bear) Mishler	**Parents:** Henry & Sarah (Lausch) Showalter
Spouse: Andrew Zug	**Spouse:** unmarried
Notes: Gravestone fragment at the location in the 1955 listing where Margaret (Mishler) Zug's was recorded.	**Notes:**

36

Grave:	4-24
Name:	Charles Renninger
Born:	5 OCT 1889
Died:	13 OCT 1889
Parents:	Barton F. & Amanda (Stark) Renninger
Spouse:	unmarried
Notes:	

Grave:	5-1
Name:	David Petticoffer
Born:	30 JAN 1838
Died:	26 MAR 1900
Parents:	John & Mary (Wise) Petticoffer

Grave:	5-2
Name:	Sarah (Lichty) Petticoffer
Born:	20 NOV 1837
Died:	27 JAN 1888
Parents:	John & Mary ( ) Lichty

Grave:	4-23
Name:	Maude Mable Renninger
Born:	5 JUN 1892
Died:	1 JUL 1892
Parents:	Barton F. & Amanda (Stark) Renninger
Spouse:	unmarried
Notes:	

David and Sarah (Lichty) Petticoffer

Poem below Sarah's inscription:

Farewell my husband and children all.

Death has tendered me a solemn call,

On earth I shall no more see you,

If you wish me again to see

Prepare for death and follow me.

Probably the maker of the Petticoffer monument

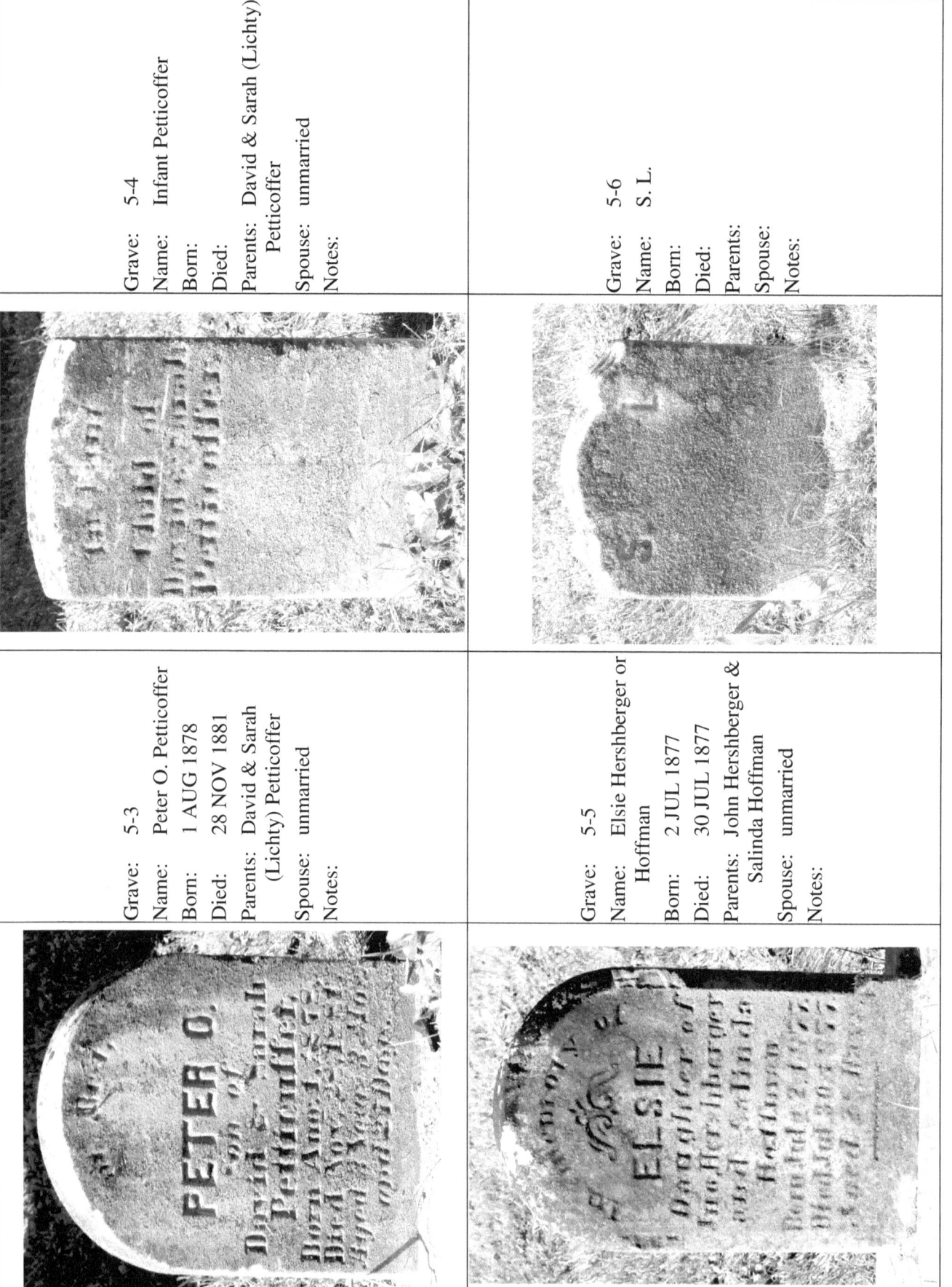

Grave: 5-4
Name: Infant Petticoffer
Born:
Died:
Parents: David & Sarah (Lichty) Petticoffer
Spouse: unmarried
Notes:

Grave: 5-6
Name: S. L.
Born:
Died:
Parents:
Spouse:
Notes:

Grave: 5-3
Name: Peter O. Petticoffer
Born: 1 AUG 1878
Died: 28 NOV 1881
Parents: David & Sarah (Lichty) Petticoffer
Spouse: unmarried
Notes:

Grave: 5-5
Name: Elsie Hershberger or Hoffman
Born: 2 JUL 1877
Died: 30 JUL 1877
Parents: John Hershberger & Salinda Hoffman
Spouse: unmarried
Notes:

Grave: 5-8 Name: H. W. Born: Died: Parents: Spouse: Notes:	Grave: 5-10 Name: Juliana (Walter) Bär [Bear] Born: 14 OCT 1753 Died: 14 AUG 1844 Parents: Henry & Charlotte () Walter Spouse: Abraham Bear Notes:
Grave: 5-7 Name: H. L. Born: Died: Parents: Spouse: Notes:	Grave: 5-9 Name: Abraham Bare [Bear] Born: 30 SEP 1747 Died: 31 MAR 1817 Parents: Michael & Magdalena () Bear Spouse: Juliana (Walter) Bear Notes:

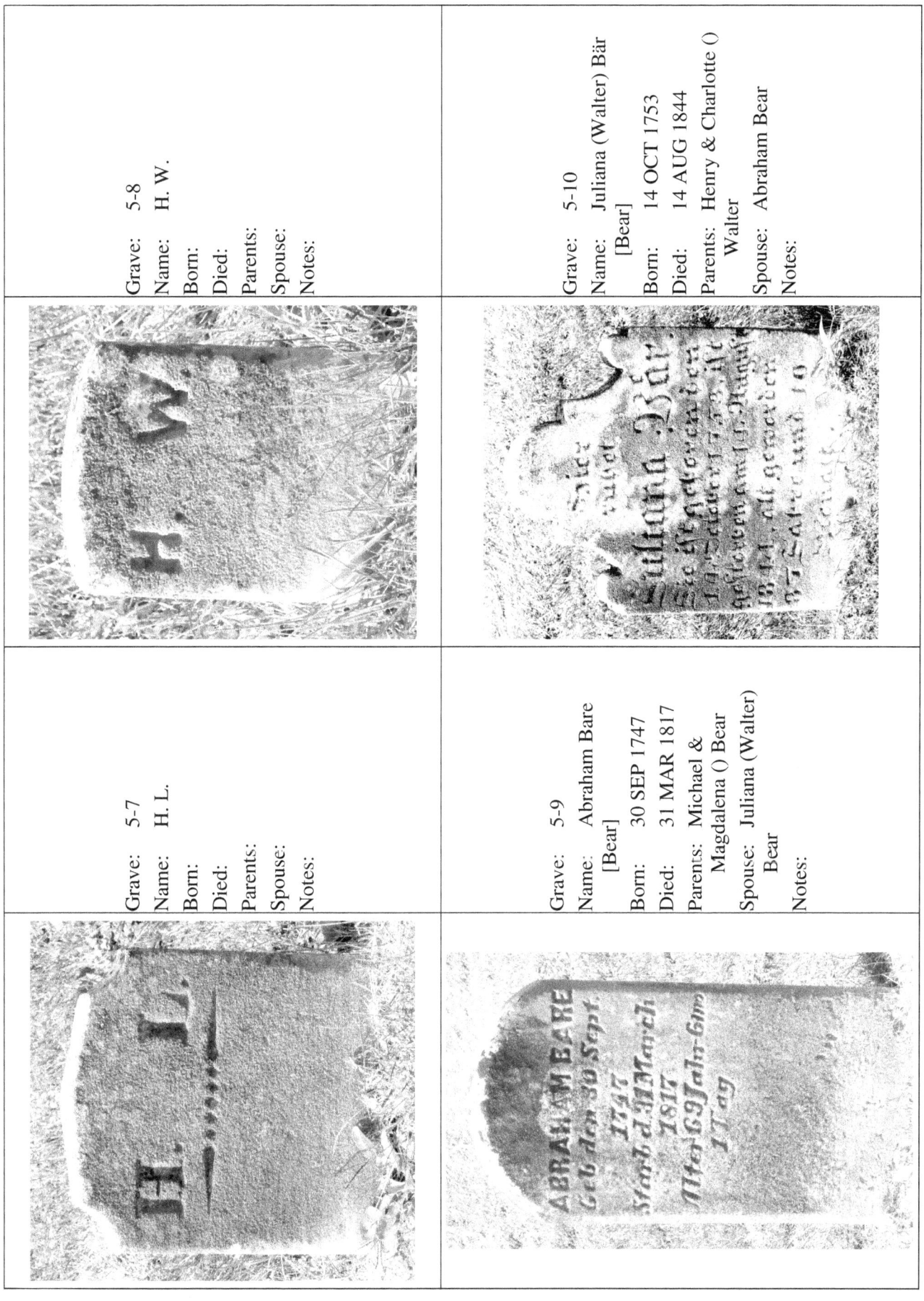

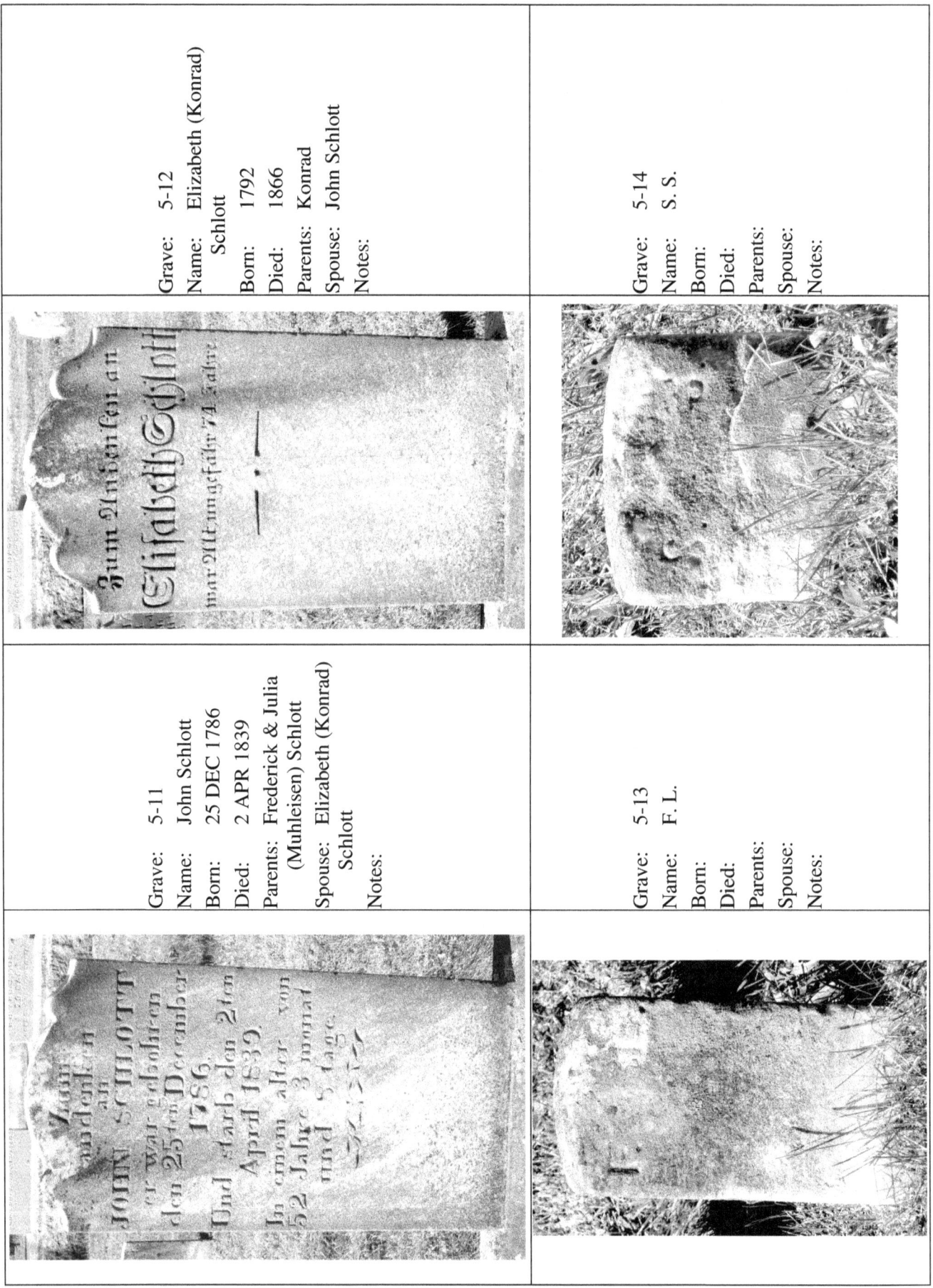

Grave: 5-12
Name: Elizabeth (Konrad) Schlott
Born: 1792
Died: 1866
Parents: Konrad
Spouse: John Schlott
Notes:

Grave: 5-14
Name: S. S.
Born:
Died:
Parents:
Spouse:
Notes:

Grave: 5-11
Name: John Schlott
Born: 25 DEC 1786
Died: 2 APR 1839
Parents: Frederick & Julia (Muhleisen) Schlott
Spouse: Elizabeth (Konrad) Schlott
Notes:

Grave: 5-13
Name: F. L.
Born:
Died:
Parents:
Spouse:
Notes:

Grave: 5-16
Name: Peter Eberly
Born: 26 OCT 1752
Died: MAR 1826
Parents: Peter & Catharine (Newcomer) Eberly
Spouse: Anna (Flickinger) Eberly
Notes:

Grave: 5-18
Name: ---
Born:
Died:
Parents:
Spouse:
Notes: Slate stone with front surface flaked off.

Grave: 5-15
Name: Anna (Flickinger) Eberly
Born: about 1754
Died: 1807
Parents: Joseph & Esther ( ) Flickinger
Spouse: Peter Eberly
Notes:

Grave: 5-17
Name: M. G.
Born:
Died:
Parents:
Spouse:
Notes:

Grave: 5-20 Name: Samuel Showalter Born: 15 OCT 1834 Died: 23 DEC 1868 Parents: Samuel & Maria (Eberly) Showalter Spouse: unmarried Notes:	Grave: 5-22 Name: Maria (Eberly) Showalter Born: 19 JUN 1807 Died: 20 FEB 1883 Parents: Samuel & Catharine (Bear) Eberly Spouse: Samuel Showalter Notes: Stone is flat on the ground.
Grave: 5-19 Name: Catharine (Bear) Eberly Born: 25 APR 1783 Died: 8 AUG 1869 Parents: Abraham & Juliana (Walter) Bear Spouse: Samuel Eberly Notes:	Grave: 5-21 Name: -- Born: Died: Parents: Spouse: Notes: Remains of slate stone with front surface flaked off.

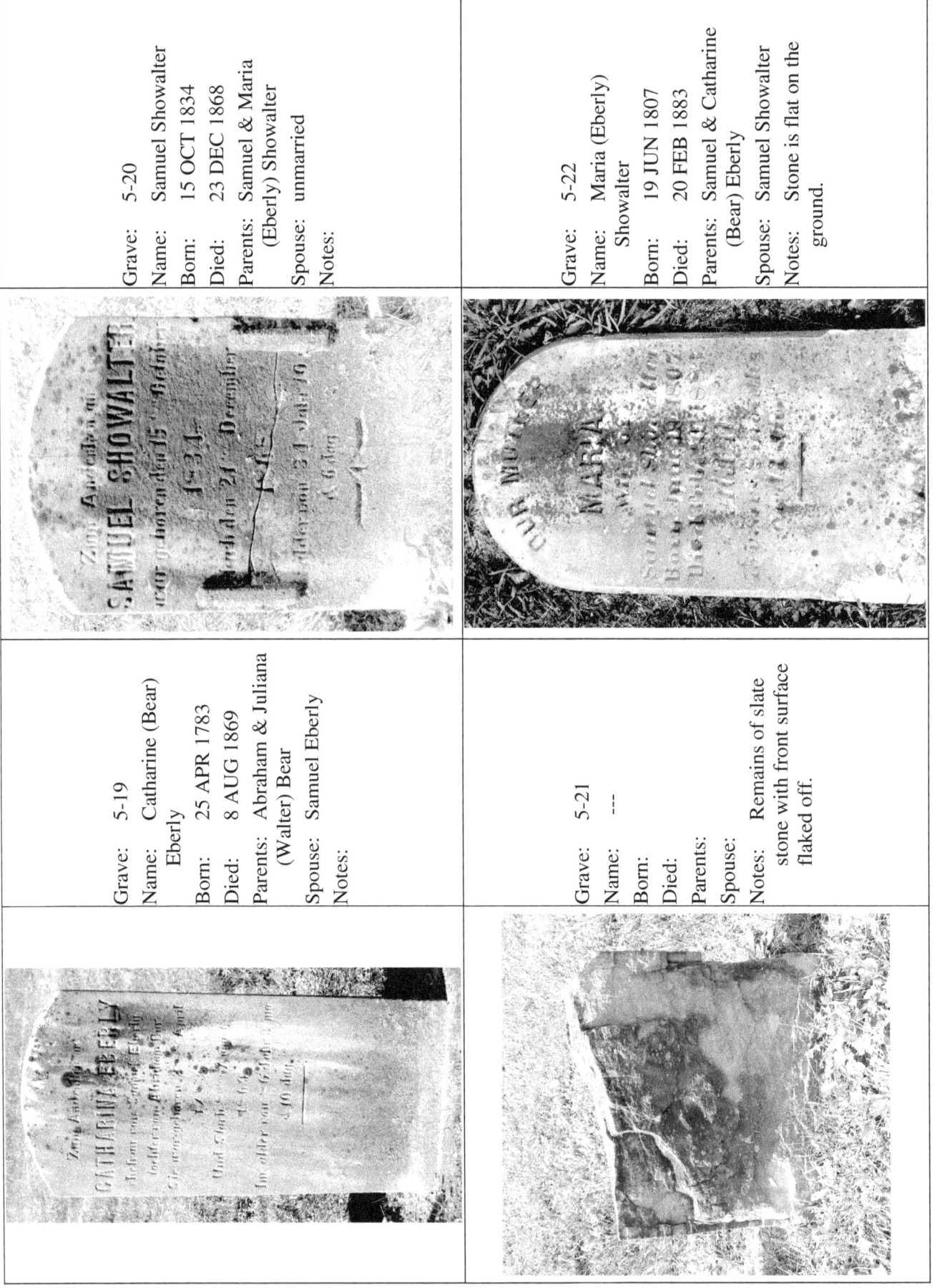

Grave: 5-24 Name: Peter Eberly Born: 15 DEC 1815 Died: 1 APR 1901 Parents: Samuel & Catharine (Bear) Eberly Spouse: Susanna (Kling) Eberly Notes:	Grave: 6-1 Name: Abraham Turner Born: AUG 1849 Died: 23 FEB 1909 Parents: Abraham & Catharine (Leisey) Turner Spouse: Emma (Sweigart) Turner Notes: Surname was usually spelled "Turner."

Grave: 5-23 Name: Henry Wolfskill Born: 28 APR 1827 Died: 9 JUN 1886 Parents: Henry & Mary (Killian) Wolfskill Spouse: Lydia (Showalter) Wolfskill Notes:	Grave: 5-25 Name: Susanna (Kling) Eberly Born: 18 FEB 1821 Died: 15 FEB 1894 Parents: Kling Spouse: Peter Eberly Notes:

Grave: 6-3
Name: Charles Turnner
Born: 10 MAR 1879
Died: 3 SEP 1882
Parents: Abraham & Emma
(Sweigart) Turner
Spouse: unmarried
Notes: Surname was usually
spelled "Turner."

Grave: 6-5
Name: Emma (Sweigart)
Turner
Born: 23 JUL 1855
Died: 25 MAY 1904
Parents: Samuel & Elizabeth
(Sweigart) Sweigart
Spouse: Abraham Turner
Notes: Surname was usually
spelled "Turner."

Grave: 6-2
Name: Stella Turnner
Born: 3 NOV 1895
Died: 3 NOV 1895
Parents: Abraham & Emma
(Sweigart) Turner
Spouse: unmarried
Notes: Surname was
usually spelled "Turner."

Grave: 6-4
Name: Ida Mengel Turner
Born: 20 APR 1876
Died: 22 JUL 1896
Parents: Abraham & Emma
(Sweigart) Turner
Spouse: unmarried
Notes:

44

Grave:	6-7	Grave:	6-9
Name:	Lizzie (Sweigart) Ludwig	Name:	Amos Ludwig
Born:	4 MAY 1854	Born:	4 MAY 1888
Died:	16 APR 1935	Died:	23 APR 1889
Parents:	Samuel & Elizabeth (Sweigart) Sweigart	Grave:	6-10
Spouse:	Samuel B. Ludwig	Name:	Daniel Ludwig
Notes:		Born:	14 FEB 1891
		Died:	20 APR 1891
		Parents:	Samuel & Lizzie (Sweigart) Ludwig
		Notes:	

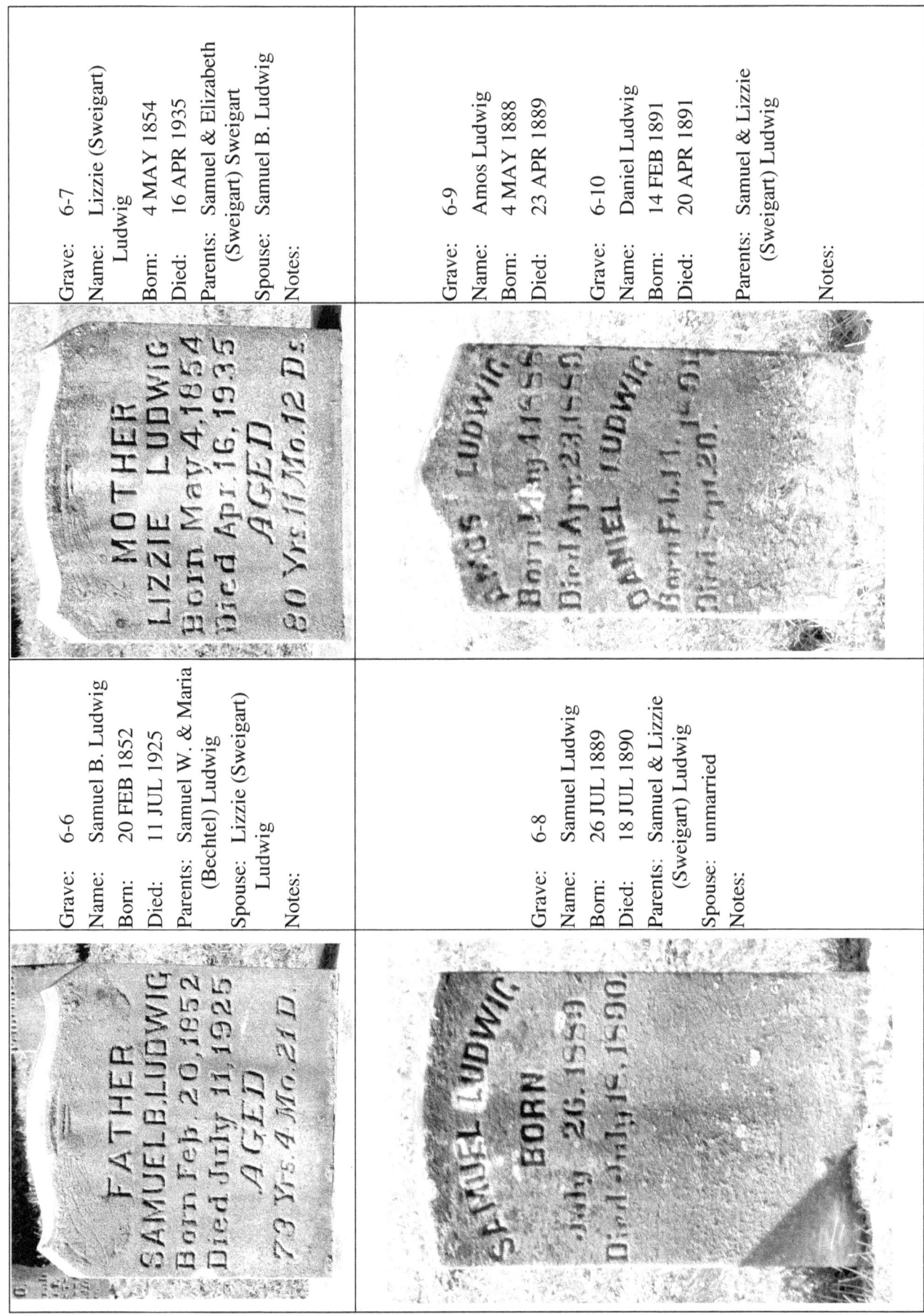

Grave:	6-6	Grave:	6-8
Name:	Samuel B. Ludwig	Name:	Samuel Ludwig
Born:	20 FEB 1852	Born:	26 JUL 1889
Died:	11 JUL 1925	Died:	18 JUL 1890
Parents:	Samuel W. & Maria (Bechtel) Ludwig	Parents:	Samuel & Lizzie (Sweigart) Ludwig
Spouse:	Lizzie (Sweigart) Ludwig	Spouse:	unmarried
Notes:		Notes:	

Grave: 6-13
Name: G. S.
Born:
Died:
Parents:
Spouse:
Notes:

Grave: 6-15
Name: ---
Born:
Died:
Parents:
Spouse:
Notes: Small stone with no writing

Grave: 6-11
Name: Anna Ludwig
Born: 17 FEB 1875
Died: 14 JAN 1876
Grave: 6-12
Name: Ida Ludwig
Born: 1 DEC 1876
Died: 5 SEP 1877
Parents: Samuel & Lizzie (Sweigart) Ludwig
Notes:

Grave: 6-14
Name: M. M. R.
Born:
Died:
Parents:
Spouse:
Notes:

Grave: 6-17
Name: Jacob Harnish
Born: 6 FEB 1793
Died: 9 NOV 1829
Parents: Jacob & Magdalena
(Wenrich) Harnish
Spouse: Anna (Gockley)
Harnish
Notes:

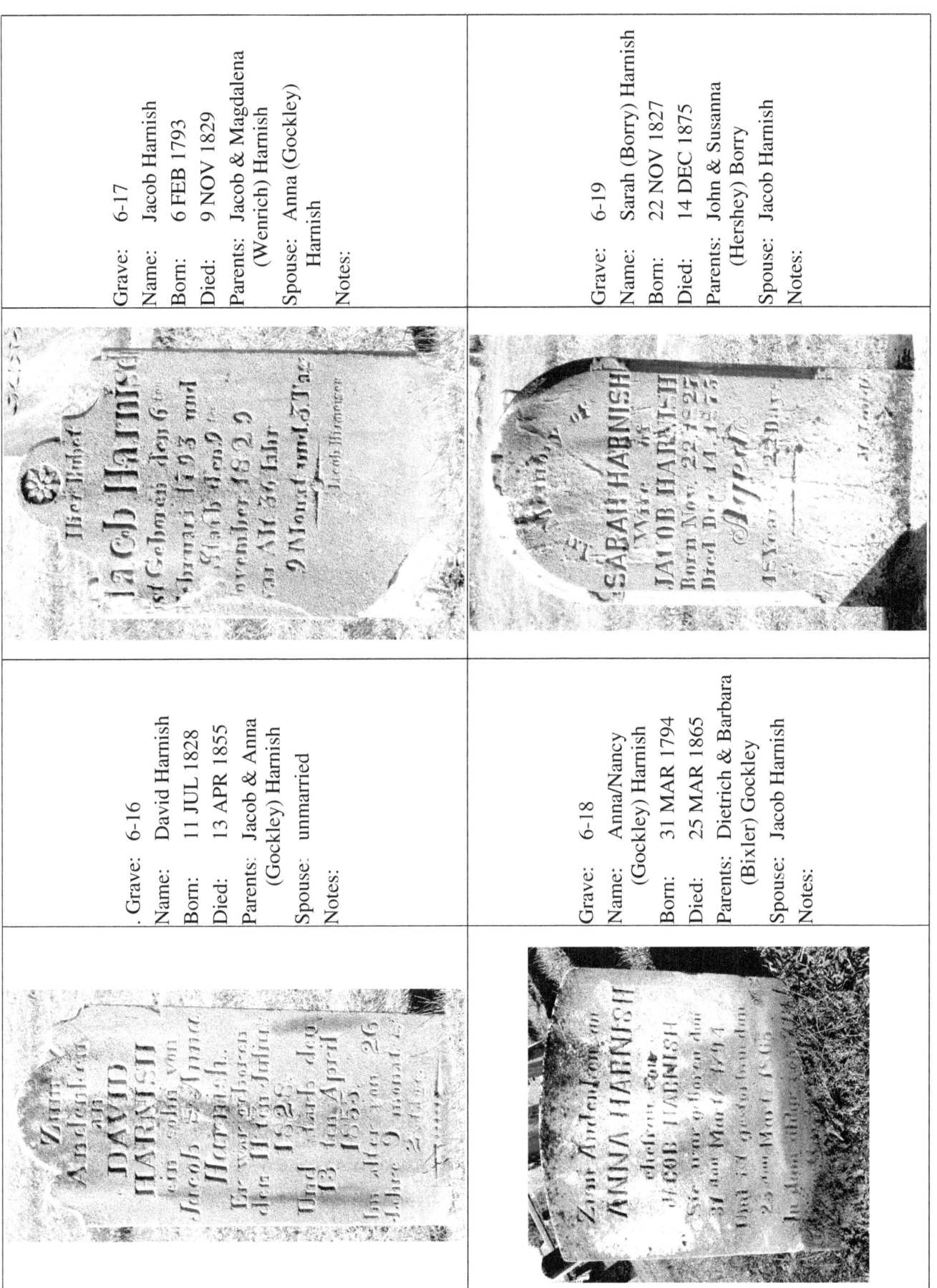

Grave: 6-19
Name: Sarah (Borry) Harnish
Born: 22 NOV 1827
Died: 14 DEC 1875
Parents: John & Susanna
(Hershey) Borry
Spouse: Jacob Harnish
Notes:

Grave: 6-16
Name: David Harnish
Born: 11 JUL 1828
Died: 13 APR 1855
Parents: Jacob & Anna
(Gockley) Harnish
Spouse: unmarried
Notes:

Grave: 6-18
Name: Anna/Nancy
(Gockley) Harnish
Born: 31 MAR 1794
Died: 25 MAR 1865
Parents: Dietrich & Barbara
(Bixler) Gockley
Spouse: Jacob Harnish
Notes:

Grave: 6-21 Name: Henry Bear Born: 21 OCT 1785 Died: 14 FEB 1837 Parents: Abraham & Juliana (Walter) Bear Spouse: Catharine (Gockley) Bear Notes:	Grave: 6-23 Name: William G. Kerling Born: 13 FEB 1843 Died: 5 JUL 1865 Parents: James & Catharine (Gockley) Kerling Spouse: unmarried Notes:
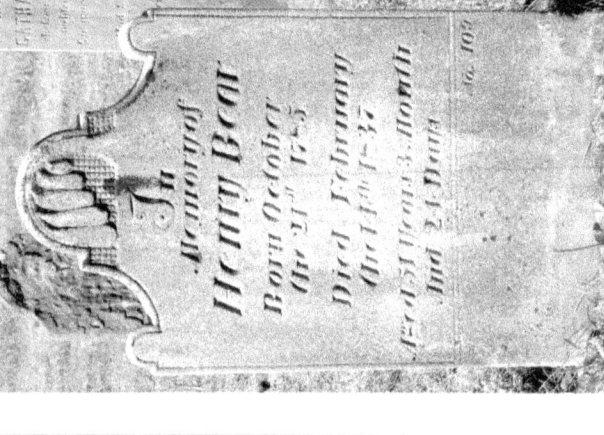	
Grave: 6-20 Name: Jacob Harnish Born: 4 NOV 1825 Died: 1 OCT 1879 Parents: Jacob & Anna (Gockley) Harnish Spouse: Sarah (Borry) Harnish Notes:	Grave: 6-22 Name: Catharine (Gockley) [Bear] Kerling Born: 12 APR 1799 Died: 9 OCT 1857 Parents: Dietrich & Barbara (Bixler) Gockley Spouse: (1) Henry Bear (2) James Kerling Notes: James and Catharine were married on 28 SEP 1837 by Rev. J. J. Strine.
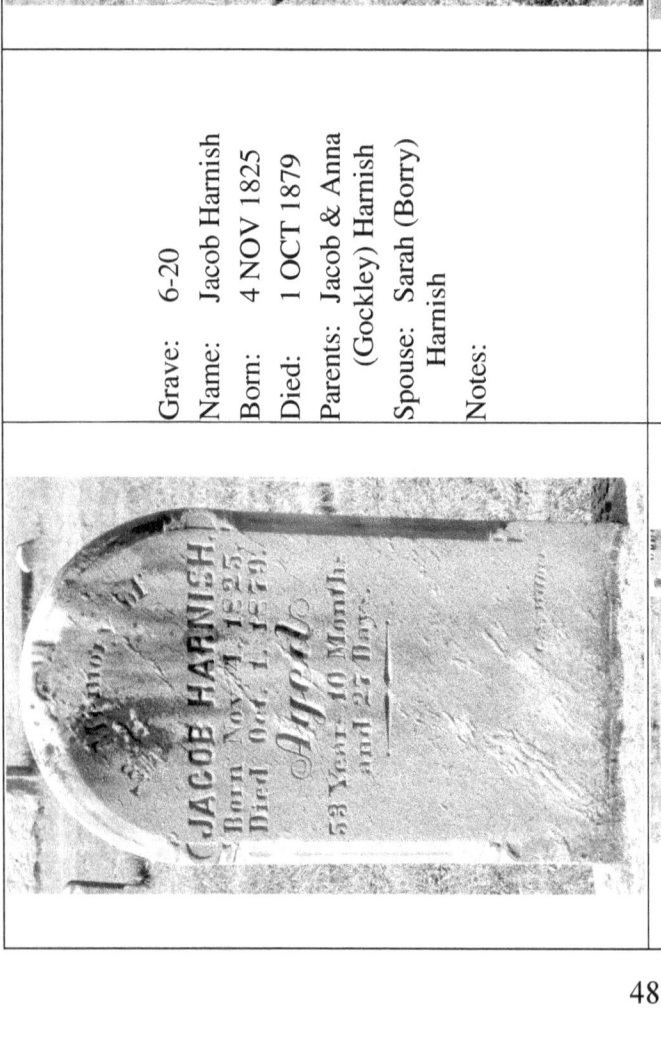	

Grave: 6-25 Name: Henry A. Kerling Born: 28 OCT 1864 Died: 14 JUL 1866 Parents: Lewis C. & Margaret S. (Ammon) Kerling Spouse: unmarried Notes:	Grave: 6-27 Name: Christian Showalter Born: 3 DEC 1853 Died: 17 APR 1934 Parents: John & Lydia (Hoffard) Showalter Spouse: (1) Addie (Harnish) Showalter (2) Mary (Smith) Showalter Notes: Christian married Mary Smith on 28 OCT 1893 at Denver, PA.

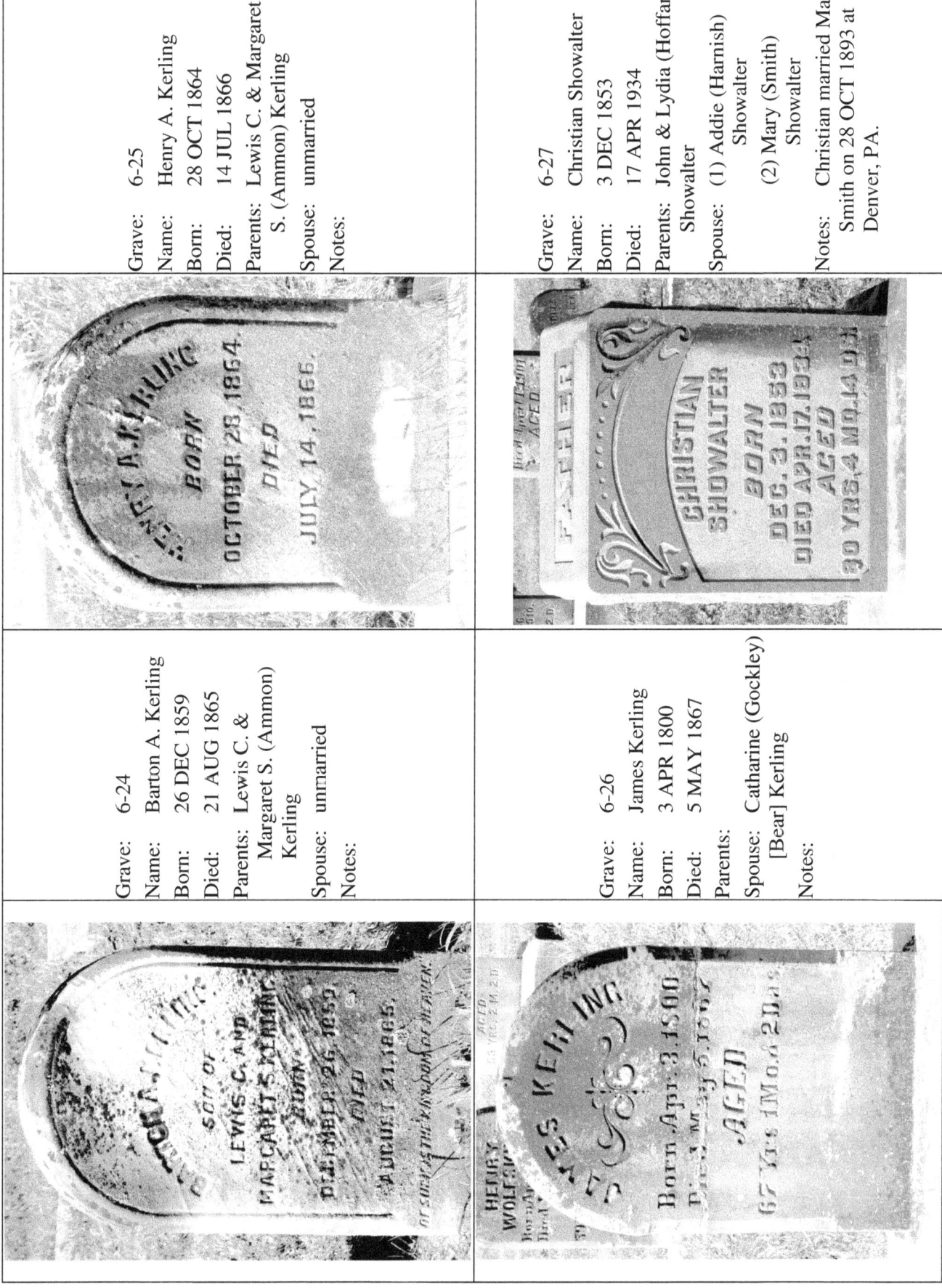

Grave: 6-24 Name: Barton A. Kerling Born: 26 DEC 1859 Died: 21 AUG 1865 Parents: Lewis C. & Margaret S. (Ammon) Kerling Spouse: unmarried Notes:	Grave: 6-26 Name: James Kerling Born: 3 APR 1800 Died: 5 MAY 1867 Parents: Spouse: Catharine (Gockley) [Bear] Kerling Notes:

Grave: 6-29
Name: Laura Mamie
       Showalter
 	
Born: 10 DEC 1869
Died: 30 AUG 1870
Parents: Christian & Addie
       (Harnish) Showalter
Spouse: unmarried
Notes:
	Grave: 7-1
	Name: Oliver Lord
	
	Born: 16 MAY 1888
	Died: 4 MAY 1963
	Parents: Jonathan P. & Matilda
	       "Tilly" (Kachel) [Lutz] Lord
	Spouse: unmarried
	Notes:

Grave: 6-28
Name: Addie (Harnish)
       Showalter
 	
Born: 17 MAR 1854
Died: 1 AUG 1887
Parents: Jacob & Sallie
       (Borry) Harnish
Spouse: Christian Showalter
Notes:
	Grave: 6-30
	Name: Jennie Mabel
	       Showalter
	
	Born: 2 OCT 1880
	Died: 26 APR 1881
	Parents: Christian & Addie
	       (Harnish) Showalter
	Spouse: unmarried
	Notes:

Grave: 7-3
Name: F. B.
Born:
Died:
Parents:
Spouse:
Notes:

Grave: 7-5
Name: J. G.
Born:
Died:
Parents:
Spouse:
Notes:

Grave: 7-2
Name: L. G.
Born:
Died:
Parents:
Spouse:
Notes:

Grave: 7-4
Name: H. B.
Born:
Died:
Parents:
Spouse:
Notes:

Grave: 7-7	Grave: 7-9
Name: Daniel Stark	Name: Barbara (Bixler) Gockley
Born: 27 NOV 1817	Born: 27 MAY 1764
Died: 6 APR 1894	Died: 27 MAR 1850
Parents: Samuel & Susanna (Sherb) Stark	Parents: Abraham & Anna ( ) Bixler
Spouse: (1) Amanda (Rupp) Stark	Spouse: Dietrich Gockley
(2) Catharine (Harnish) Stark	Notes: Spelled "Gackly" on gravestone.
Notes:	

Grave: 7-6	Grave: 7-8
Name: Josiah Stark	Name: Dietrich Gockley
Born: 7 AUG 1841	Born: 3 SEP 1767
Died: 9 SEP 1885	Died: 13 JUN 1828
Parents: Daniel & Catharine (Harnish) Stark	Parents: John Nicholas & Magdalena (Eberly) Gockley
Spouse: unmarried	Spouse: Barbara (Bixler) Gockley
Notes:	Notes: Spelled "Gackli" on gravestone.

Grave: 7-11 Name: Mary (Lied) Gockley Born: 14 JAN 1805 Died: 30 MAR 1883 Parents: George & Margaret (Glaze) Lied Spouse: John Gockley Notes:	Grave: 7-13 Name: Abraham Gackli Born: 21 JUL 1796 Died: 13 SEP 1839 Parents: Dietrich & Barbara (Bixler) Gockley Spouse: Catharine (Bear) Gockley Notes: Surname was usually spelled "Gockley."

Grave: 7-10 Name: John Gockley Born: 14 OCT 1792 Died: 5 AUG 1882 Parents: Dietrich & Barbara (Bixler) Gockley Spouse: Mary (Lied) Gockley Notes:	Grave: 7-12 Name: David Gockley Born: 10 DEC 1828 Died: 22 SEP 1829 Parents: Abraham & Catharina (Bear) Gockley Spouse: unmarried Notes:

Grave: 7-15
Name: John Gockley
Born: 21 OCT 1859
Died: 28 JUN 1860
Parents: Levi & Maria (Lutz)
         Gockley
Spouse: unmarried
Notes:
	Grave: 7-17
	Name: Catharine (Harnish)
	         Stark
	Born: 31 JUL 1818
	Died: 19 SEP 1890
	Parents: Jacob & Nancy
	         (Gockley) Harnish
	Spouse: (1) John Zern
	         (2) Daniel Stark
	Notes:

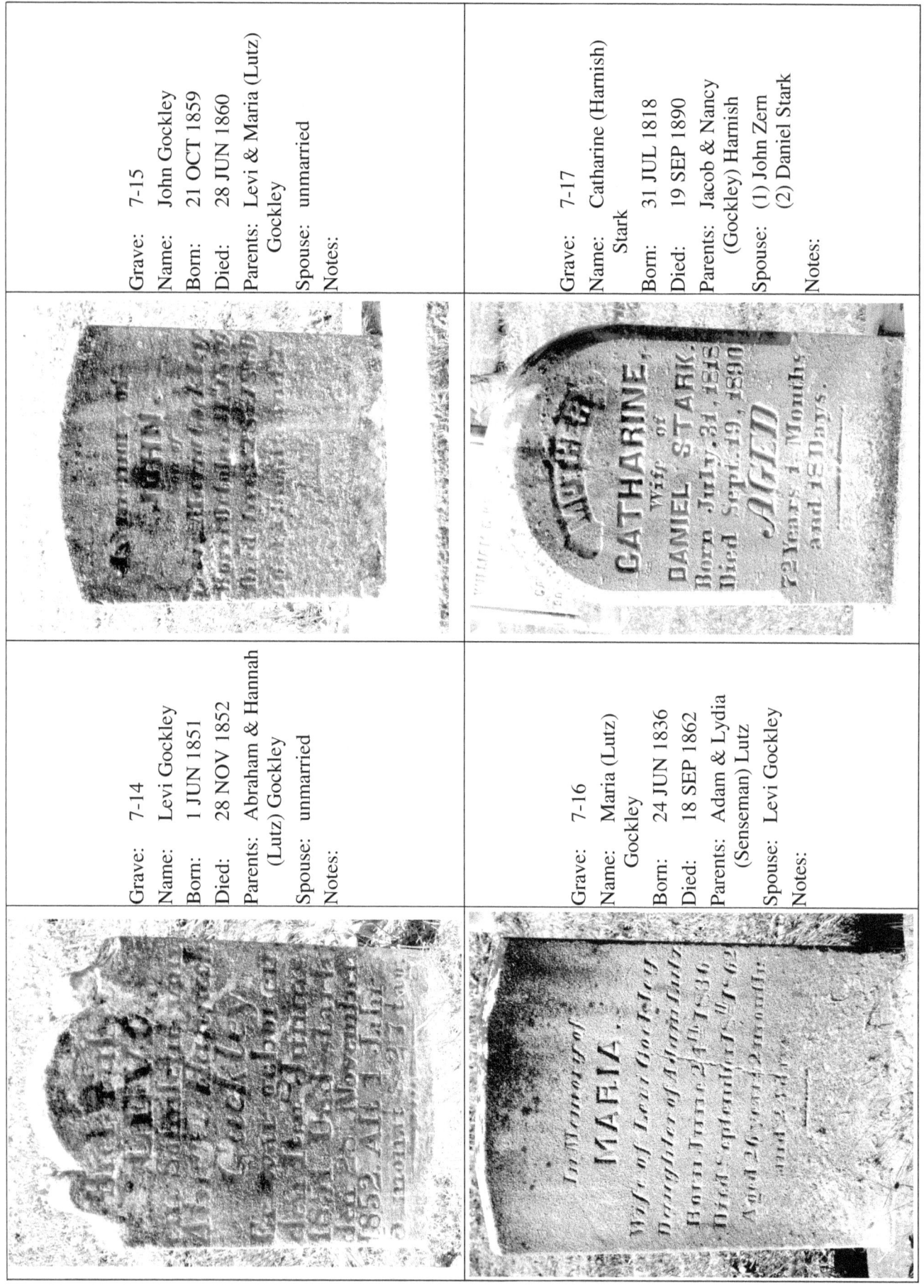

Grave: 7-14
Name: Levi Gockley
Born: 1 JUN 1851
Died: 28 NOV 1852
Parents: Abraham & Hannah
         (Lutz) Gockley
Spouse: unmarried
Notes:
	Grave: 7-16
	Name: Maria (Lutz)
	         Gockley
	Born: 24 JUN 1836
	Died: 18 SEP 1862
	Parents: Adam & Lydia
	         (Senseman) Lutz
	Spouse: Levi Gockley
	Notes:

Grave: 7-19 Name: Susanna Zern Born: 14 APR 1835 Died: 30 APR 1835 Parents: John & Catharine (Harnish) Zern Spouse: unmarried Notes:	Grave: 7-21 Name: Levi Harnish Born: 23 NOV 1850 Died: 5 JAN 1852 Parents: Jacob & Sarah (Borry) Harnish Spouse: unmarried Notes:

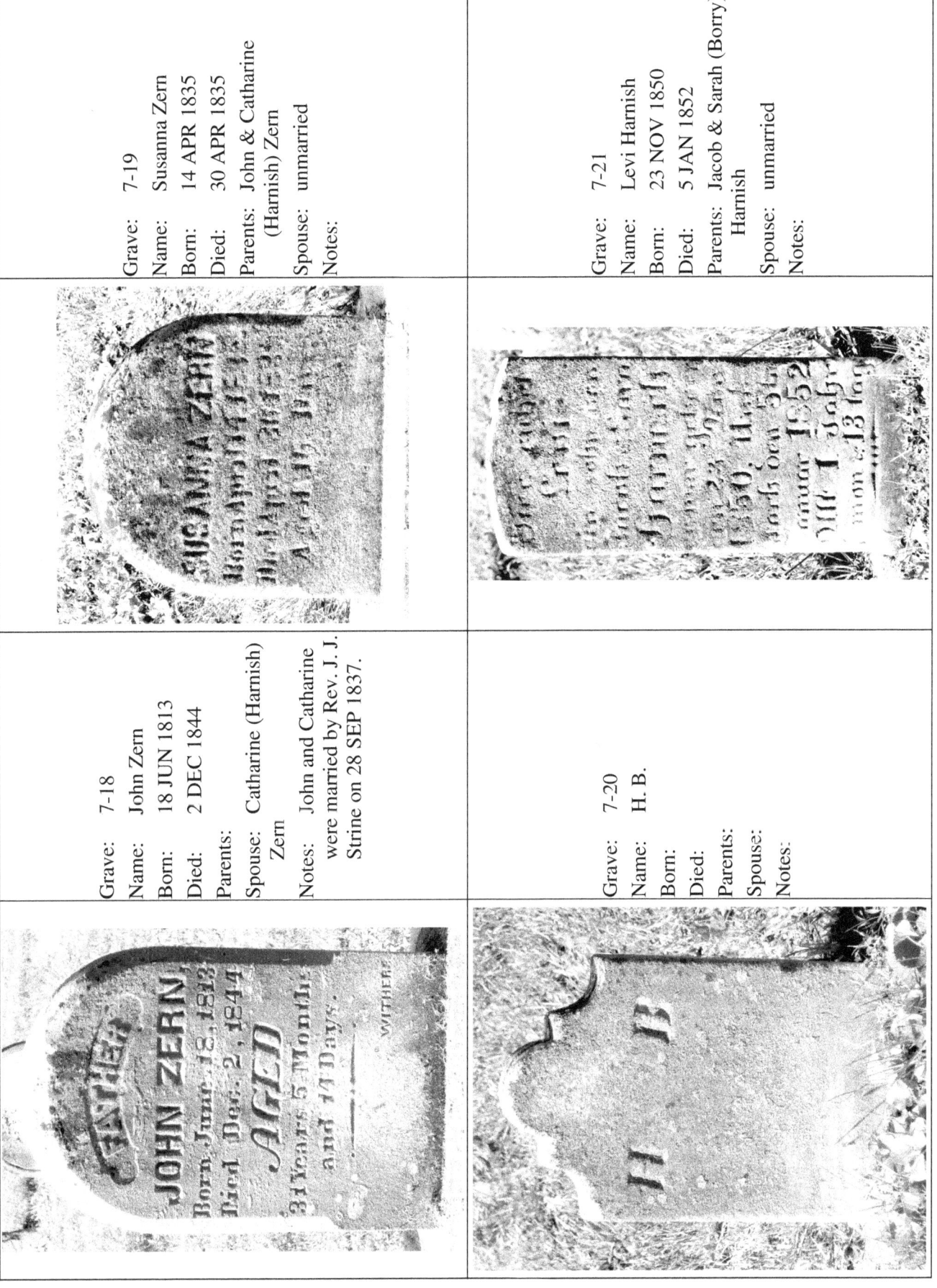

Grave: 7-18 Name: John Zern Born: 18 JUN 1813 Died: 2 DEC 1844 Parents: Spouse: Catharine (Harnish) Zern Notes: John and Catharine were married by Rev. J. J. Strine on 28 SEP 1837.	Grave: 7-20 Name: H. B. Born: Died: Parents: Spouse: Notes:

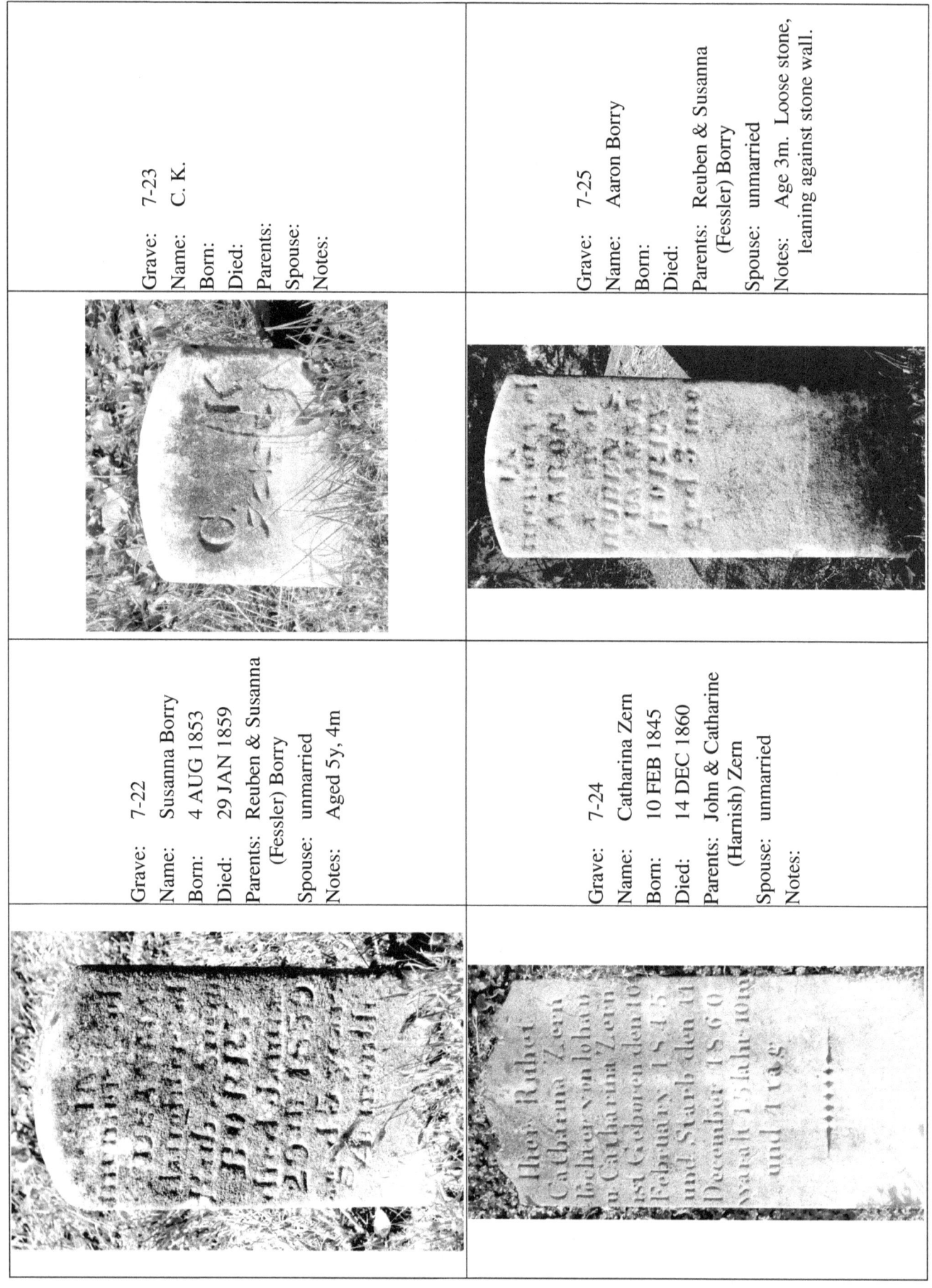

Grave: 7-23
Name: C. K.
Born:
Died:
Parents:
Spouse:
Notes:

Grave: 7-25
Name: Aaron Borry
Born:
Died:
Parents: Reuben & Susanna
(Fessler) Borry
Spouse: unmarried
Notes: Age 3m. Loose stone,
leaning against stone wall.

Grave: 7-22
Name: Susanna Borry
Born: 4 AUG 1853
Died: 29 JAN 1859
Parents: Reuben & Susanna
(Fessler) Borry
Spouse: unmarried
Notes: Aged 5y, 4m

Grave: 7-24
Name: Catharina Zern
Born: 10 FEB 1845
Died: 14 DEC 1860
Parents: John & Catharine
(Harnish) Zern
Spouse: unmarried
Notes:

Grave:	8-2	Grave:	8-4
Name:	Elizabeth "Eliza" (Lutz) Bixler	Name:	Tilly (Kachel) Lutz
Born:	13 JAN 1859	Born:	26 DEC 1856
Died:	30 JAN 1921	Died:	19 JUL 1914
Parents:	Daniel & Elizabeth (Macwate) Lutz	Parents:	Jacob & Louisa () Kachel
Spouse:	Jacob D. Bixler	Spouse:	William M. Lutz
Notes:		Notes:	After the death of William Lutz, Tilly married John P. Lord and was divorced in 1892, then married William Fessler in 1900.

Grave:	8-1	Grave:	8-3
Name:	Jacob D. Bixler	Name:	William M. Lutz
Born:	7 APR 1854	Born:	20 APR 1856
Died:	5 FEB 1934	Died:	15 NOV 1885
Parents:	Jacob & Lydia (Rupp) Bixler	Parents:	Daniel & Elizabeth (Macwate) Lutz
Spouse:	Elizabeth (Lutz) Bixler	Spouse:	Tilly (Kachel) Lutz
Notes:		Notes:	

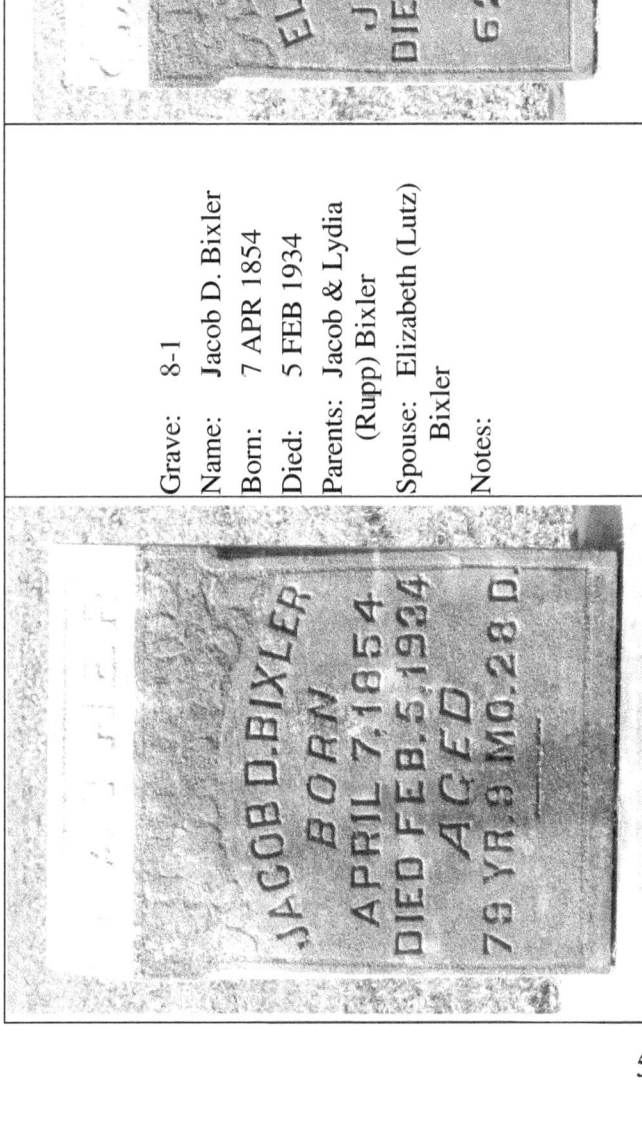

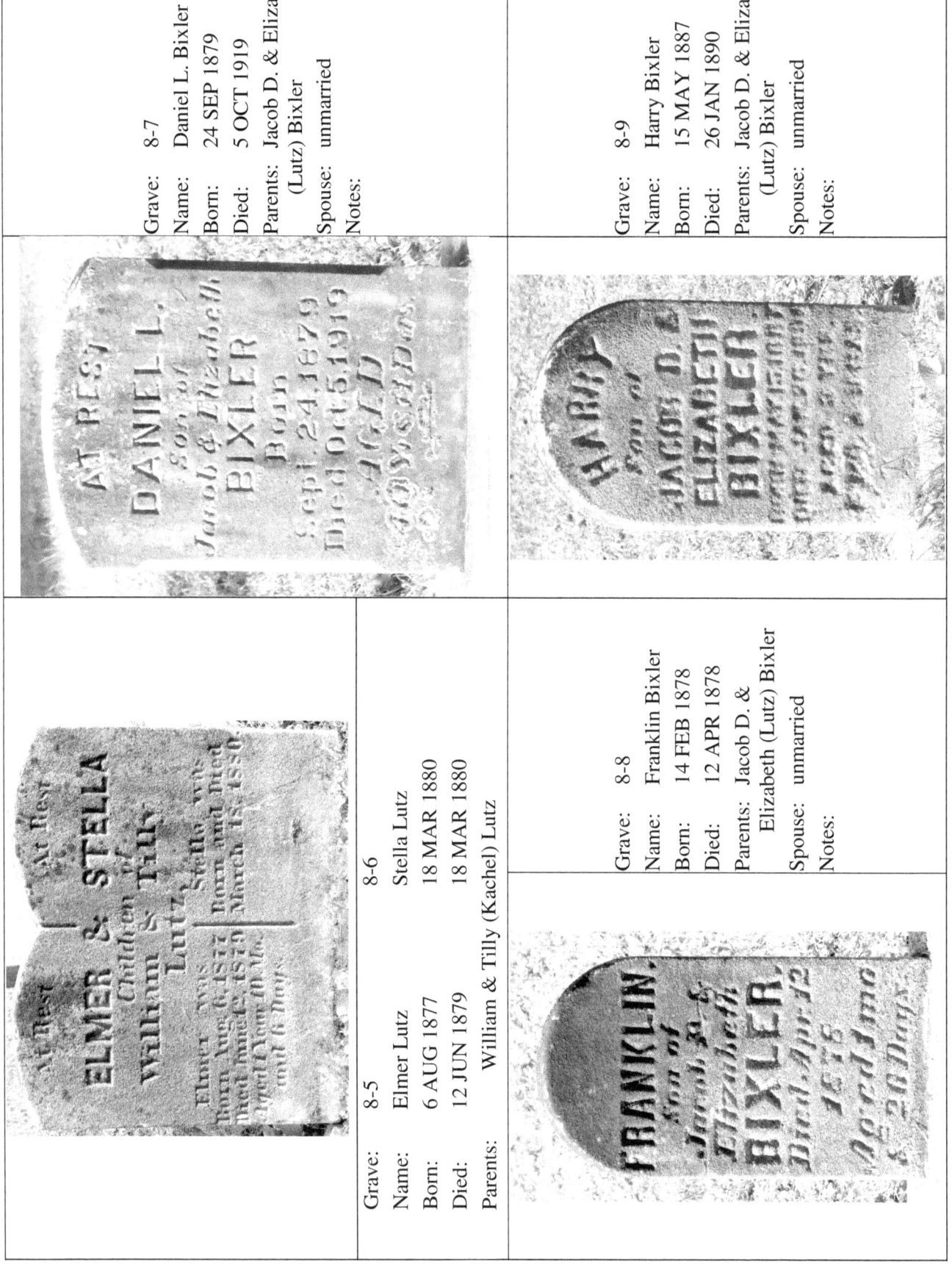

Grave: 8-7
Name: Daniel L. Bixler
Born: 24 SEP 1879
Died: 5 OCT 1919
Parents: Jacob D. & Elizabeth
(Lutz) Bixler
Spouse: unmarried
Notes:

Grave: 8-9
Name: Harry Bixler
Born: 15 MAY 1887
Died: 26 JAN 1890
Parents: Jacob D. & Elizabeth
(Lutz) Bixler
Spouse: unmarried
Notes:

Grave: 8-5
Name: Elmer Lutz
Born: 6 AUG 1877
Died: 12 JUN 1879
Parents: William & Tilly (Kachel) Lutz

Grave: 8-6
Name: Stella Lutz
Born: 18 MAR 1880
Died: 18 MAR 1880

Grave: 8-8
Name: Franklin Bixler
Born: 14 FEB 1878
Died: 12 APR 1878
Parents: Jacob D. &
Elizabeth (Lutz) Bixler
Spouse: unmarried
Notes:

Grave:	8-11	Grave:	8-13
Name:	Henry Lutz	Name:	Susanna (Royer) Lutz
Born:	20 DEC 1843	Born:	17 FEB 1773
Died:	25 JAN 1844	Died:	8 MAR 1858
Parents:	Daniel & Elizabeth (Macwate) Lutz	Parents:	Peter & Catharine (Stump) Royer
Spouse:	unmarried	Spouse:	Henry Lutz
Notes:		Notes:	

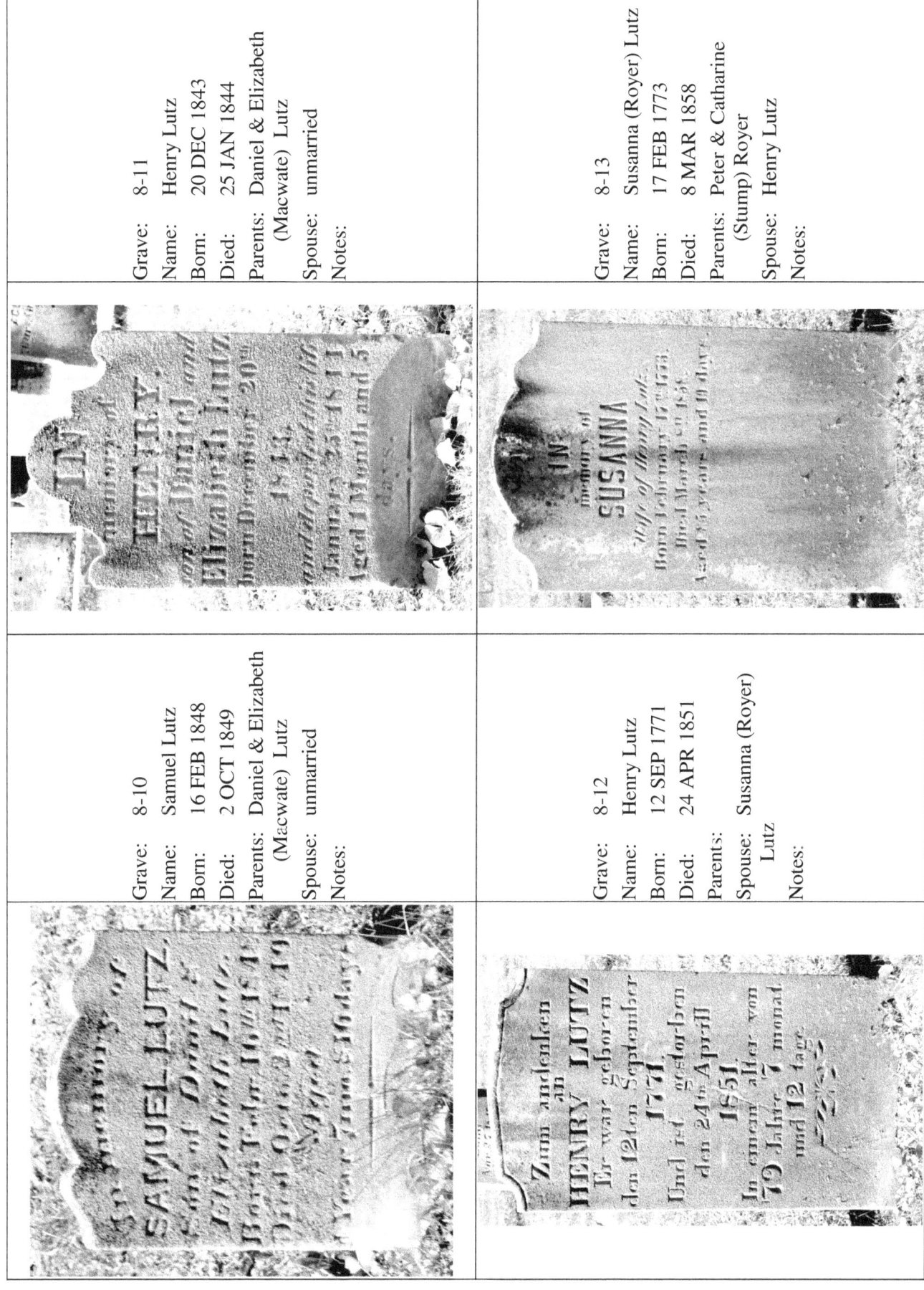

Grave:	8-10	Grave:	8-12
Name:	Samuel Lutz	Name:	Henry Lutz
Born:	16 FEB 1848	Born:	12 SEP 1771
Died:	2 OCT 1849	Died:	24 APR 1851
Parents:	Daniel & Elizabeth (Macwate) Lutz	Parents:	
Spouse:	unmarried	Spouse:	Susanna (Royer) Lutz
Notes:		Notes:	

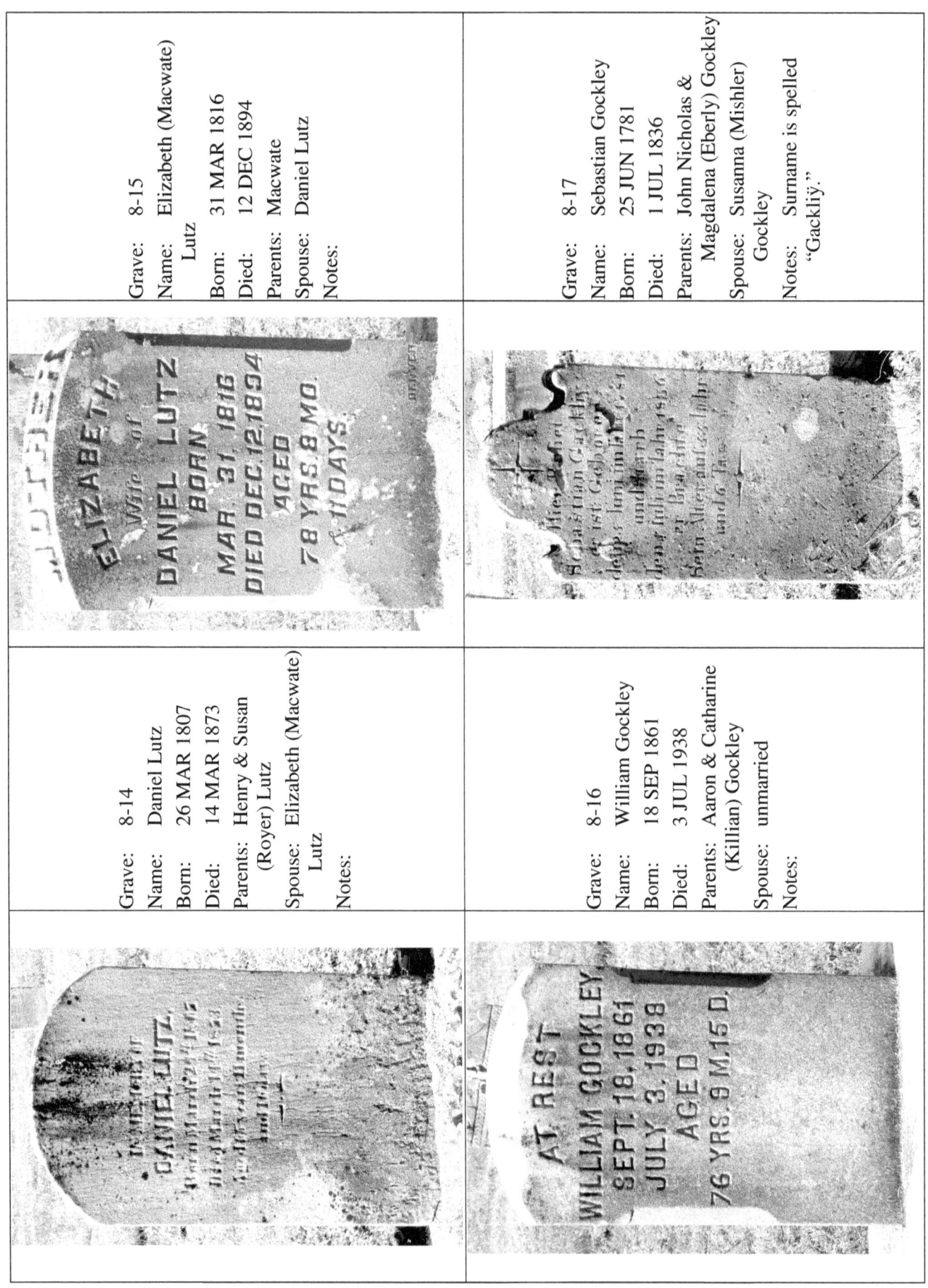

Grave: 8-15
Name: Elizabeth (Macwate) Lutz
Born: 31 MAR 1816
Died: 12 DEC 1894
Parents: Macwate
Spouse: Daniel Lutz
Notes:

Grave: 8-17
Name: Sebastian Gockley
Born: 25 JUN 1781
Died: 1 JUL 1836
Parents: John Nicholas & Magdalena (Eberly) Gockley
Spouse: Susanna (Mishler) Gockley
Notes: Surname is spelled "Gackliy."

Grave: 8-14
Name: Daniel Lutz
Born: 26 MAR 1807
Died: 14 MAR 1873
Parents: Henry & Susan (Royer) Lutz
Spouse: Elizabeth (Macwate) Lutz
Notes:

Grave: 8-16
Name: William Gockley
Born: 18 SEP 1861
Died: 3 JUL 1938
Parents: Aaron & Catharine (Killian) Gockley
Spouse: unmarried
Notes:

Grave: 8-18 Name: Susanna (Mishler) Gockley Born: 2 APR 1802 Died: 18 JAN 1865 Parents: Joseph & Margaret (Bear) Mishler Spouse: Sebastian Gockley Notes:	Grave: 8-19 Name: Jacob Gockley Born: 6 MAR 1850 Died: 30 MAY 1851 Parents: Aaron & Casia [Catharine] (Killian) Gockley Spouse: unmarried Notes:
Grave: 8-20 Name: Susanna Gockley Born: 22 JAN 1848 Died: 6 FEB 1856 Parents: Aaron & Catharine (Killian) Gockley Spouse: unmarried Notes:	Grave: 8-21 Name: Aaron Gockley Born: 11 OCT 1823 Died: 14 OCT 1890 Parents: Sebastian & Susanna (Mishler) Gockley Spouse: Catharine (Killian) Gockley Notes:

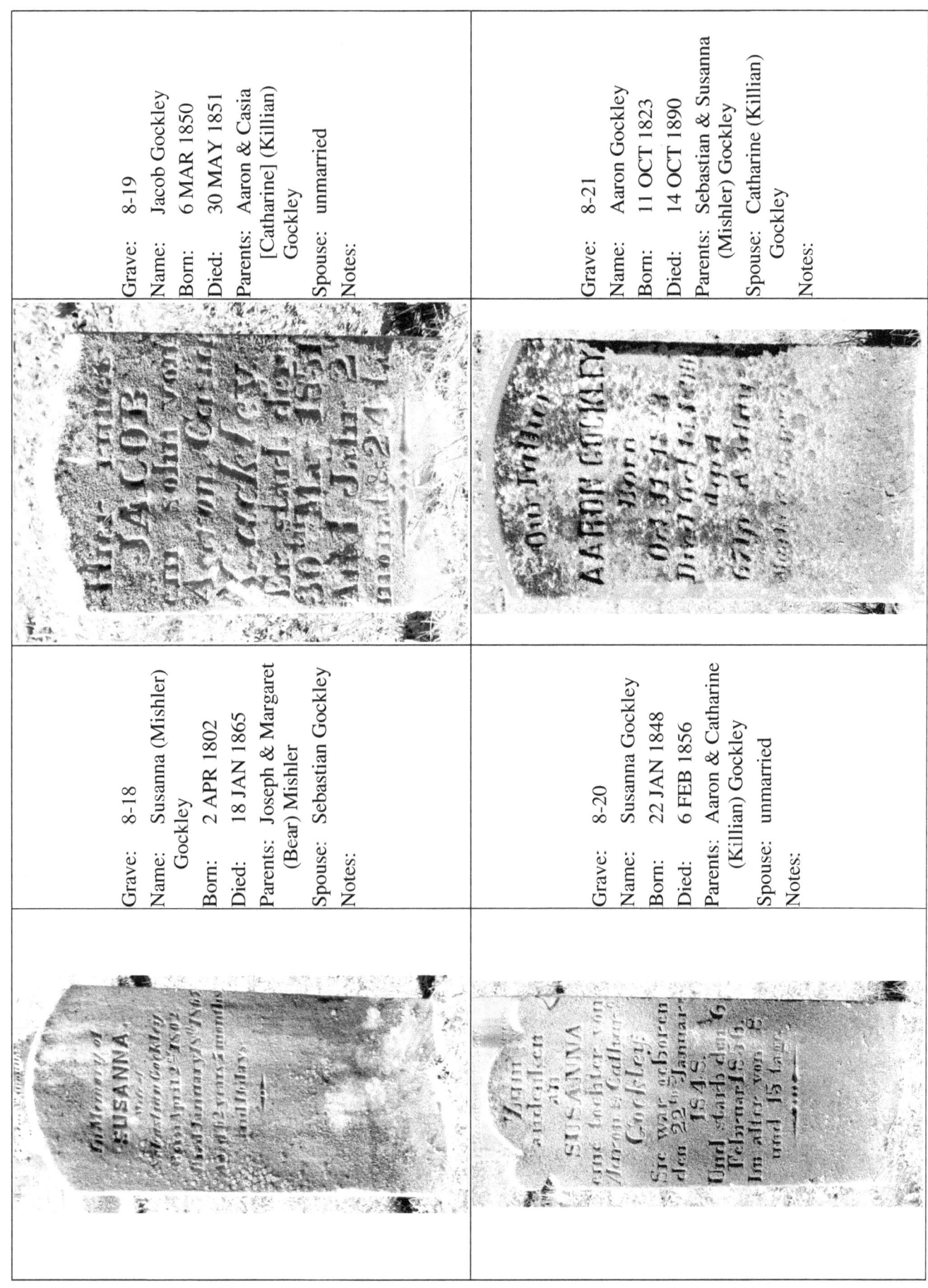

Grave: 8-23
Name: Anna Gockley
Born: 19 MAY 1850
Died: 6 SEP 1863
Parents: John B. & Sarah (Lutz)
   Gockley
Spouse: unmarried
Notes:
	Grave: 8-25
	Name: John B. Gockley
	Born: 3 NOV 1825
	Died: 25 JUN 1882
	Parents: Abraham & Catharine
	   (Bear) Gockley
	Spouse: Sarah (Lutz) Gockley
	Notes:

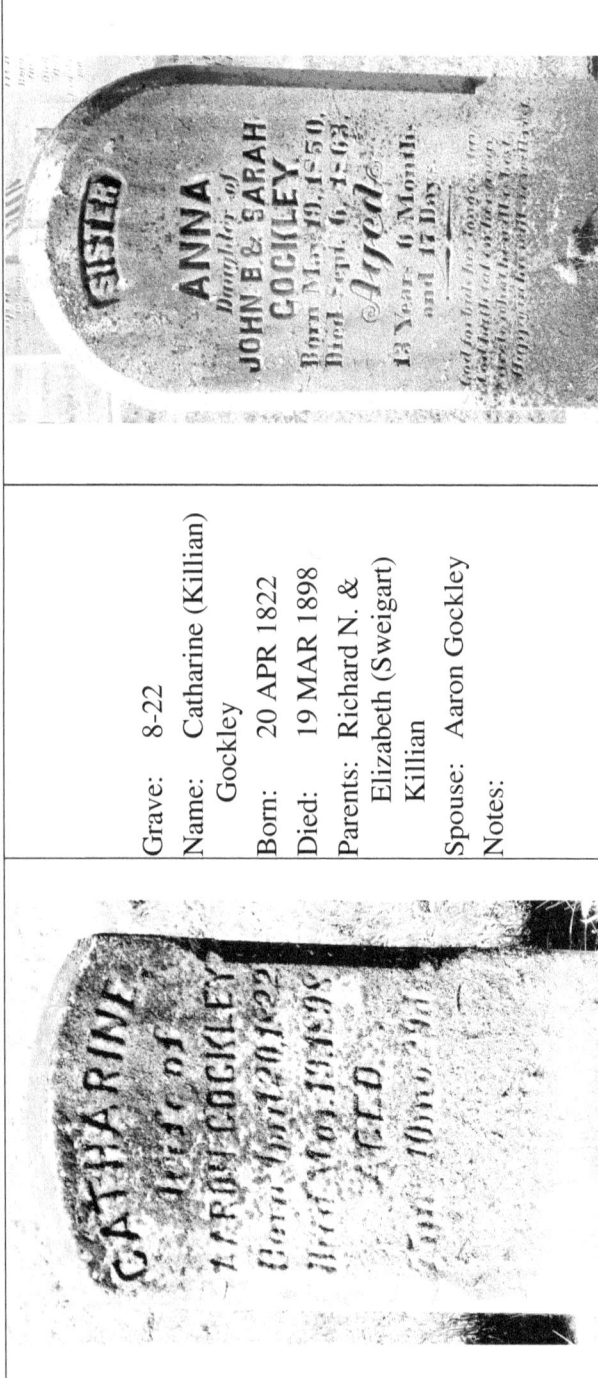	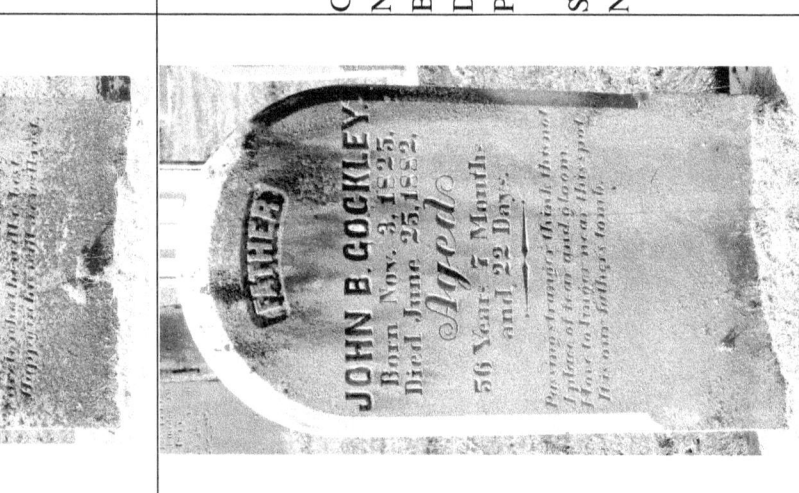

Grave: 8-22
Name: Catharine (Killian)
   Gockley
Born: 20 APR 1822
Died: 19 MAR 1898
Parents: Richard N. &
   Elizabeth (Sweigart)
   Killian
Spouse: Aaron Gockley
Notes:
	Grave: 8-24
	Name: Sarah (Lutz)
	   Gockley
	Born: 20 MAY 1830
	Died: 17 OCT 1863
	Parents: John & Susanna
	   (Swarr) Lutz
	Spouse: John B. Gockley
	Notes:

Grave: 9-2 Name: Bertha M. Lutz Born: 11 MAR 1881 Died: 26 FEB 1885 Parents: Daniel M. & Anna C. (Frecht) Lutz Spouse: unmarried Notes:	Grave: 9-4 Name: Mary C. Lutz Born: 29 MAR 1874 Died: 5 APR 1878 Parents: Daniel M. & Anna C. (Frecht) Lutz Spouse: unmarried Notes:

Grave: 9-1 Name: Frances S. Lutz Born: 27 SEP 1876 Died: 5 MAR 1885 Parents: Daniel M. & Anna C. (Frecht) Lutz Spouse: unmarried Notes:	Grave: 9-3 Name: Clara Louise Lutz Born: 31 JAN 1879 Died: 23 FEB 1885 Parents: Daniel M. & Anna C. (Frecht) Lutz Spouse: unmarried Notes:

Grave: 9-7 Name: Evan E. Lutz Born: 25 MAR 1848 Died: 25 JAN 1879 Parents: Jacob & Sarah (Eberly) Lutz Spouse: Elizabeth (Flickinger) Lutz Notes:	Grave: 9-9 Name: Eduard Lutz Born: 11 DEC 1830 Died: 22 JUN 1849 Parents: Jacob & Salme [=Sarah] (Eberly) Lutz Spouse: unmarried Notes:

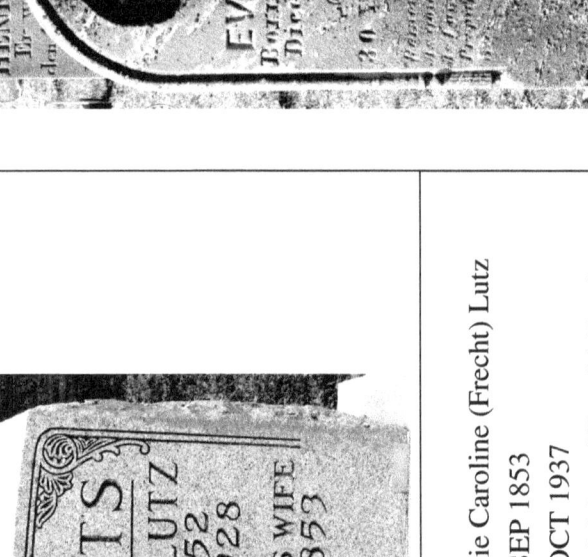

PARENTS DANIEL M. LUTZ NOV. 2, 1852 DEC. 29, 1928 ANNIE C. HIS WIFE SEPT. 14, 1853	Grave: 9-8 Name: Adda Lutz Born: Died: Parents: Spouse: Notes: The inscription includes the year 1878, but it is unclear if that is a birth or death year.

	9-6 Annie Caroline (Frecht) Lutz 14 SEP 1853 13 OCT 1937 John & Mary (Rhoads) Frecht
Grave: 9-5 Name: Daniel M. Lutz Born: 2 NOV 1852 Died: 29 DEC 1928 Parents: Daniel & Elizabeth (Macwate) Lutz	

Grave: 9-11	Grave: 9-13
Name: Sarah (Eberly) Lutz	Name: Adam Lutz
Born: 3 JUN 1809	Born: 28 NOV 1800
Died: 16 DEC 1893	Died: 14 APR 1865
Parents: Henry & Mary (Hagy) Eberly	Parents: Adam & Magdalena (Ream) Lutz
Spouse: Jacob Lutz	Spouse: Lydia (Senseman) Lutz
Notes:	Notes:

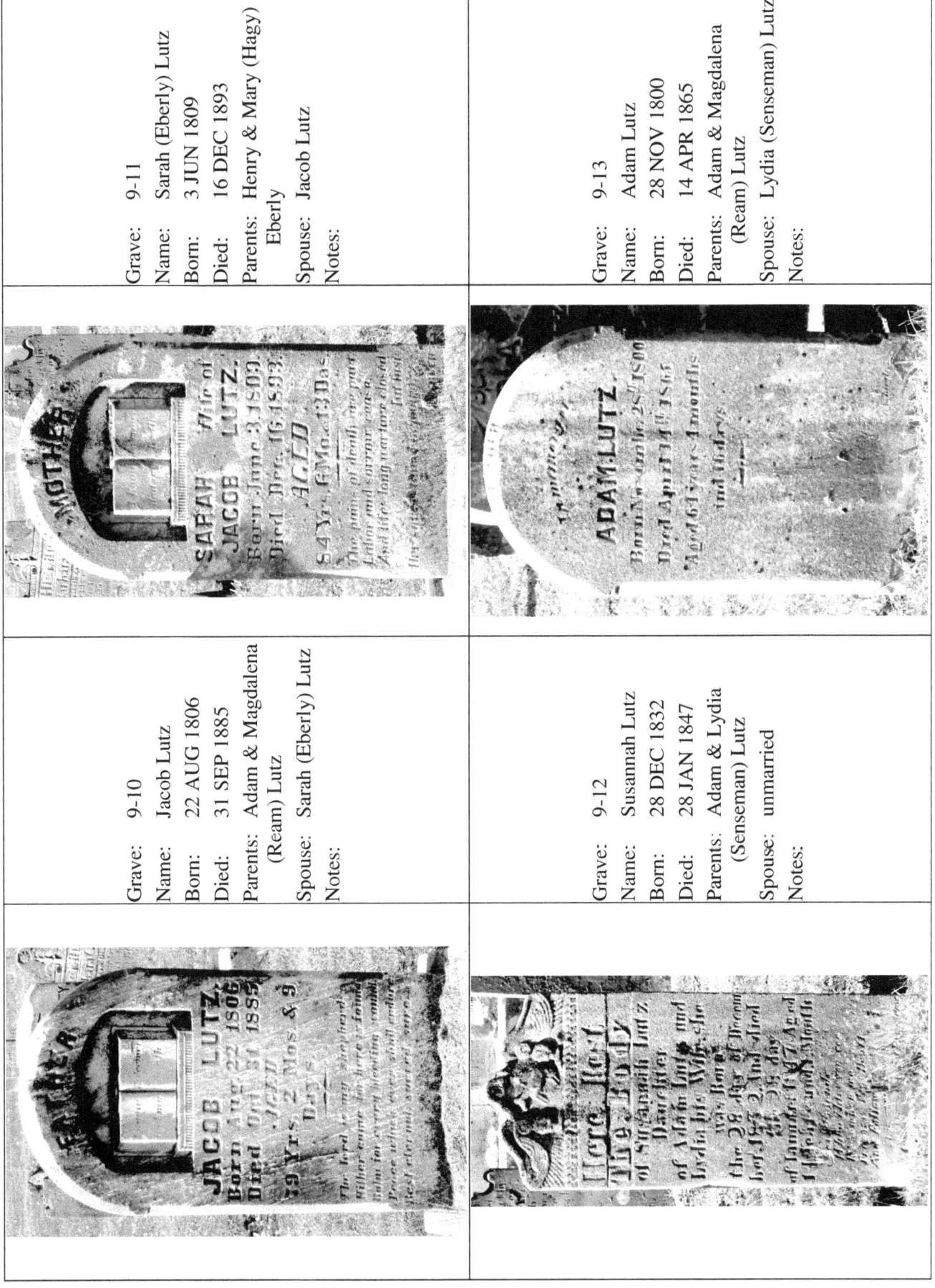

Grave: 9-10	Grave: 9-12
Name: Jacob Lutz	Name: Susannah Lutz
Born: 22 AUG 1806	Born: 28 DEC 1832
Died: 31 SEP 1885	Died: 28 JAN 1847
Parents: Adam & Magdalena (Ream) Lutz	Parents: Adam & Lydia (Senseman) Lutz
Spouse: Sarah (Eberly) Lutz	Spouse: unmarried
Notes:	Notes:

Grave: 9-15	Grave: 9-17
Name: Henry Lutz	Name: Susanna (Swarr) Lutz
Born: 3 MAY 1803	Born: 28 FEB 1804
Died: 14 SEP 1863	Died: 9 JUN 1875
Parents: Adam & Magdalena (Ream) Lutz	Parents: John & Margaret (Hernley) Swarr
Spouse: unmarried	Spouse: John Lutz
Notes:	Notes:

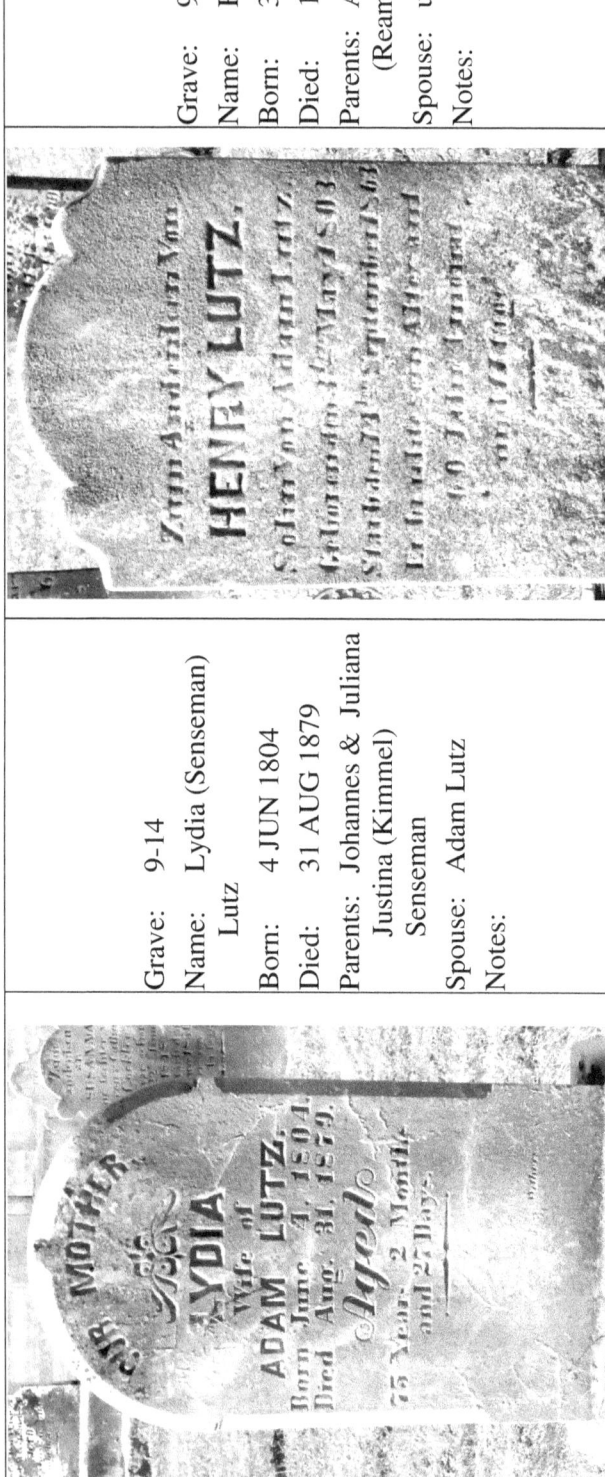

Grave: 9-14	Grave: 9-16
Name: Lydia (Senseman) Lutz	Name: John Lutz
Born: 4 JUN 1804	Born: 8 AUG 1797
Died: 31 AUG 1879	Died: 4 APR 1870
Parents: Johannes & Juliana Justina (Kimmel) Senseman	Parents: Adam & Magdalena (Ream) Lutz
Spouse: Adam Lutz	Spouse: Susanna (Swarr) Lutz
Notes:	Notes:

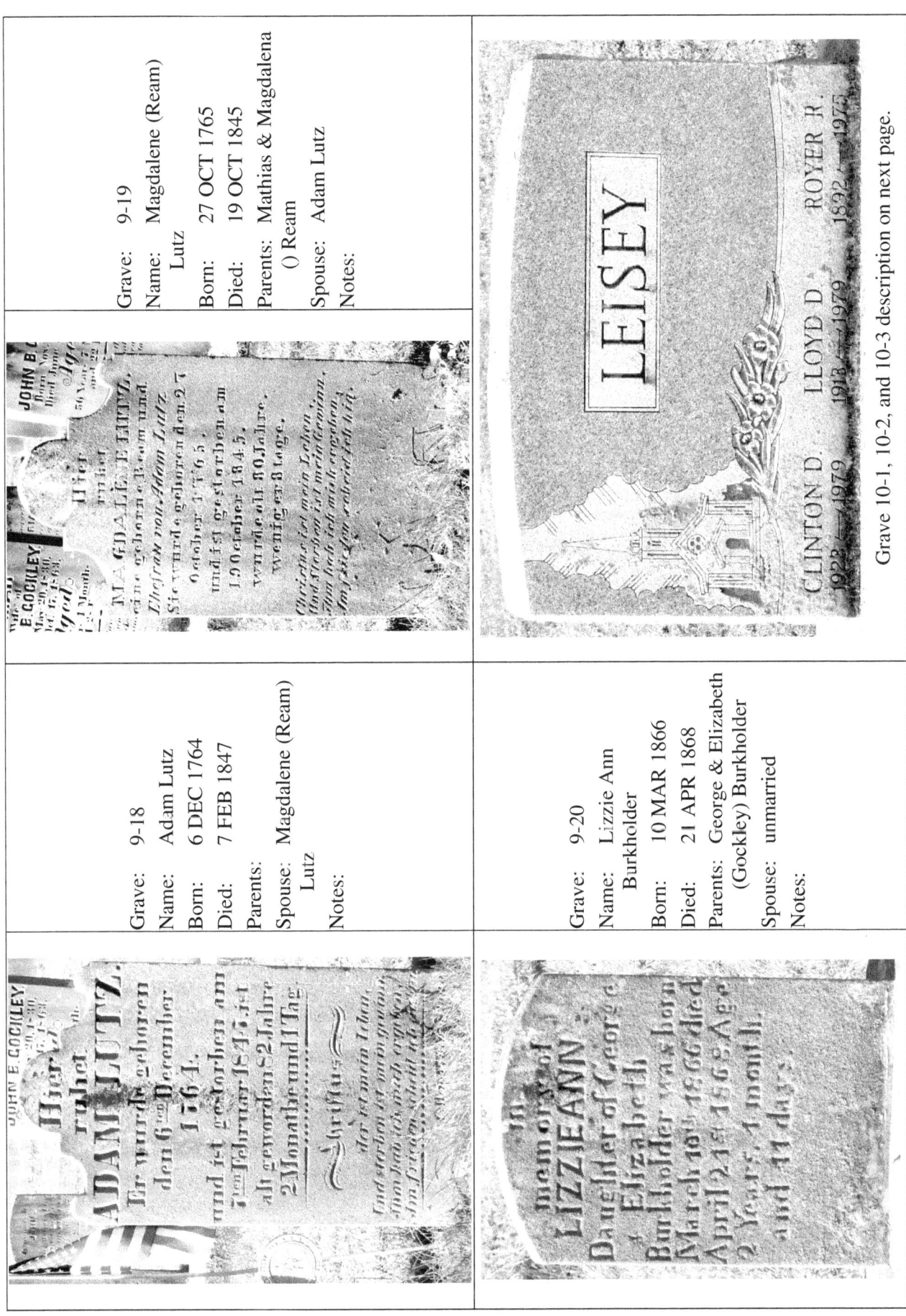

Grave: 9-18
Name: Adam Lutz
Born: 6 DEC 1764
Died: 7 FEB 1847
Parents:
Spouse: Magdalene (Ream) Lutz
Notes:

Grave: 9-19
Name: Magdalene (Ream) Lutz
Born: 27 OCT 1765
Died: 19 OCT 1845
Parents: Mathias & Magdalena () Ream
Spouse: Adam Lutz
Notes:

Grave: 9-20
Name: Lizzie Ann Burkholder
Born: 10 MAR 1866
Died: 21 APR 1868
Parents: George & Elizabeth (Gockley) Burkholder
Spouse: unmarried
Notes:

Grave 10-1, 10-2, and 10-3 description on next page.

67

Grave:	10-3
Name:	Royer R. Leisey
Born:	21 DEC 1892
Died:	29 MAR 1975
Parents:	Abraham G. & Matilda (Royer) Leisey
Spouse:	Ella S. (Dissinger) Leisey
Notes:	

Grave:	10-5
Name:	Esrom Althouse
Born:	10 JAN 1827
Died:	19 FEB 1899
Parents:	John & Elizabeth (Musser) Althouse
Spouse:	Rachel (Fry) Althouse
Notes:	

Grave:	10-2
Name:	Lloyd D. Leisey
Born:	22 DEC 1913
Died:	8 JAN 1979
Parents:	Royer & Ella (Dissinger) Leisey
Spouse:	unmarried
Notes:	

Grave:	10-4
Name:	Ella S. (Dissinger) Leisey
Born:	9 JUL 1883
Died:	13 FEB 1937
Parents:	Harry & Priscilla (Sloat) Dissinger
Spouse:	Royer Leisey
Notes:	

Grave:	10-1
Name:	Clinton D. Leisey
Born:	30 APR 1923
Died:	10 JAN 1979
Parents:	Royer & Ella (Dissinger) Leisey
Spouse:	June (Heister) Leisey
Notes:	

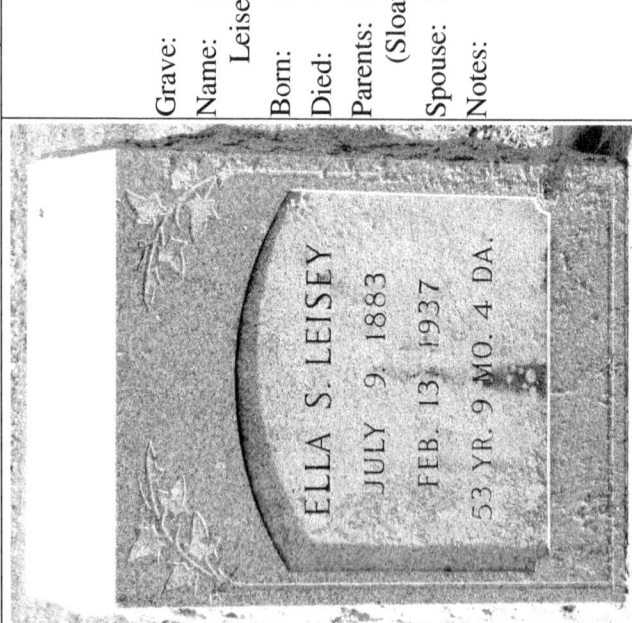

Grave: 10-7	Grave: 10-9
Name: Franklin Lutz	Name: Kate (Lorah) Lutz
Born: 18 OCT 1878	Born: 24 JUN 1845
Died: 9 JAN 1879	Died: 3 NOV 1895
Parents: John & Kate (Lorah) Lutz	Parents: Jacob & Sarah (Eberly) Lorah
Spouse: unmarried	Spouse: John M. Lutz
Notes:	Notes:

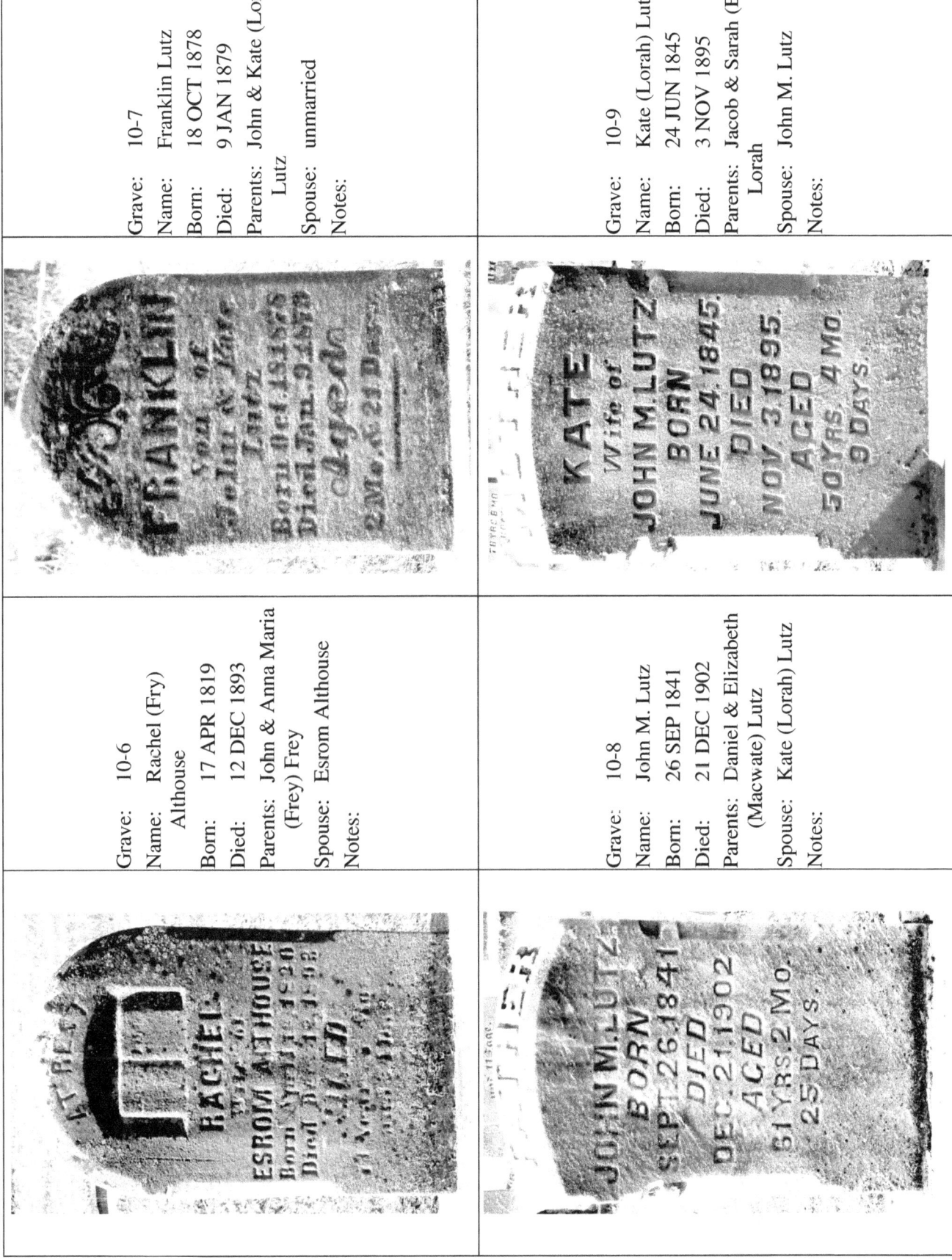

Grave: 10-6	Grave: 10-8
Name: Rachel (Fry) Althouse	Name: John M. Lutz
Born: 17 APR 1819	Born: 26 SEP 1841
Died: 12 DEC 1893	Died: 21 DEC 1902
Parents: John & Anna Maria (Frey) Frey	Parents: Daniel & Elizabeth (Macwate) Lutz
Spouse: Esrom Althouse	Spouse: Kate (Lorah) Lutz
Notes:	Notes:

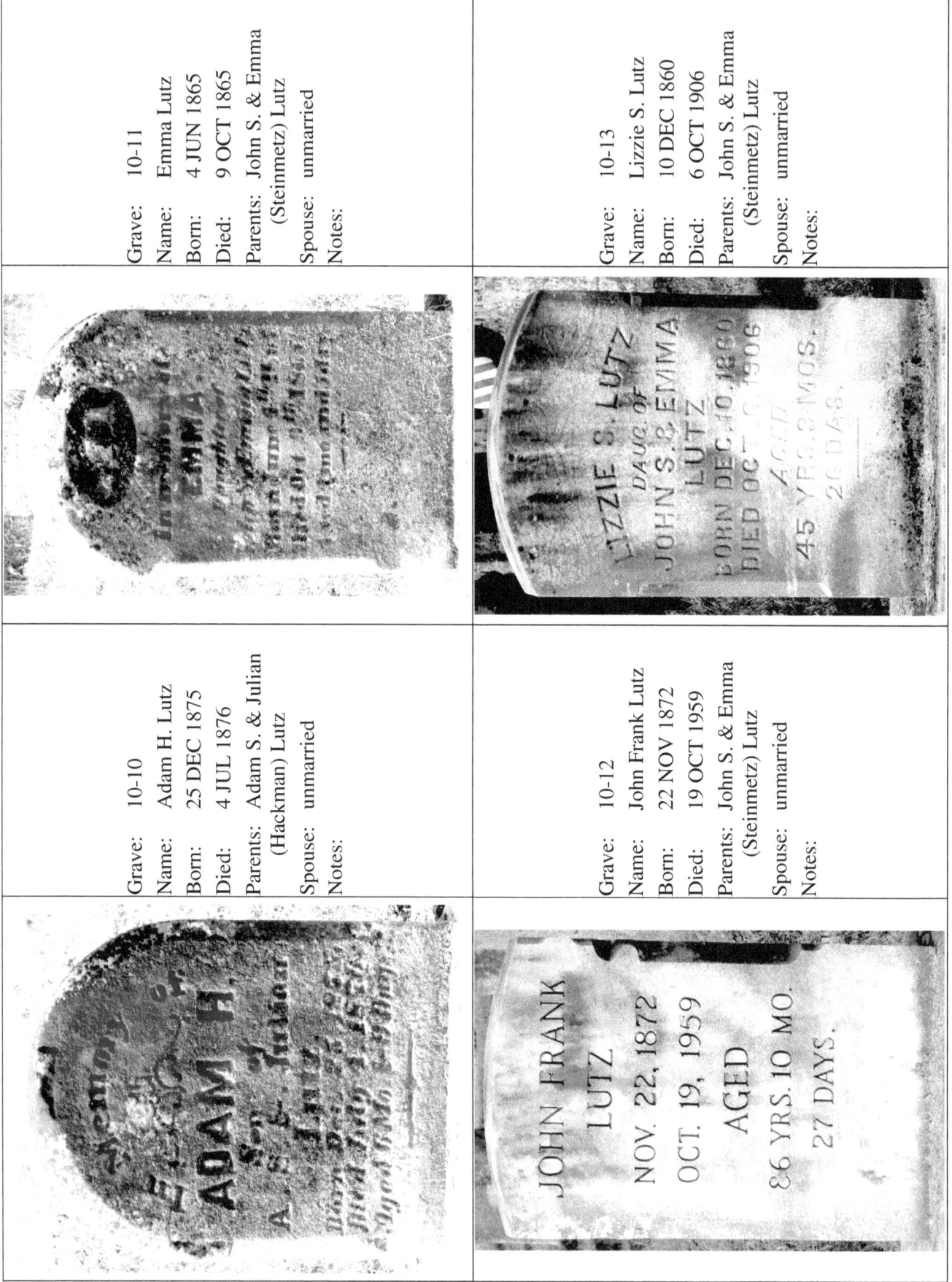

Grave: 10-11
Name: Emma Lutz
Born: 4 JUN 1865
Died: 9 OCT 1865
Parents: John S. & Emma (Steinmetz) Lutz
Spouse: unmarried
Notes:

Grave: 10-13
Name: Lizzie S. Lutz
Born: 10 DEC 1860
Died: 6 OCT 1906
Parents: John S. & Emma (Steinmetz) Lutz
Spouse: unmarried
Notes:

Grave: 10-10
Name: Adam H. Lutz
Born: 25 DEC 1875
Died: 4 JUL 1876
Parents: Adam S. & Julian (Hackman) Lutz
Spouse: unmarried
Notes:

Grave: 10-12
Name: John Frank Lutz
Born: 22 NOV 1872
Died: 19 OCT 1959
Parents: John S. & Emma (Steinmetz) Lutz
Spouse: unmarried
Notes:

70

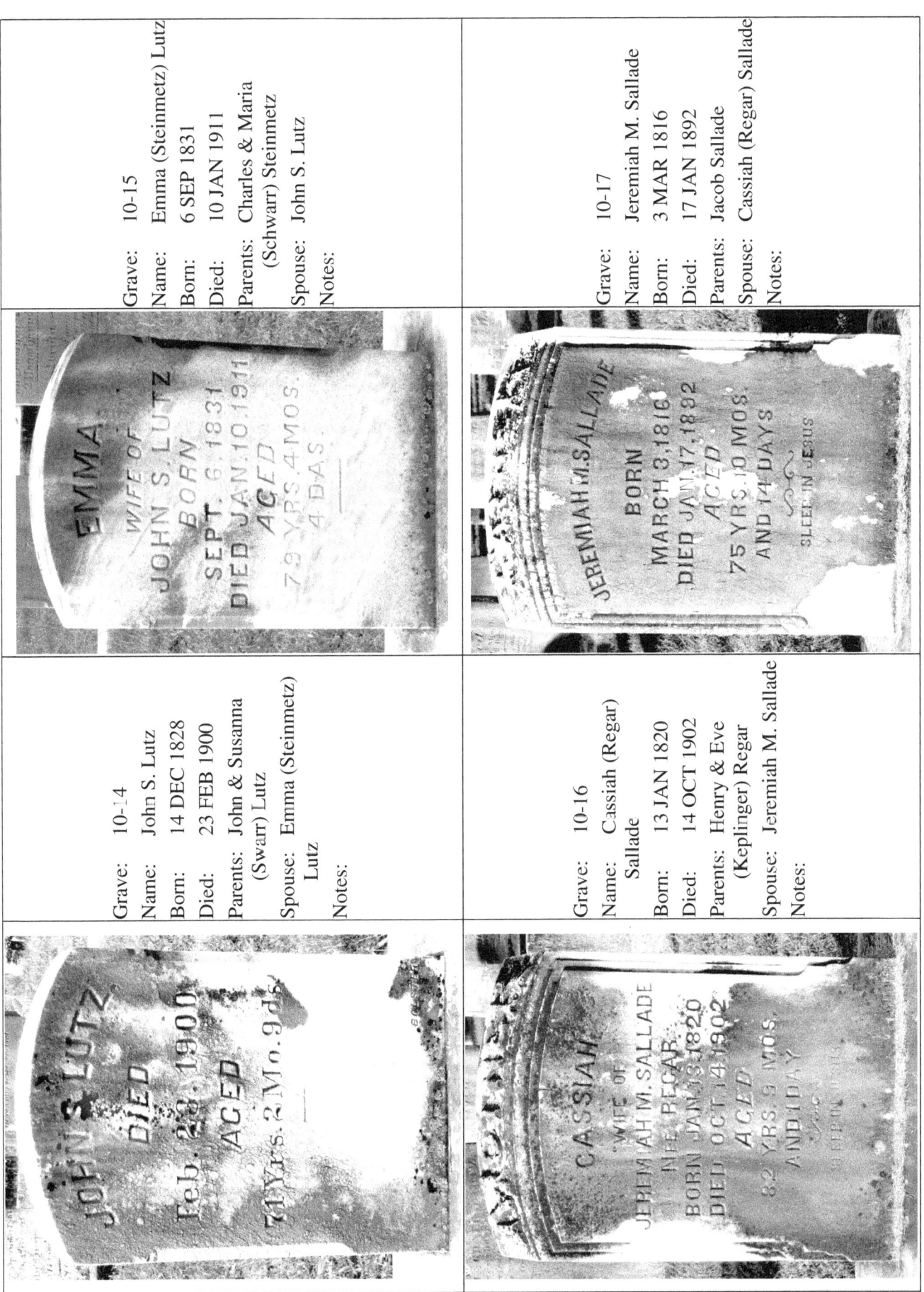

Grave: 10-15
Name: Emma (Steinmetz) Lutz
Born: 6 SEP 1831
Died: 10 JAN 1911
Parents: Charles & Maria (Schwarr) Steinmetz
Spouse: John S. Lutz
Notes:

Grave: 10-17
Name: Jeremiah M. Sallade
Born: 3 MAR 1816
Died: 17 JAN 1892
Parents: Jacob Sallade
Spouse: Cassiah (Regar) Sallade
Notes:

Grave: 10-14
Name: John S. Lutz
Born: 14 DEC 1828
Died: 23 FEB 1900
Parents: John & Susanna (Swarr) Lutz
Spouse: Emma (Steinmetz) Lutz
Notes:

Grave: 10-16
Name: Cassiah (Regar) Sallade
Born: 13 JAN 1820
Died: 14 OCT 1902
Parents: Henry & Eve (Keplinger) Regar
Spouse: Jeremiah M. Sallade
Notes:

Grave: 10-19 Name: John S. Nolde Born: 23 OCT 1844 Died: 11 JAN 1891 Parents: Lawrence &Martha (Strube) Nolde Spouse: Emma (Sallade) [Rhoads] Nolde [Grosh] Notes:	Grave: 10-21 Name: infant daughter Sallade Born: 1856 Died: 1856 Parents: Jeremiah M. & Cassiah (Regar) Sallade Spouse: unmarried Notes:
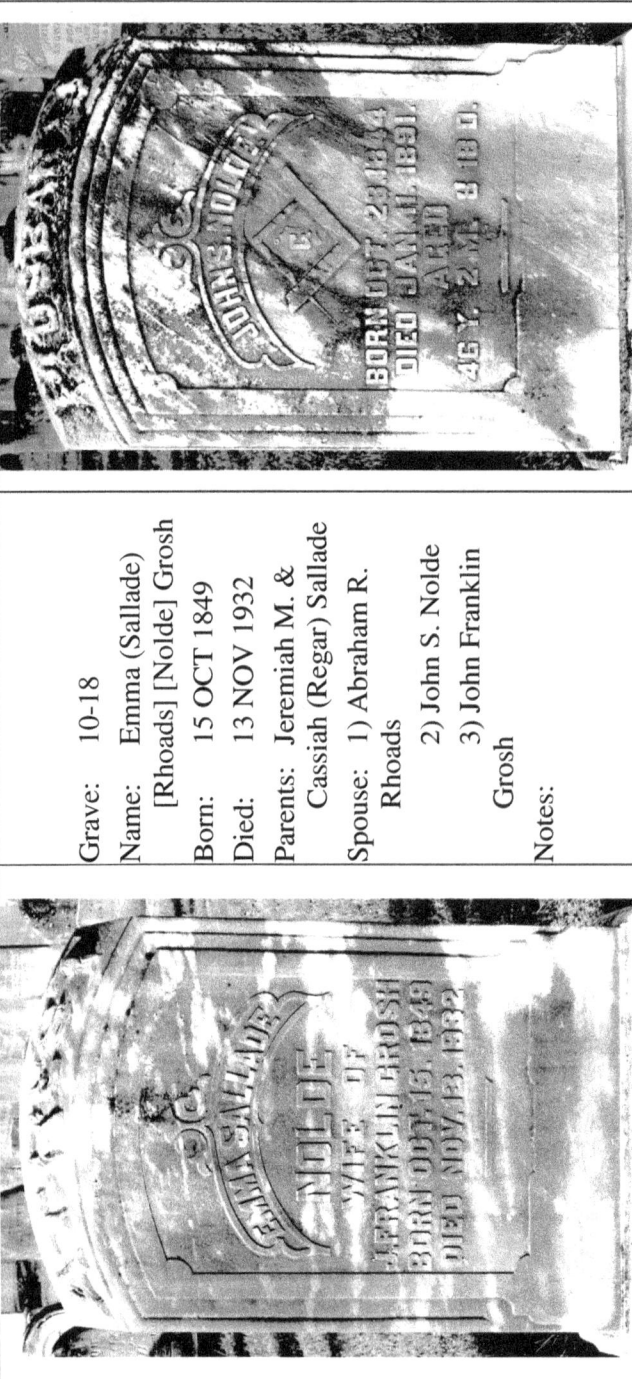	
Grave: 10-18 Name: Emma (Sallade) [Rhoads] [Nolde] Grosh Born: 15 OCT 1849 Died: 13 NOV 1932 Parents: Jeremiah M. & Cassiah (Regar) Sallade Spouse: 1) Abraham R. Rhoads 2) John S. Nolde 3) John Franklin Grosh Notes:	Grave: 10-20 Name: Alma S. Nolde Born: 5 MAY 1882 Died: 11 MAY 1888 Parents: John S. & Emma (Sallade) Nolde Spouse: unmarried Notes:

Grave: 10-24
Name: ---

Grave: 10-23
Name: ---

Notes: Gravestones have been broken off and base is against the stone wall around the cemetery.

Grave: 11-1
Name: Ada Emma Frankhouser
Born: 13 DEC 1877
Died: 11 SEP 1883
Parents: Byram L. & Sarah J. (Root) Frankhouser
Spouse: unmarried
Notes:

Grave: 10-22
Name: infant son Nolde
Born: 1830
Died: 1830
Parents: John S. & Emma (Sallade) Nolde
Spouse: unmarried
Notes: stillborn

Grave: 10-25
Name: J. H. O.
Born:
Died:
Parents:
Spouse:
Notes: Loose small gravestone leaning up against the stone wall around the cemetery.

Grave: 11-3 Name: Sarah J. (Root) Frankhouser Born: 26 JAN 1842 Died: 6 OCT 1911 Parents: Allen & Nancy Anna (Getz) Root Spouse: Byram L. Frankhouser Notes:	Grave: 11-5 Name: Fianna E. Lutz Born: 12 OCT 1845 Died: 29 JUL 1909 Parents: Jacob & Sarah (Eberly) Lutz Spouse: unmarried Notes:
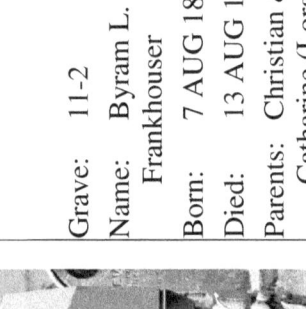	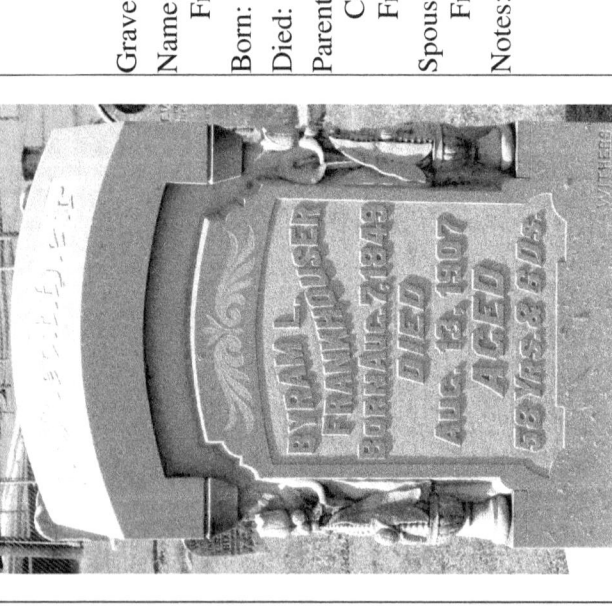
Grave: 11-2 Name: Byram L. Frankhouser Born: 7 AUG 1849 Died: 13 AUG 1907 Parents: Christian & Catharine (Lorah) Frankhouser Spouse: Sarah J. (Root) Frankhouser Notes:	Grave: 11-4 Name: Henry E. Lutz Born: 18 AUG 1840 Died: 16 FEB 1887 Parents: Jacob & Sarah (Eberly) Lutz Spouse: Katharine () Lutz Notes:

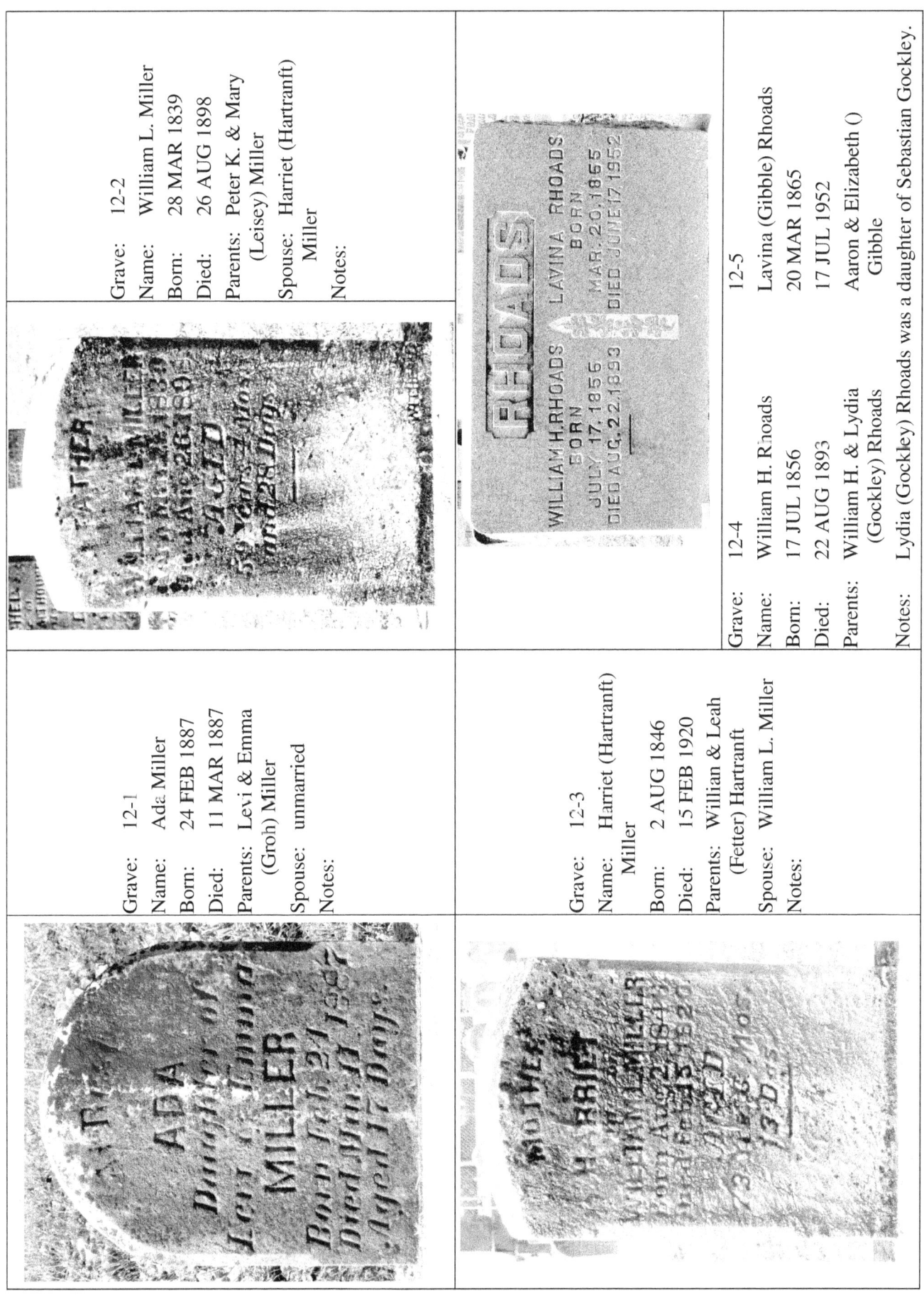

Grave: 12-2
Name: William L. Miller
Born: 28 MAR 1839
Died: 26 AUG 1898
Parents: Peter K. & Mary (Leisey) Miller
Spouse: Harriet (Hartranft) Miller
Notes:

Grave: 12-5
Name: Lavina (Gibble) Rhoads
Born: 20 MAR 1865
Died: 17 JUL 1952
Parents: Aaron & Elizabeth () Gibble
Notes:

Grave: 12-4
Name: William H. Rhoads
Born: 17 JUL 1856
Died: 22 AUG 1893
Parents: William H. & Lydia (Gockley) Rhoads
Notes: Lydia (Gockley) Rhoads was a daughter of Sebastian Gockley.

Grave: 12-1
Name: Ada Miller
Born: 24 FEB 1887
Died: 11 MAR 1887
Parents: Levi & Emma (Groh) Miller
Spouse: unmarried
Notes:

Grave: 12-3
Name: Harriet (Hartranft) Miller
Born: 2 AUG 1846
Died: 15 FEB 1920
Parents: Willian & Leah (Fetter) Hartranft
Spouse: William L. Miller
Notes:

Grave: 12-7 Name: William H. Rhoads Born: 28 DEC 1891 Died: 8 AUG 1972 Parents: William H. & Lavina (Gibble) Rhoads Spouse: Bessie B. (Beck) Rhoads Notes:	Grave: 12-9 Name: Mayme R. Shiffer Born: 14 NOV 1888 Died: 16 MAR 1974 Parents: William H. & Lavina (Gibble) Rhoads Spouse: Elmer R. Shiffer Notes:
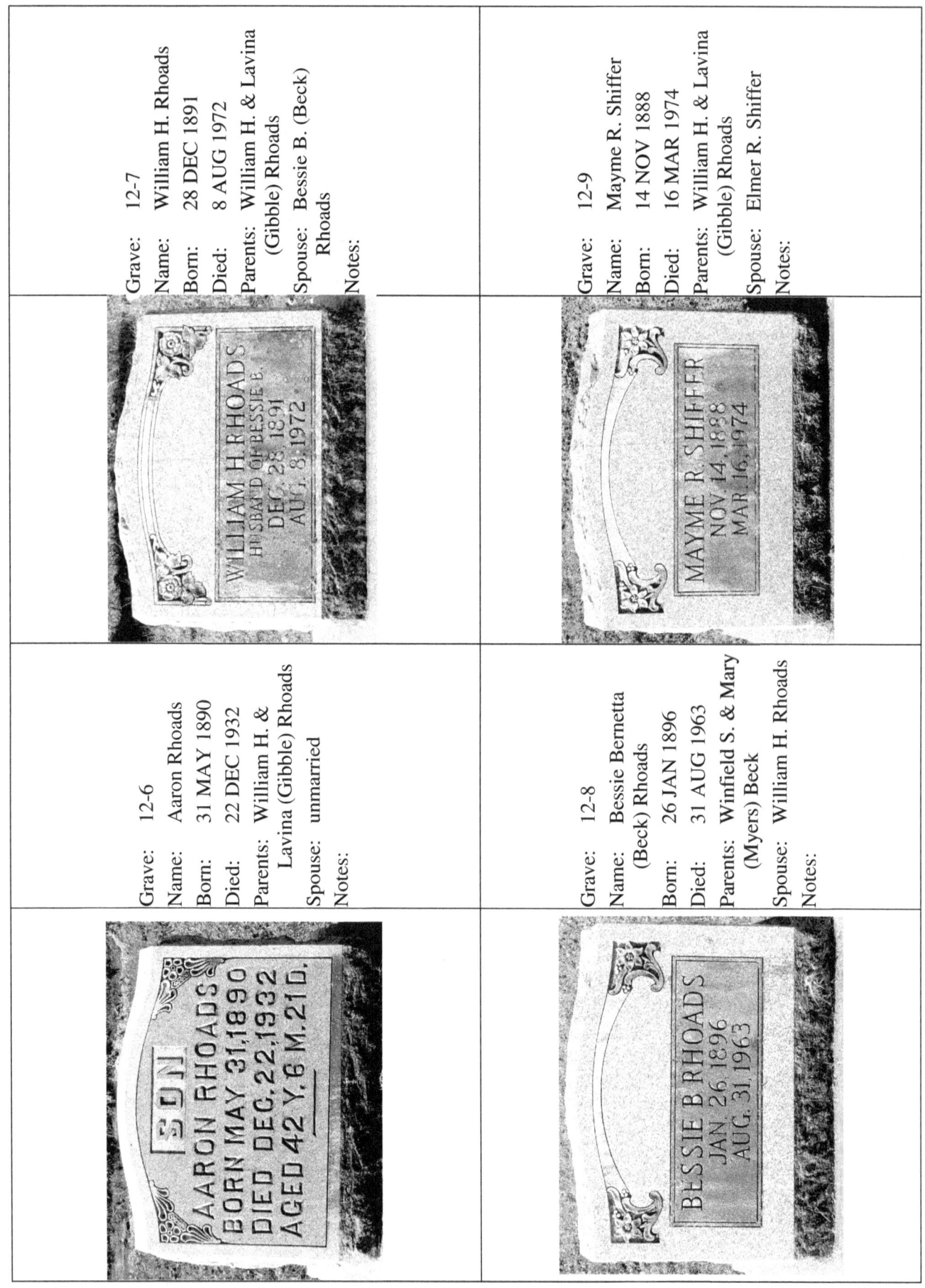	
Grave: 12-6 Name: Aaron Rhoads Born: 31 MAY 1890 Died: 22 DEC 1932 Parents: William H. & Lavina (Gibble) Rhoads Spouse: unmarried Notes:	Grave: 12-8 Name: Bessie Bernetta (Beck) Rhoads Born: 26 JAN 1896 Died: 31 AUG 1963 Parents: Winfield S. & Mary (Myers) Beck Spouse: William H. Rhoads Notes:

Grave: 12-11 Name: Annie (Haldeman) Miller Born: 5 JAN 1877 Died: 20 DEC 1897 Parents: Samuel G. & Mahala (Reynold) Haldeman Spouse: Edwin O. Miller Notes:	Grave: 12-13 Name: Peter L. Miller Born: 7 MAR 1849 Died: 3 MAR 1916 Parents: Peter K. & Mary (Ludwig) Miller Spouse: Clementine (Ott) Miller Notes:
 ANNIE Wife of EDWIN O MILLER Nee Born Haldeman BORN JAN 5, 1877 DIED DEC 20 1897 AGED 20 YRS 11 MO 15 DAS	FATHER PETER L MILLER BORN MARCH 7 1849 DIED MARCH 3 1916 AGED 66 YRS 11 M 26 D
Grave: 12-10 Name: Edwin O. Miller Born: 20 MAR 1873 Died: 1 JUN 1918 Parents: Peter L. & Clementine (Ott) Miller Spouse: (1) Annie (Haldeman) Miller (2) Cora (Haller) Miller Notes:	Grave: 12-12 Name: Edwin Miller Born: 2 DEC 1897 Died: 17 DEC 1897 Parents: Edwin O. & Annie (Haldeman) Miller Spouse: unmarried Notes:
HUSBAND EDWIN O MILLER BORN MARCH 20, 1873 DIED JUNE 1 1918 AGED 45 YR 2 MO 11 L	

Grave: 12-15 Name: Michael L. Miller Born: 28 JAN 1841 Died: 5 FEB 1916 Parents: Peter K. & Mary (Ludwig) Miller Spouse: Polly (Garner) Miller Notes:	Grave: 12-17 Name: Peter K. Miller Born: 2 MAY 1810 Died: 28 SEP 1879 Parents: Rudy & Mary (Krick) Miller Spouse: Mary (Ludwig) Miller Notes: Baptized at Muddy Creek Reformed Church on 2 SEP 1810.
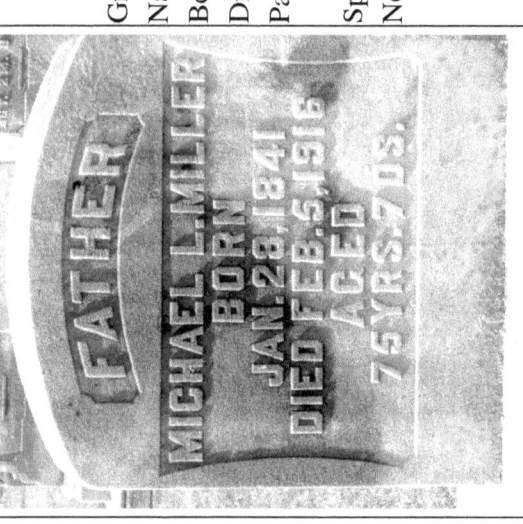	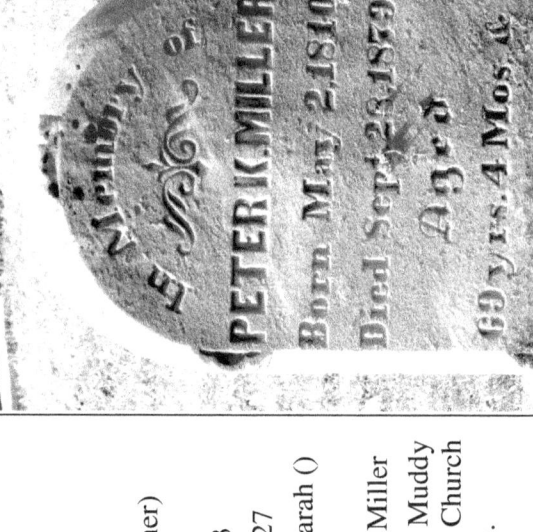
Grave: 12-14 Name: Clementine (Ott) Miller Born: 8 NOV 1851 Died: 24 MAY 1933 Parents: John & --- () Ott Spouse: Peter L. Miller Notes:	Grave: 12-16 Name: Polly (Garner) Miller Born: 8 SEP 1843 Died: 15 JAN 1927 Parents: Daniel & Sarah () Garner Spouse: Michael L. Miller Notes: Baptized at Muddy Creek Reformed Church on 15 OCT 1843.
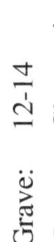	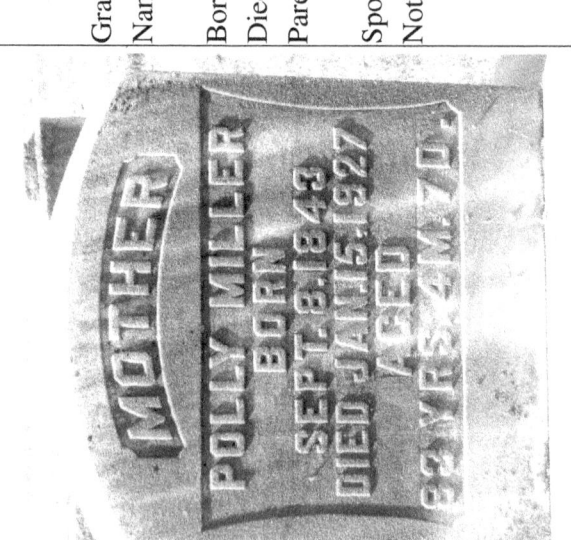

Grave: 13-1
Name: Franklin K. Kilhafner
Born: 18 MAR 1856
Died: 15 SEP 1936
Parents: Christ & Lydia
          (Kemper) Kilhafner
Spouse: Lucetta (Troupe)
          Kilhafner
Notes:

Grave: 13-3
Name: Isaac Trupe
Born: 14 MAY 1827
Died: 12 AUG 1915
Parents: Philip & Barbara
          (Frankhouser) Trupe
Spouse: Catharine (Deamer)
          Trupe
Notes:

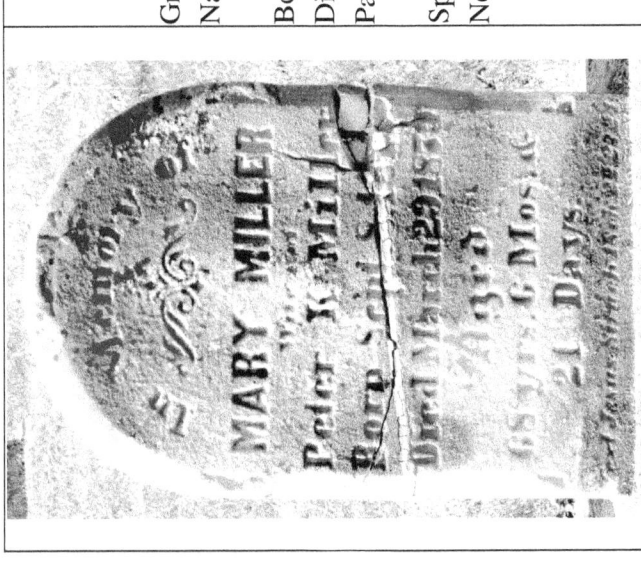

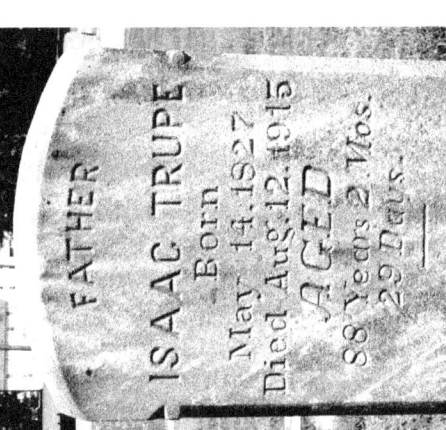

Grave: 12-18
Name: Mary (Ludwig)
          Miller
Born: 8 SEP 1819
Died: 29 MAR 1879
Parents: George & Rachel M.
          (Wendel) Ludwig
Spouse: Peter K. Miller
Notes:

Grave: 13-2
Name: Lucetta (Troupe)
          Kilhafner
Born: 31 JAN 1856
Died: 6 SEP 1942
Parents: Isaac & Catharine
          (Deamer) Troupe
Spouse: Franklin K.
          Kilhafner
Notes:

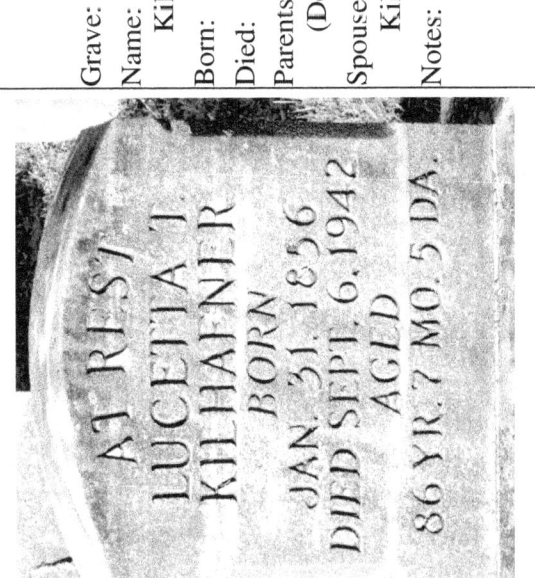

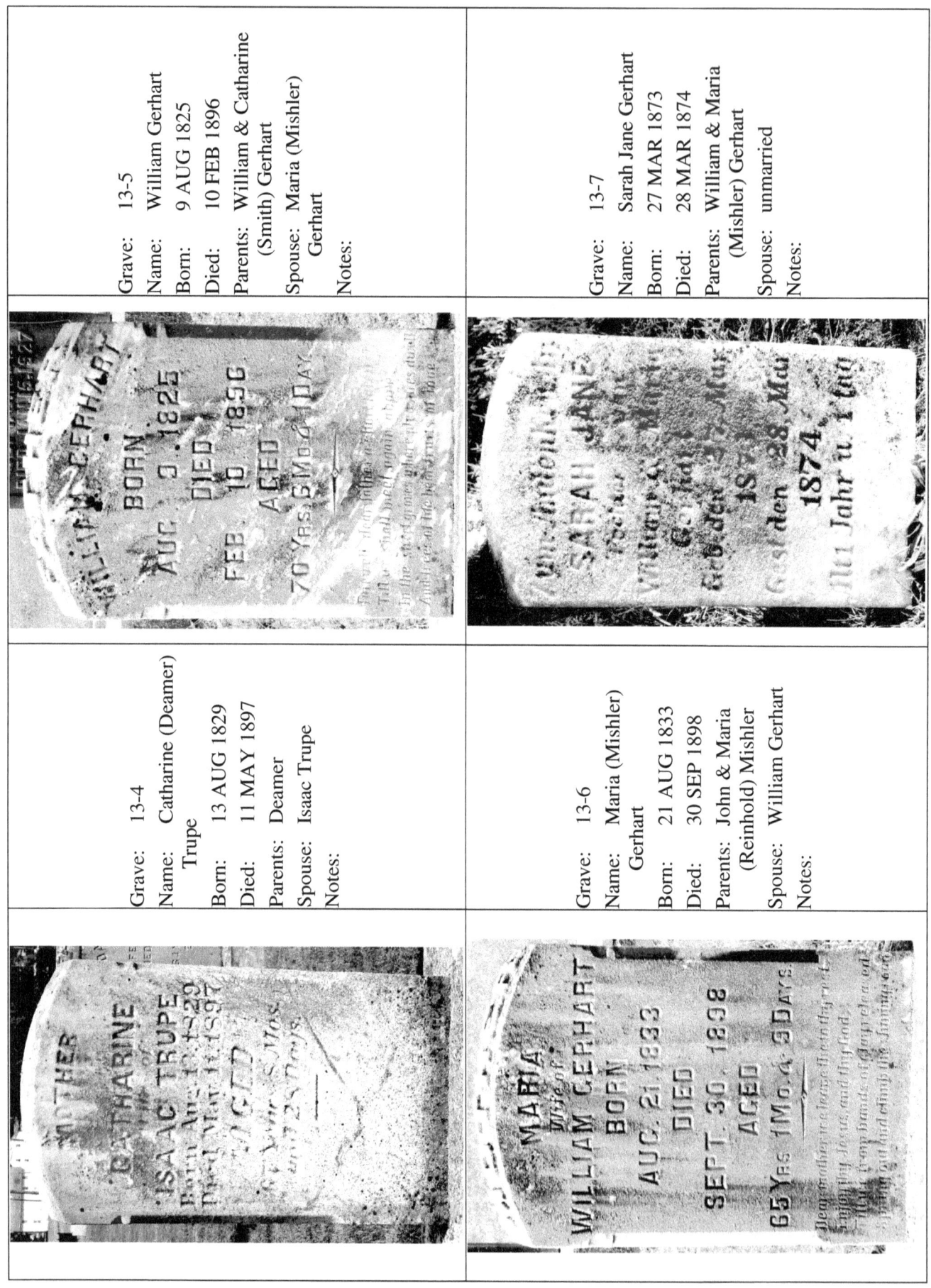

Grave: 13-5
Name: William Gerhart
Born: 9 AUG 1825
Died: 10 FEB 1896
Parents: William & Catharine
(Smith) Gerhart
Spouse: Maria (Mishler)
Gerhart
Notes:

Grave: 13-7
Name: Sarah Jane Gerhart
Born: 27 MAR 1873
Died: 28 MAR 1874
Parents: William & Maria
(Mishler) Gerhart
Spouse: unmarried
Notes:

Grave: 13-4
Name: Catharine (Deamer)
Trupe
Born: 13 AUG 1829
Died: 11 MAY 1897
Parents: Deamer
Spouse: Isaac Trupe
Notes:

Grave: 13-6
Name: Maria (Mishler)
Gerhart
Born: 21 AUG 1833
Died: 30 SEP 1898
Parents: John & Maria
(Reinhold) Mishler
Spouse: William Gerhart
Notes:

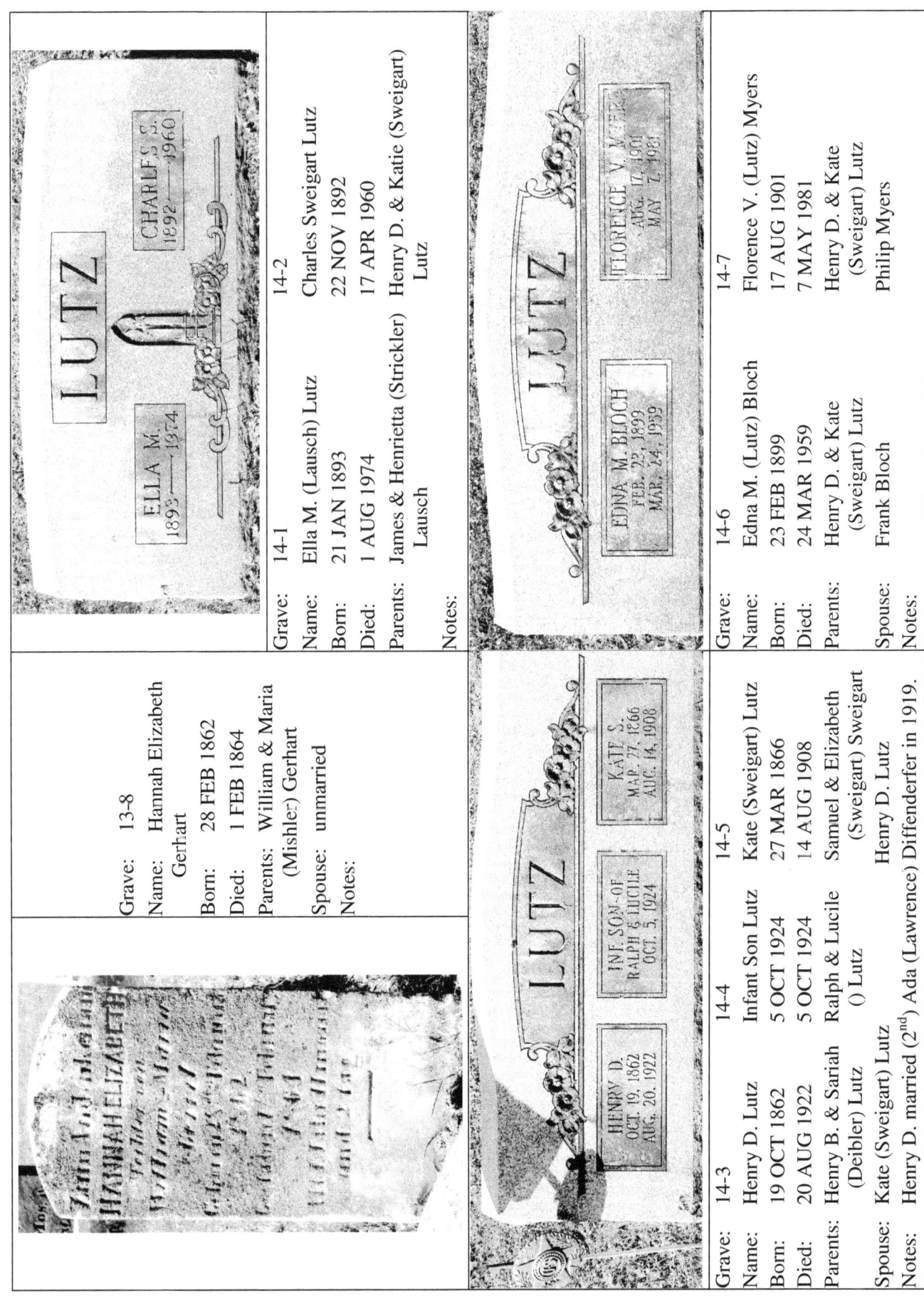

Grave:	13-8	
Name:	Hannah Elizabeth Gerhart	
Born:	28 FEB 1862	
Died:	1 FEB 1864	
Parents:	William & Maria (Mishler) Gerhart	
Spouse:	unmarried	
Notes:		

Grave:	14-1
Name:	Ella M. (Lausch) Lutz
Born:	21 JAN 1893
Died:	1 AUG 1974
Parents:	James & Henrietta (Strickler) Lausch
Notes:	

Grave:	14-2
Name:	Charles Sweigart Lutz
Born:	22 NOV 1892
Died:	17 APR 1960
Parents:	Henry D. & Katie (Sweigart) Lutz

Grave:	14-3
Name:	Henry D. Lutz
Born:	19 OCT 1862
Died:	20 AUG 1922
Parents:	Henry B. & Sariah (Deibler) Lutz
Spouse:	Kate (Sweigart) Lutz
Notes:	Henry D. married (2nd) Ada (Lawrence) Diffenderfer in 1919.

Grave:	14-4
Name:	Infant Son Lutz
Born:	5 OCT 1924
Died:	5 OCT 1924
Parents:	Ralph & Lucile () Lutz

Grave:	14-5
Name:	Kate (Sweigart) Lutz
Born:	27 MAR 1866
Died:	14 AUG 1908
Parents:	Samuel & Elizabeth (Sweigart) Sweigart
Spouse:	Henry D. Lutz

Grave:	14-6
Name:	Edna M. (Lutz) Bloch
Born:	23 FEB 1899
Died:	24 MAR 1959
Parents:	Henry D. & Kate (Sweigart) Lutz
Spouse:	Frank Bloch
Notes:	

Grave:	14-7
Name:	Florence V. (Lutz) Myers
Born:	17 AUG 1901
Died:	7 MAY 1981
Parents:	Henry D. & Kate (Sweigart) Lutz
Spouse:	Philip Myers
Notes:	

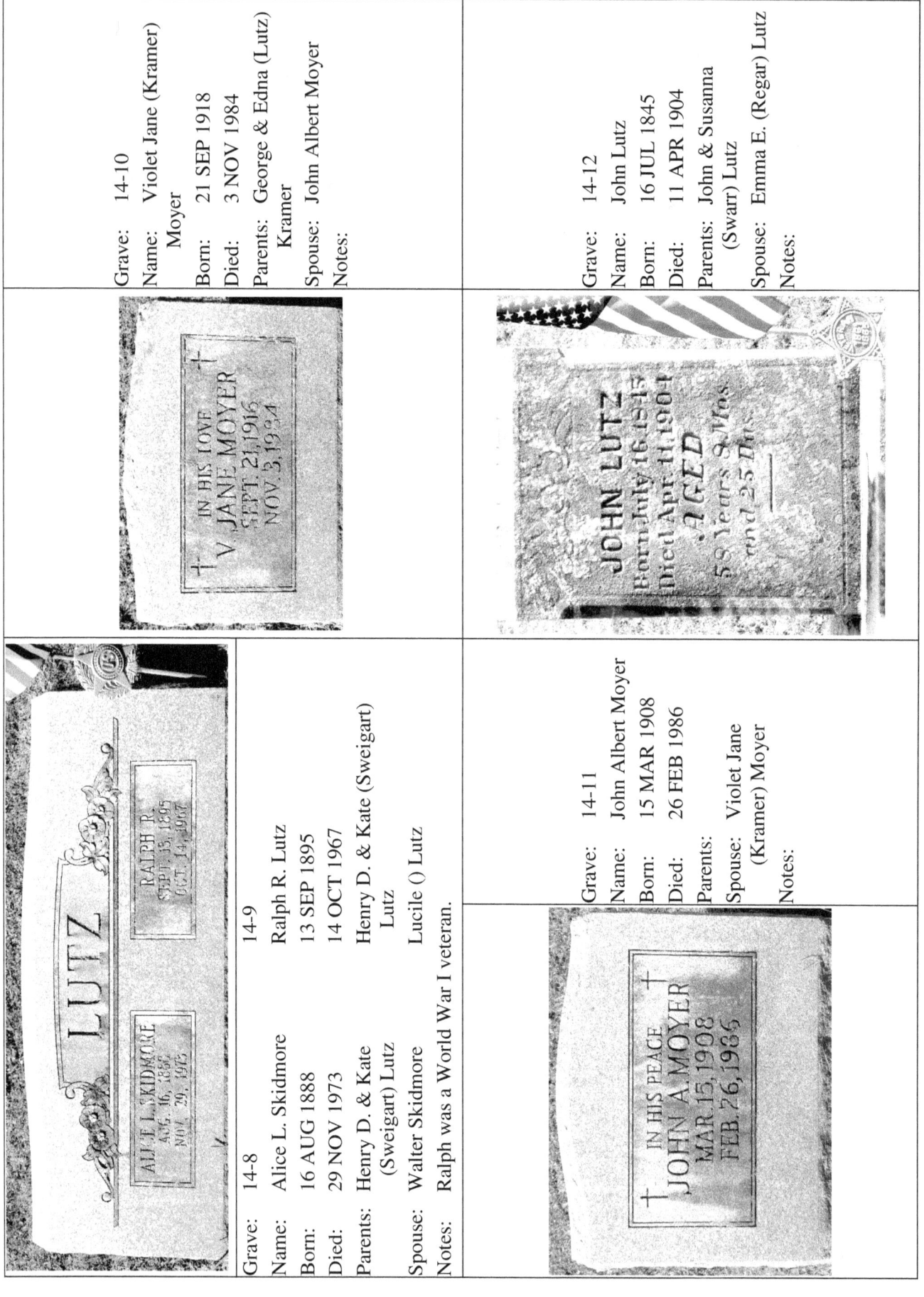

Grave: 14-10
Name: Violet Jane (Kramer) Moyer
Born: 21 SEP 1918
Died: 3 NOV 1984
Parents: George & Edna (Lutz) Kramer
Spouse: John Albert Moyer
Notes:

Grave: 14-12
Name: John Lutz
Born: 16 JUL 1845
Died: 11 APR 1904
Parents: John & Susanna (Swarr) Lutz
Spouse: Emma E. (Regar) Lutz
Notes:

Grave: 14-8
Name: Alice L. Skidmore
Born: 16 AUG 1888
Died: 29 NOV 1973
Parents: Henry D. & Kate (Sweigart) Lutz
Spouse: Walter Skidmore
Notes:

Grave: 14-9
Name: Ralph R. Lutz
Born: 13 SEP 1895
Died: 14 OCT 1967
Parents: Henry D. & Kate (Sweigart) Lutz
Spouse: Lucile () Lutz
Notes: Ralph was a World War I veteran.

Grave: 14-11
Name: John Albert Moyer
Born: 15 MAR 1908
Died: 26 FEB 1986
Parents:
Spouse: Violet Jane (Kramer) Moyer
Notes:

82

Grave: 14-14
Name: Elmer R. Lutz
Born: 5 MAR 1884
Died: 18 AUG 1942
Parents: John & Emma E.
         (Regar) Lutz
Spouse: unmarried
Notes:

Grave: 14-16
Name: Louisa K. (Regar) Lutz
Born: 26 OCT 1828
Died: 16 JUN 1892
Parents: Henry & Eve
         (Keplinger) Regar
Spouse: Adam S. Lutz
Notes:

Grave: 14-13
Name: Emma E. (Regar)
       Lutz
Born: 7 MAY 1853
Died: 20 FEB 1906
Parents: Cyrus K. & Eliza
         (Hornberger) Regar
Spouse: John Lutz
Notes:

Grave: 14-15
Name: Adam S. Lutz
Born: 28 FEB 1827
Died: 26 OCT 1891
Parents: John & Susanna
         (Swarr) Lutz
Spouse: Louisa K. (Regar)
         Lutz
Notes:

Grave:	14-18
Name:	Louisa (Zern) Artz
Born:	15 MAY 1839
Died:	5 SEP 1910
Parents:	John & Catharine (Harnish) Zern
Spouse:	William Artz
Notes:	

Grave:	15-1
Name:	Dorothy M. (Lutz) Hagy
Born:	15 AUG 1914
Died:	24 OCT 1989
Parents:	Barton S. & Alice (Harding) Lutz
Spouse:	John F. Hagy
Notes:	Married in Berks County, PA in November 1935.

Grave:	14-17
Name:	William Artz
Born:	29 MAY 1830
Died:	25 JAN 1914
Parents:	John & Magdalena ( ) Artz
Spouse:	Louisa (Zern) Artz
Notes:	Baptized at Muddy Creek Reformed Church on 12 OCT 1831.

Grave:	14-19
Name:	Christian Ziegler
Born:	28 NOV 1797
Died:	14 FEB 1881
Parents:	
Spouse:	
Notes:	

Grave:
Name: Paul Henry Lutz
Born: 21 MAR 1913
Died: 23 APR 1914
Parents: Barton & Alice (Harting) Lutz
Notes:

15-3

Grave: 15-2
Name: Alice (Harding) Lutz
Born: 21 AUG 1893
Died: 13 DEC 1916
Parents: Jacob & Annie (Barsch) Harding
Spouse: Barton S. Lutz
Notes:

15-5
Name: Miriam Jane (Bowman) Snyder
Born: 4 JUN 1930
Died: 13 NOV 1982
Parents: Harry & Lydia (Sweigart) Bowman
Notes:

Grave: 15-6
Name: Robert Charles Snyder
Born: 15 APR 1927
Died: 2 APR 2013
Parents: William & Ada (Snyder) Snyder
Notes:

Grave:
Name: William R. Lutz
Born: 29 APR 1916
Died: 29 APR 1916
Parents: Barton & Alice (Harting) Lutz
Notes:

15-4

Grave: 15-8	Grave: 16-1
Name: Florence Lutz	Name: Samuel Givler
Born: 30 DEC 1896	Born: 24 DEC 1825
Died: 24 AUG 1897	Died: 25 DEC 1899
Parents: Martin R. & Mary J. (Keener) Lutz	Parents: Peter & Mollie (Faust) Givler
Spouse: unmarried	Spouse: Catharine (Zell) Givler
Notes:	Notes: Samuel and Catharine were married on 11 DEC 1853 in Ephrata, Lancaster County, PA.

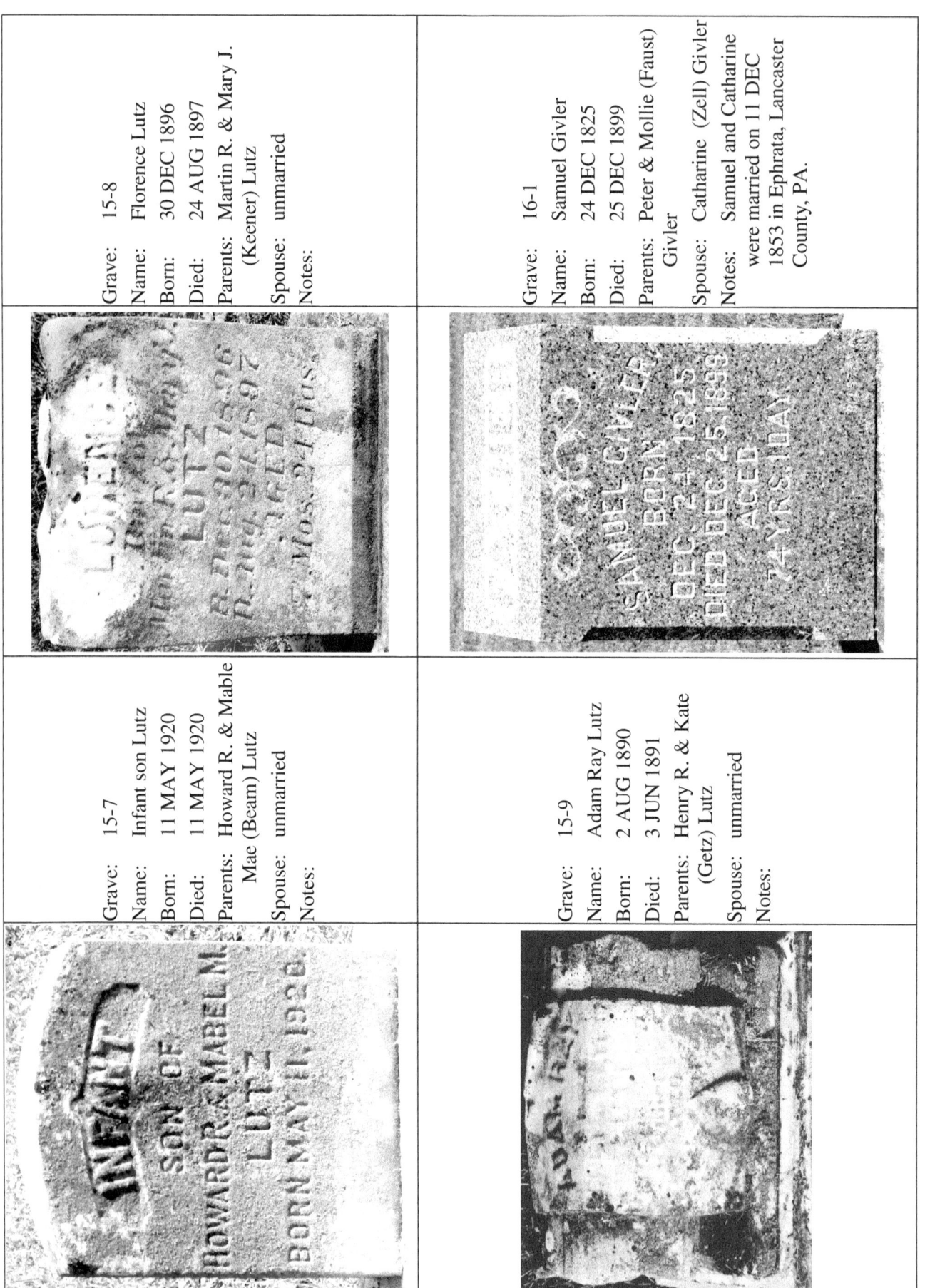

Grave: 15-7	Grave: 15-9
Name: Infant son Lutz	Name: Adam Ray Lutz
Born: 11 MAY 1920	Born: 2 AUG 1890
Died: 11 MAY 1920	Died: 3 JUN 1891
Parents: Howard R. & Mable Mae (Beam) Lutz	Parents: Henry R. & Kate (Getz) Lutz
Spouse: unmarried	Spouse: unmarried
Notes:	Notes:

Grave: 16-3
Name: John M. Schlegel
Born: 26 APR 1851
Died: 22 NOV 1923
Parents: Jacob & Mary (Matz)
          Schlegel
Spouse: Leah L. (Ludwig)
          Schlegel
Notes:

Grave: 16-5
Name: Jacob L. Schlegel
Born: 3 APR 1879
Died: 7 DEC 1888
Parents: John M. & Leah L.
          (Ludwig) Schlegel
Spouse: unmarried
Notes:

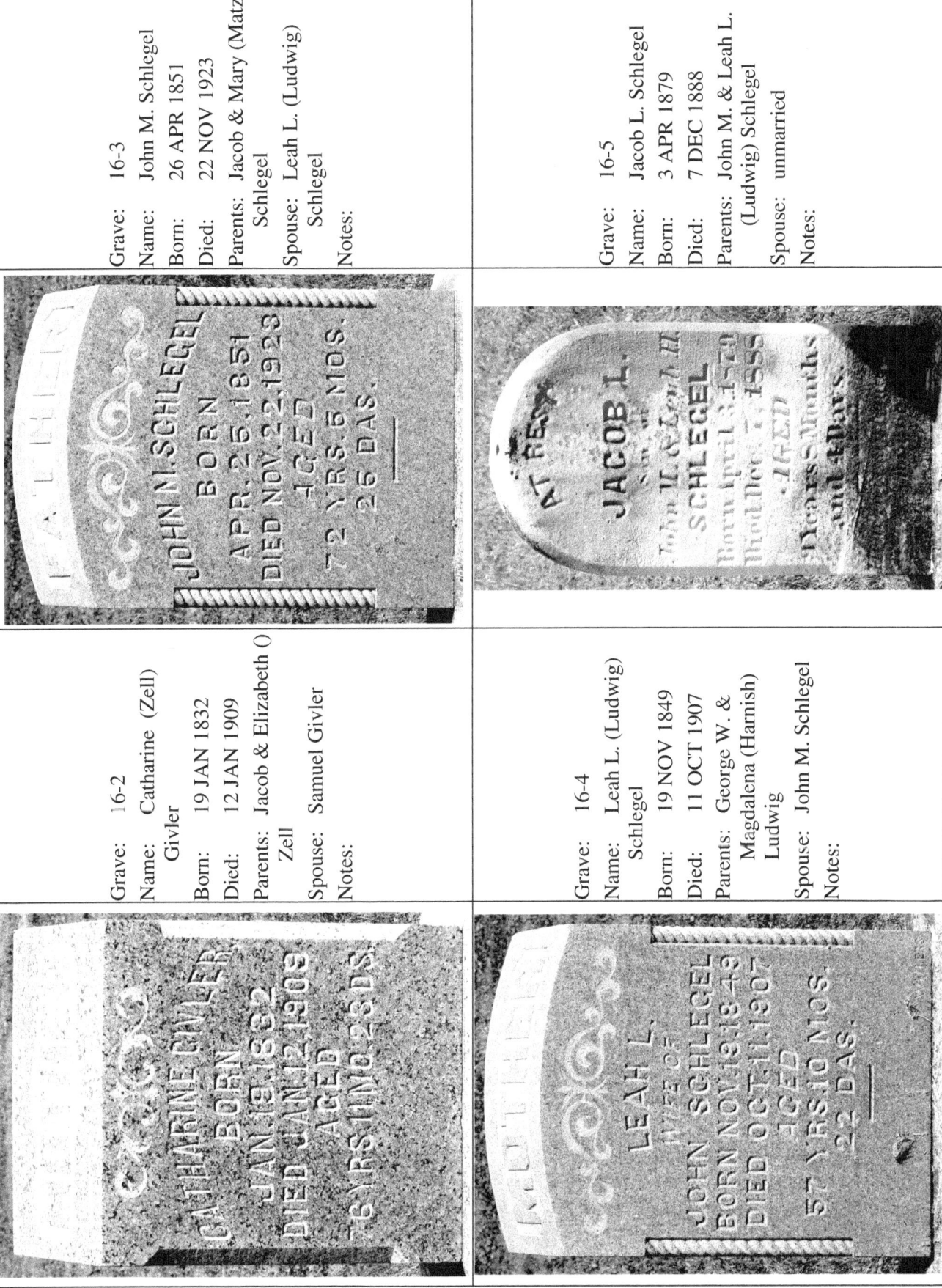

Grave: 16-2
Name: Catharine (Zell)
          Givler
Born: 19 JAN 1832
Died: 12 JAN 1909
Parents: Jacob & Elizabeth ()
          Zell
Spouse: Samuel Givler
Notes:

Grave: 16-4
Name: Leah L. (Ludwig)
          Schlegel
Born: 19 NOV 1849
Died: 11 OCT 1907
Parents: George W. &
          Magdalena (Harnish)
          Ludwig
Spouse: John M. Schlegel
Notes:

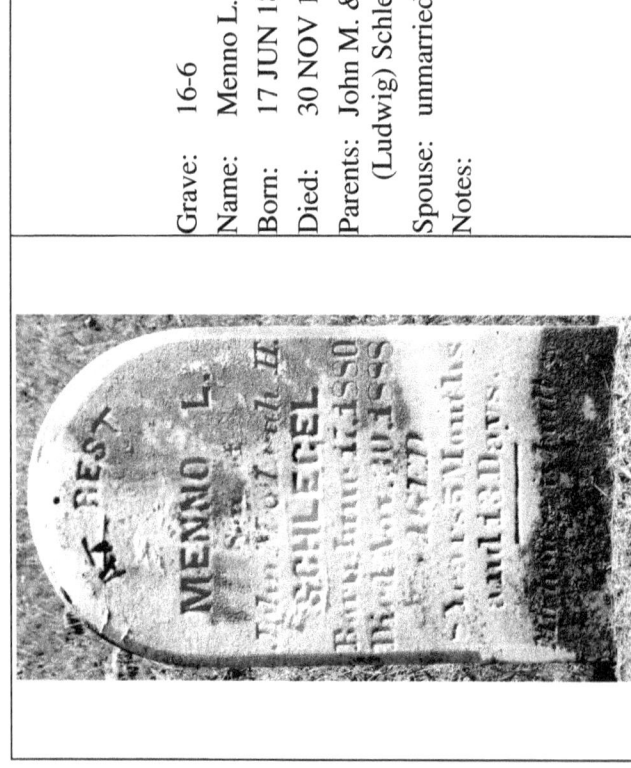

CHRISTINE W.
DAU. OF
ELWOOD B. AND RUTH A.
GROFF
DEC. 23, 1968

Grave: 17-1
Name: Christine W. Groff
Born: 23 DEC 1968
Died: 23 DEC 1968
Parents: Elwood B. & Ruth Ann (Weaver) Groff
Notes:

RONALD A.
INFANT SON OF
CALEB S. AND MABEL S.
ZIMMERMAN
JUNE 26, 1965
JUNE 28, 1965

Grave: 18-3
Name: Ronald A. Zimmerman
Born: 26 JUN 1965
Died: 28 JUN 1965
Parents: Caleb S. & Mabel S. (Auker) Zimmerman
Notes:

MENNO L. SCHLEGEL

Grave: 16-6
Name: Menno L. Schlegel
Born: 17 JUN 1880
Died: 30 NOV 1888
Parents: John M. & Leah L. (Ludwig) Schlegel
Spouse: unmarried
Notes:

ZIMMERMAN
CALEB S.
SEPT. 23, 1938
JULY 5, 2003
MABEL S. (AUKER)
[MARRIED OCT 26 1963]

Grave: 18-1
Name: Caleb S. Zimmerman
Born: 23 SEP 1938
Died: 5 JUL 2003
Parents: Levi F. & Emma B. (Stauffer) Zimmerman
Notes: Married on 26 OCT 1963 at Akron, PA.

Grave: 18-2
Name: Mabel S. (Auker) Zimmerman
Born: [Living in 2013]
Died: ---
Parents: Auker
Notes:

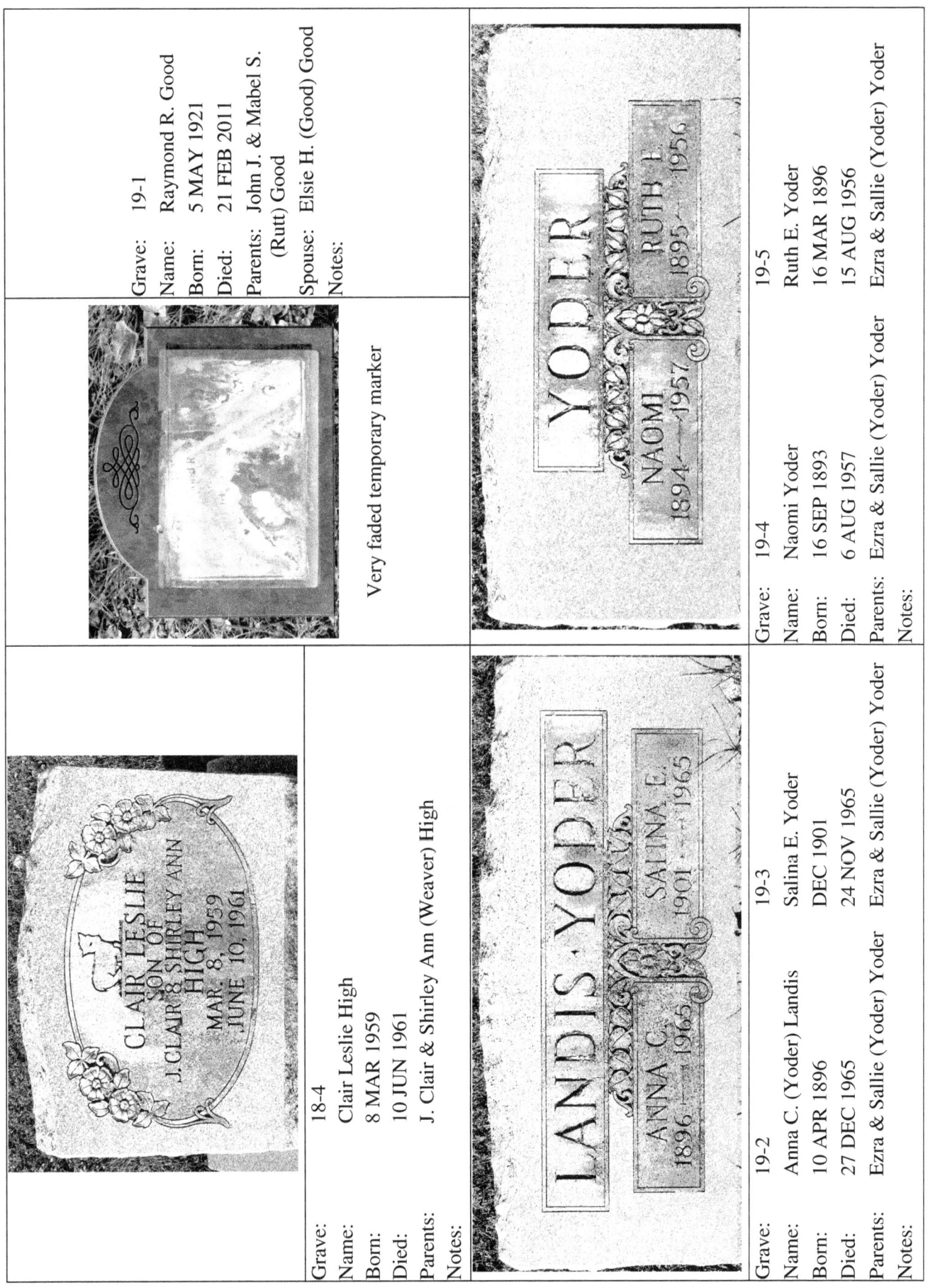

Grave: 19-1
Name: Raymond R. Good
Born: 5 MAY 1921
Died: 21 FEB 2011
Parents: John J. & Mabel S. (Rutt) Good
Spouse: Elsie H. (Good) Good
Notes:

Very faded temporary marker

Grave: 19-5
Name: Ruth E. Yoder
Born: 16 MAR 1896
Died: 15 AUG 1956
Parents: Ezra & Sallie (Yoder) Yoder
Notes:

Grave: 19-4
Name: Naomi Yoder
Born: 16 SEP 1893
Died: 6 AUG 1957
Parents: Ezra & Sallie (Yoder) Yoder
Notes:

Grave: 18-4
Name: Clair Leslie High
Born: 8 MAR 1959
Died: 10 JUN 1961
Parents: J. Clair & Shirley Ann (Weaver) High
Notes:

Grave: 19-3
Name: Salina E. Yoder
Born: DEC 1901
Died: 24 NOV 1965
Parents: Ezra & Sallie (Yoder) Yoder
Notes:

Grave: 19-2
Name: Anna C. (Yoder) Landis
Born: 10 APR 1896
Died: 27 DEC 1965
Parents: Ezra & Sallie (Yoder) Yoder
Notes:

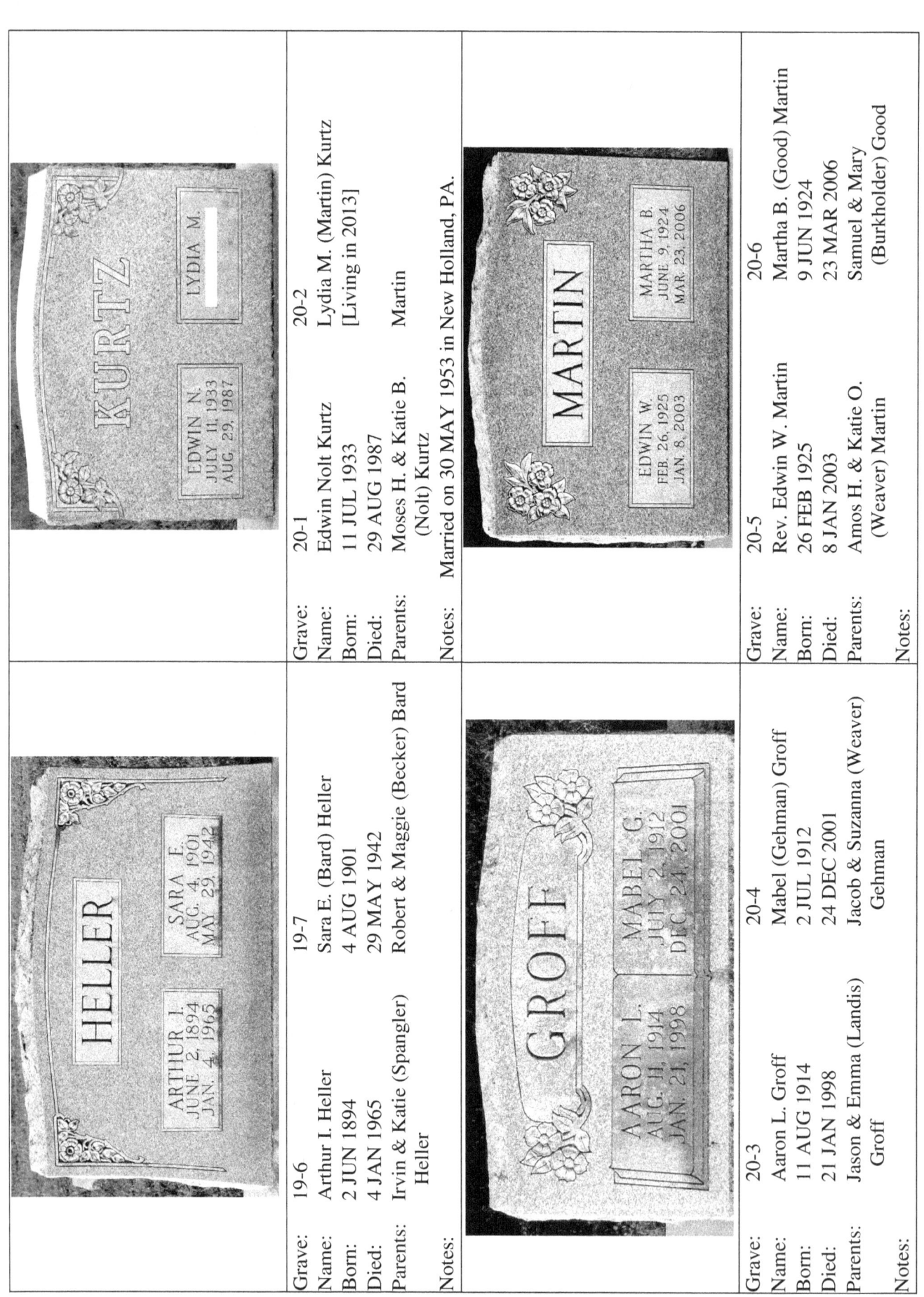

Grave:	19-6
Name:	Arthur I. Heller
Born:	2 JUN 1894
Died:	4 JAN 1965
Parents:	Irvin & Katie (Spangler) Heller
Notes:	

Grave:	19-7
Name:	Sara E. (Bard) Heller
Born:	4 AUG 1901
Died:	29 MAY 1942
Parents:	Robert & Maggie (Becker) Bard
Notes:	

Grave:	20-1
Name:	Edwin Nolt Kurtz
Born:	11 JUL 1933
Died:	29 AUG 1987
Parents:	Moses H. & Katie B. (Nolt) Kurtz
Notes:	Married on 30 MAY 1953 in New Holland, PA.

Grave:	20-2
Name:	Lydia M. (Martin) Kurtz
	[Living in 2013]
	Martin
Parents:	

Grave:	20-3
Name:	Aaron L. Groff
Born:	11 AUG 1914
Died:	21 JAN 1998
Parents:	Jason & Emma (Landis) Groff
Notes:	

Grave:	20-4
Name:	Mabel (Gehman) Groff
Born:	2 JUL 1912
Died:	24 DEC 2001
Parents:	Jacob & Suzanna (Weaver) Gehman
Notes:	

Grave:	20-5
Name:	Rev. Edwin W. Martin
Born:	26 FEB 1925
Died:	8 JAN 2003
Parents:	Amos H. & Katie O. (Weaver) Martin
Notes:	

Grave:	20-6
Name:	Martha B. (Good) Martin
Born:	9 JUN 1924
Died:	23 MAR 2006
Parents:	Samuel & Mary (Burkholder) Good
Notes:	

BARD
ROBERT E.
1874 — 1961
MAGGIE B.
1877 — 1956

Grave:	20-10
Name:	Maggie (Becker) Bard
Born:	1877
Died:	8 JUN 1956
Parents:	Samuel & Elizabeth (Shirk) Becker
Notes:	

Grave:	20-9
Name:	Robert E. Bard
Born:	1874
Died:	6 FEB 1961
Parents:	Absalom & Susan (Eberly) Bard
Notes:	Married on 30 Jan 1897 at Denver, PA.

WEAVER
RUFUS M.
NOV. 7, 1917
DEC. 23, 1983
ELLA MAE
DEC. 27, 1919
JUNE 14, 1992
I KNOW, MY REDEEMER LIVETH

Grave:	21-2
Name:	Ella Mae (Good) Weaver
Born:	27 DEC 1919
Died:	14 JUN 1992
Parents:	Barton H. & Lizzie (Geigley) Good
Notes:	

Grave:	21-1
Name:	Rufus M. Weaver
Born:	7 NOV 1917
Died:	23 DEC 1983
Parents:	David O. & Lizzie (Martin) Weaver
Notes:	

GEHMAN
PAUL H.
OCT 25, 1927
JAN 20, 1990
BARBARA K.
SEPT. 28, 1930
MAY 7, 2005

Grave:	20-8
Name:	Barbara Kilmer (Ringler) Gehman
Born:	28 SEP 1930
Died:	7 MAY 2005
Parents:	Abraham & Fannie S. (Kilmer) Ringler
Notes:	Married on 8 FEB 1951 at Bowmansville, PA.

Grave:	20-7
Name:	Paul Hursh Gehman
Born:	25 OCT 1927
Died:	20 JAN 1990
Parents:	Peter H. & Elsie (Hursh) Gehman
Notes:	

Grave:	20-11
Name:	Harry S. Lefever
Born:	1906
Died:	23 MAR 1954
Parents:	Lizzie G. Lefever & --- Schweager

Grave:	20-12
Name:	Mary M. (Althouse) Lefever
Born:	22 OCT 1909
Died:	19 APR 1984
Paren:s:	Wayne & Susan (Wenrich) Althouse

Grave:	20-13
Name:	stillborn girl
Parents:	Harry S. & Mary M. (Althouse) Lefever

LEFEVER
HARRY S.
1906 — 1954
MARY M.
1909 — 1984
STILL BORN GIRL

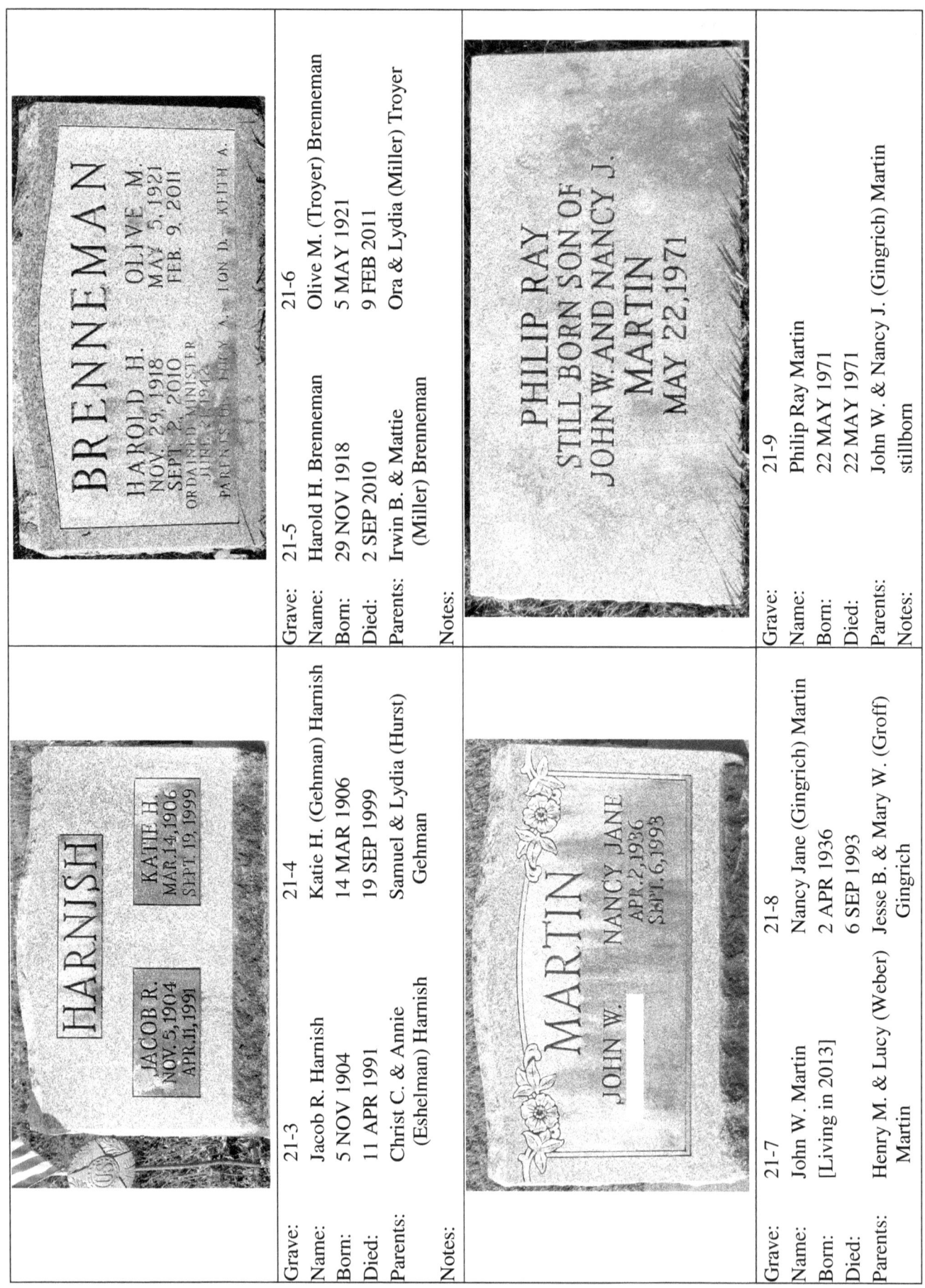

Grave: 21-3	Grave: 21-5
Name: Jacob R. Harnish	Name: Harold H. Brenneman
Born: 5 NOV 1904	Born: 29 NOV 1918
Died: 11 APR 1991	Died: 2 SEP 2010
Parents: Christ C. & Annie (Eshelman) Harnish	Parents: Irwin B. & Mattie (Miller) Brenneman
Notes:	Notes:

Grave: 21-4	Grave: 21-6
Name: Katie H. (Gehman) Harnish	Name: Olive M. (Troyer) Brenneman
Born: 14 MAR 1906	Born: 5 MAY 1921
Died: 19 SEP 1999	Died: 9 FEB 2011
Parents: Samuel & Lydia (Hurst) Gehman	Parents: Ora & Lydia (Miller) Troyer

Grave: 21-7	Grave: 21-9
Name: John W. Martin	Name: Philip Ray Martin
Born: [Living in 2013]	Born: 22 MAY 1971
Died:	Died: 22 MAY 1971
Parents: Henry M. & Lucy (Weber) Martin	Parents: John W. & Nancy J. (Gingrich) Martin
	Notes: stillborn

Grave: 21-8
Name: Nancy Jane (Gingrich) Martin
Born: 2 APR 1936
Died: 6 SEP 1993
Parents: Jesse B. & Mary W. (Groff) Gingrich

NOLL

1862 JACOB B. 1938
1863 CATHRINE R. 1936

Grave:	21-13
Name:	Cathrine R. (Painter) Noll
Born:	1863
Died:	17 JAN 1936
Parents:	Jacob & Catharine (Rathman) Painter
Notes:	

Grave:	21-12
Name:	Jacob B. Noll
Born:	1862
Died:	15 SEP 1938
Parents:	Michael D. & Carolina (Bell) Noll

MARTIN

ESTHER A.
MAY 14, 1931
MAR 10, 2004

WEAVER B.
DEC. 4, 1932
JULY 2, 2003

Grave:	22-2
Name:	Esther A. (Yoder) Martin
Born:	14 MAY 1931
Died:	10 MAR 2004
Parents:	John B. & Lena (Hoffman) Yoder

Grave:	22-1
Name:	Weaver B. Martin
Born:	4 DEC 1932
Died:	2 JUL 2003
Parents:	John F. & Edna (Burkholder) Martin

FRY

WAYNE Z.
1878 — 1946

SALLIE L.
1879 — 1960

Grave:	21-11
Name:	Wayne Z. Fry
Born:	JUN 1878
Died:	7 OCT 1946
Parents:	Jacob & Salinda (Zwally) Fry

Grave:	21-10
Name:	Sallie L. (Brubaker) Fry
Born:	1879
Died:	14 OCT 1960
Parents:	Benjamin & Mary M. (Leisey) Brubaker
Notes:	Married 19 JAN 1900 at Reamstown, PA.

Grave:	21-14
Name:	Robert P. Noll
Born:	18 JUL 1884
Died:	6 FEB 1906
Parents:	Jacob B. & Catharine (Painter) Noll
Spouse:	unmarried
Notes:	

OUR SON
ROBERT P.
SON OF
JACOB B. & CATHARINE
NOLL
BORN JULY 18, 1884
DIED FEB. 8, 1906
AGED
21 YRS. 6 MO. 18 DA.

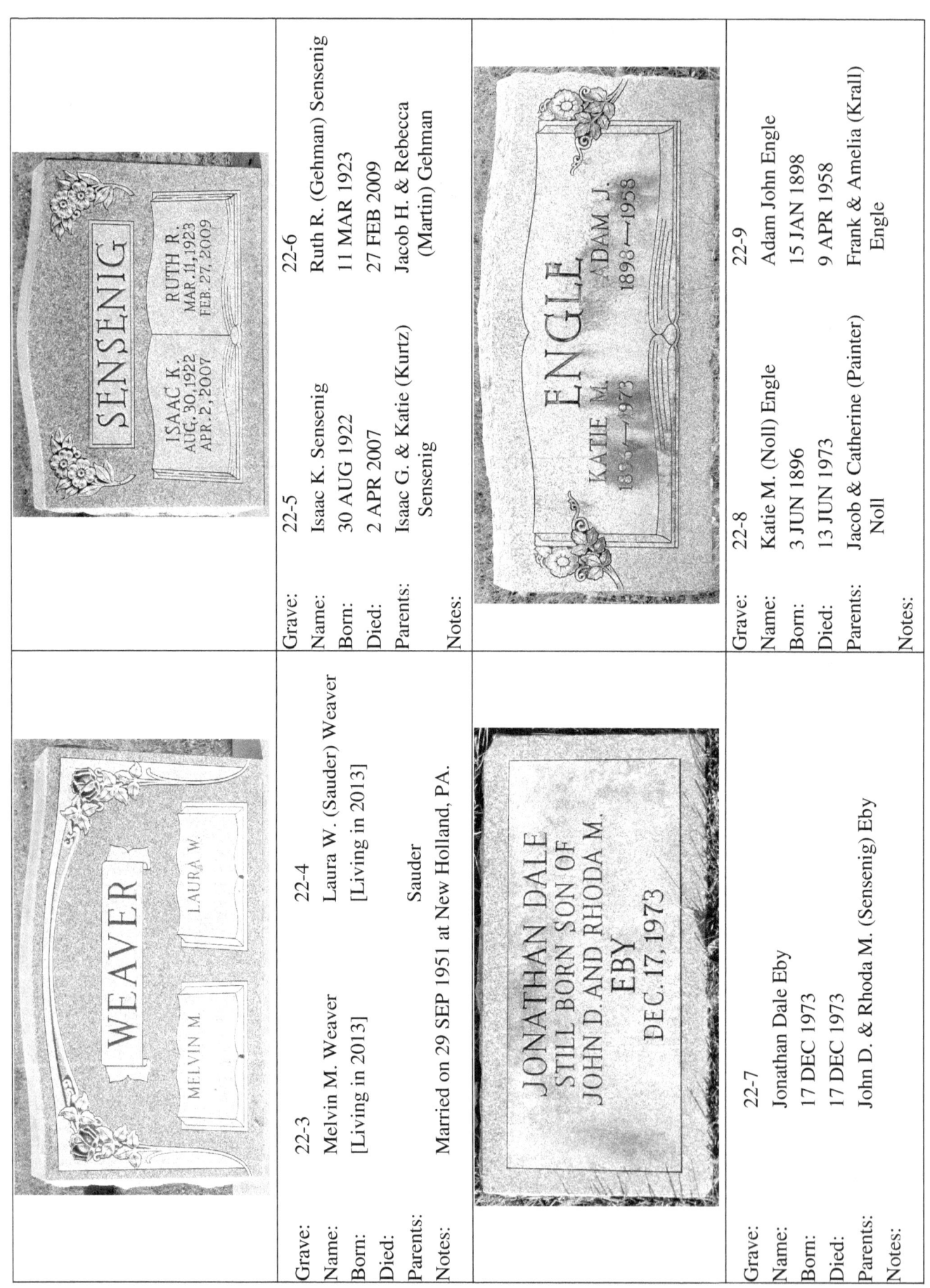

WEAVER — LAURA W. / MELVIN M

Grave: 22-3
Name: Melvin M. Weaver
Born: [Living in 2013]
Died:
Parents:
Notes: Married on 29 SEP 1951 at New Holland, PA.

Grave: 22-4
Name: Laura W. (Sauder) Weaver
Born: [Living in 2013]
Died:
Parents: Sauder
Notes:

SENSENIG — ISAAC K. AUG. 30, 1922 APR. 2, 2007 / RUTH R. MAR. 11, 1923 FEB. 27, 2009

Grave: 22-5
Name: Isaac K. Sensenig
Born: 30 AUG 1922
Died: 2 APR 2007
Parents: Isaac G. & Katie (Kurtz) Sensenig
Notes:

Grave: 22-6
Name: Ruth R. (Gehman) Sensenig
Born: 11 MAR 1923
Died: 27 FEB 2009
Parents: Jacob H. & Rebecca (Martin) Gehman
Notes:

JONATHAN DALE
STILL BORN SON OF
JOHN D. AND RHODA M.
EBY
DEC. 17, 1973

Grave: 22-7
Name: Jonathan Dale Eby
Born: 17 DEC 1973
Died: 17 DEC 1973
Parents: John D. & Rhoda M. (Sensenig) Eby
Notes:

ENGLE — ADAM J. 1898—1958 / KATIE M. 1896—1973

Grave: 22-8
Name: Katie M. (Noll) Engle
Born: 3 JUN 1896
Died: 13 JUN 1973
Parents: Jacob & Catherine (Painter) Noll
Notes:

Grave: 22-9
Name: Adam John Engle
Born: 15 JAN 1898
Died: 9 APR 1958
Parents: Frank & Amelia (Krall) Engle
Notes:

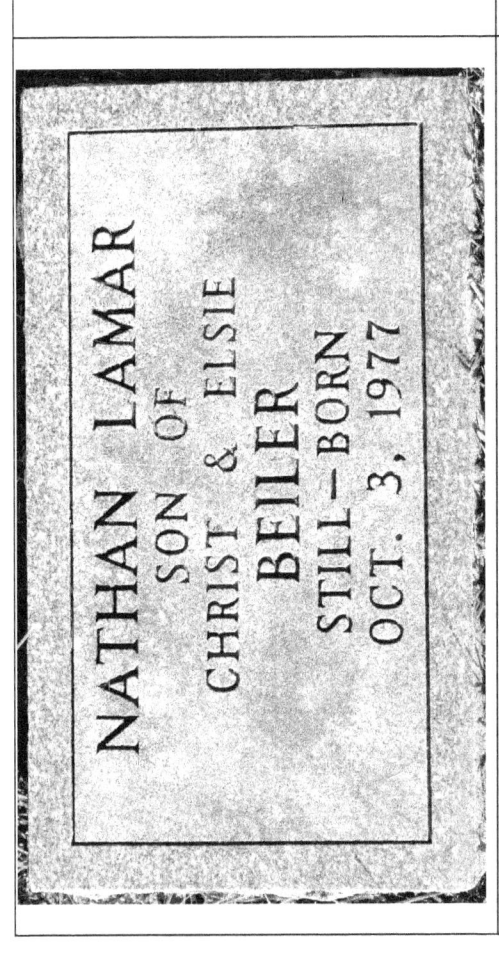

Grave:	23-1
Name:	Nathan Lamar Beiler
Born:	3 OCT 1977
Died:	3 OCT 1977
Parents:	Christ & Elsie Ann (Redcay) Beiler
Notes:	stillborn

Grave:	23-2
Name:	Phares H. Miller
Born:	23 DEC 1910
Died:	19 MAY 1992
Parents:	James & Mamie (Hoaster) Miller
Notes:	

	23-3
Name:	Amanda B. (Drybread) Miller
Born:	7 NOV 1907
Died:	6 AUG 1989
Parents:	William & Laura (Blimline) Drybread

Grave:	23-5
Name:	Henry E. Miller
Born:	10 JAN 1934
Died:	20 FEB 1992
Parents:	Phares H. & Amanda B. (Drybread) Miller
Notes:	

Grave:	23-4
Name:	Charles "Carl" R. Showalter
Born:	1929
Died:	10 JUL 1948
Parents:	Charles & Daisy (Regar) Showalter
Notes:	Died from a fall from a 3rd story roof.

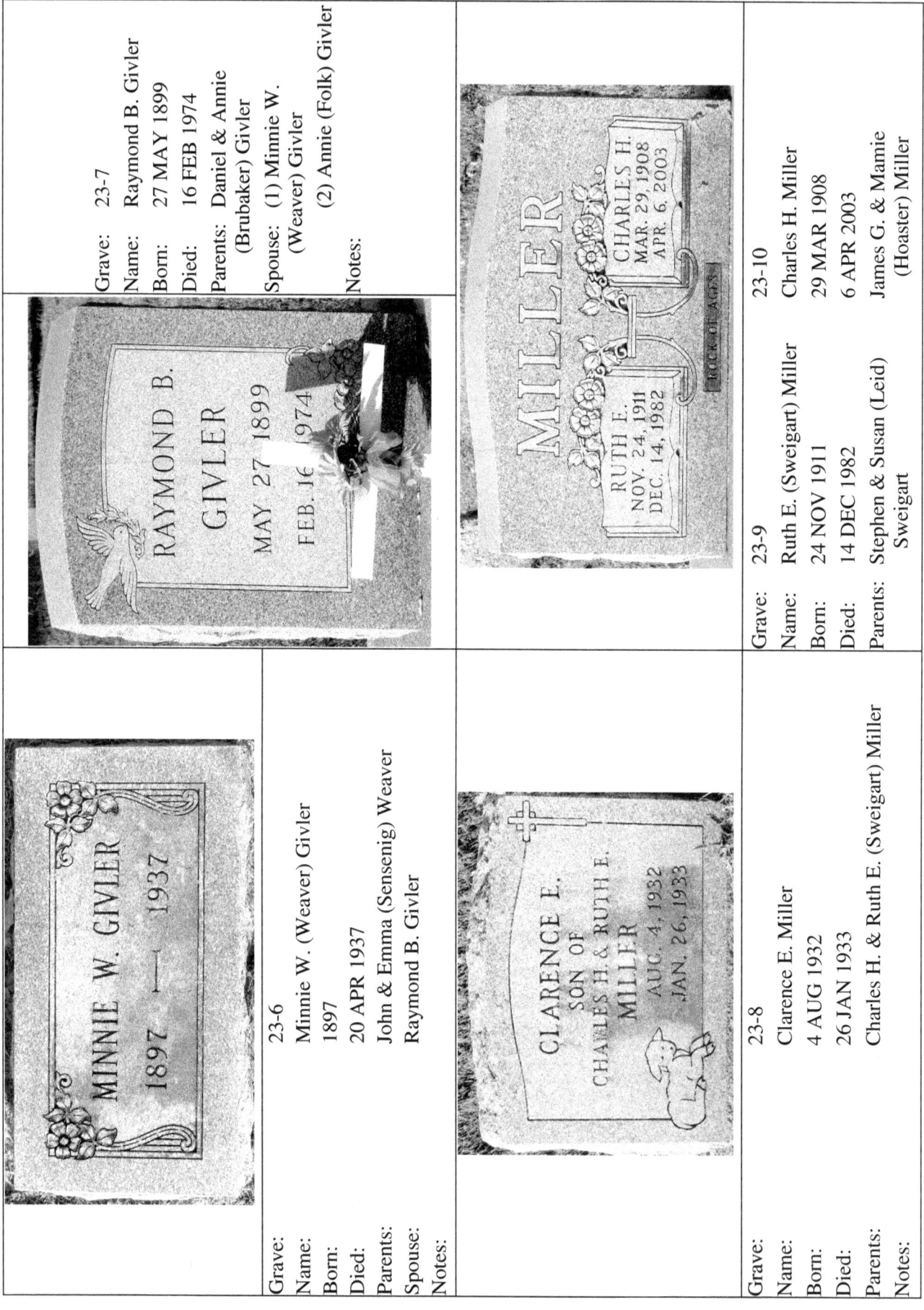

Grave: 23-7
Name: Raymond B. Givler
Born: 27 MAY 1899
Died: 16 FEB 1974
Parents: Daniel & Annie (Brubaker) Givler
Spouse: (1) Minnie W. (Weaver) Givler
(2) Annie (Folk) Givler
Notes:

Grave: 23-9
Name: Ruth E. (Sweigart) Miller
Born: 24 NOV 1911
Died: 14 DEC 1982
Parents: Stephen & Susan (Leid) Sweigart

Grave: 23-10
Name: Charles H. Miller
Born: 29 MAR 1908
Died: 6 APR 2003
Parents: James G. & Mamie (Hoaster) Miller

Grave: 23-6
Name: Minnie W. (Weaver) Givler
Born: 1897
Died: 20 APR 1937
Parents: John & Emma (Sensenig) Weaver
Spouse: Raymond B. Givler
Notes:

Grave: 23-8
Name: Clarence E. Miller
Born: 4 AUG 1932
Died: 26 JAN 1933
Parents: Charles H. & Ruth E. (Sweigart) Miller
Notes:

Grave: 24-2
Name: Raymond Givler
Born: 20 JUN 1923
Died: 2 AUG 1923
Parents: Raymond & Minnie
            (Weaver) Givler
Notes:

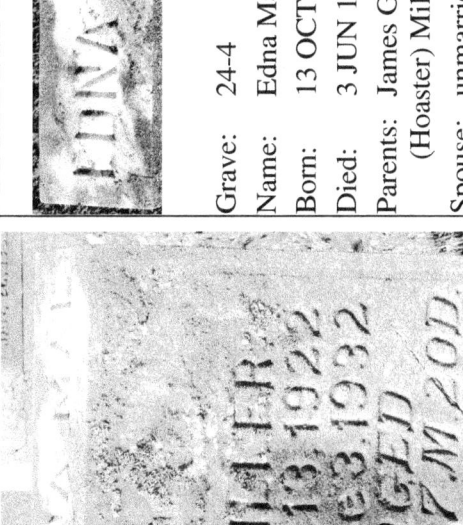

Grave: 24-4
Name: Edna Mae Miller
Born: 13 OCT 1922
Died: 3 JUN 1932
Parents: James G. & Mamie
            (Hoaster) Miller
Spouse: unmarried
Notes:

Grave:
Name: Dianne Marie Clark
Born: 1 JAN 1952
Died: 11 APR 2000
Parents:
Notes: Shirley M. (Miller) Lefever

24-1

Grave: 24-3
Name: Annie F. (Folk)
            Givler
Born: 7 OCT 1895
Died: 16 MAR 1974
Parents: William & Ellen
            (Schwoyer) Folk
Spouse: Raymond B. Givler
Notes:

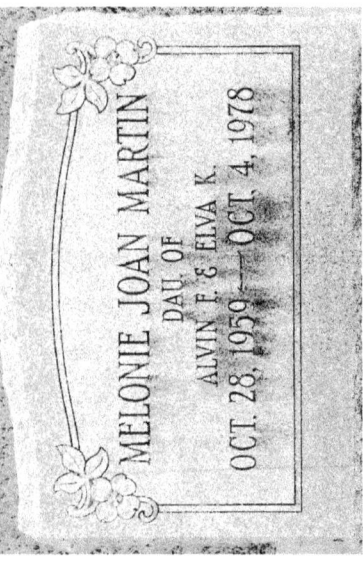

Grave: 24-5
Name: James G. Miller
Born: 1869
Died: 5 MAR 1937
Parents: Michael L. & Polly (Garner) Miller
Notes: Married on 16 NOV 1901 in Denver, PA.

Grave: 24-6
Name: Mamie S. (Hoaster) Miller
Born: 1880
Died: 28 MAY 1940
Parents: William & Elizabeth (Workman) Hoaster
Notes:

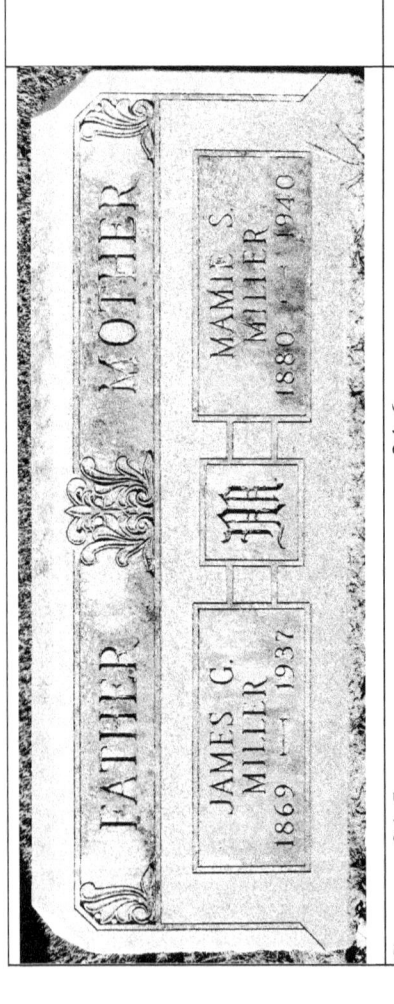

Grave: 25-1
Name: Melonie Joan Martin
Born: 28 OCT 1959
Died: 4 OCT 1978
Parents: Alvin F. & Elva Kilhefner (Kreider) Martin
Notes: Alvin & Elva were married on 14 JUN 1952 at Ephrata, PA.

Grave: 26-1
Name: Moses M. Weaver
Born: 17 JUL 1915
Died: 19 SEP 2004
Parents: Joseph M. & Maria Z. (Martin) Weaver
Notes:

Grave: 26-2
Name: Verna M. (Gehman) Weaver
Born: 26 NOV 1916
Died: 5 APR 2013
Parents: Jacob H. & Rebecca (Martin) Gehman

Grave: 26-3
Name: John S. Stauffer
Born: [Living in 2013]
Parents:

Grave: 26-4
Name: Lena S. (Weaver) Stauffer
Born: [Living in 2013]
Parents: Weaver

Grave: 26-5
Name: Percy W. Stauffer
Born: 14 MAY 1961
Died: 12 MAY 1983
Parents: John S. & Lena S. (Weaver) Stauffer

Grave: 26-6
Name: Samuel W. Stauffer
Born: 24 OCT 1956
Died: 24 OCT 1956
Parents: John S. & Lena S. (Weaver) Stauffer
Notes: John & Lena were married on 25 DEC 1955 in Hinkletown, PA.

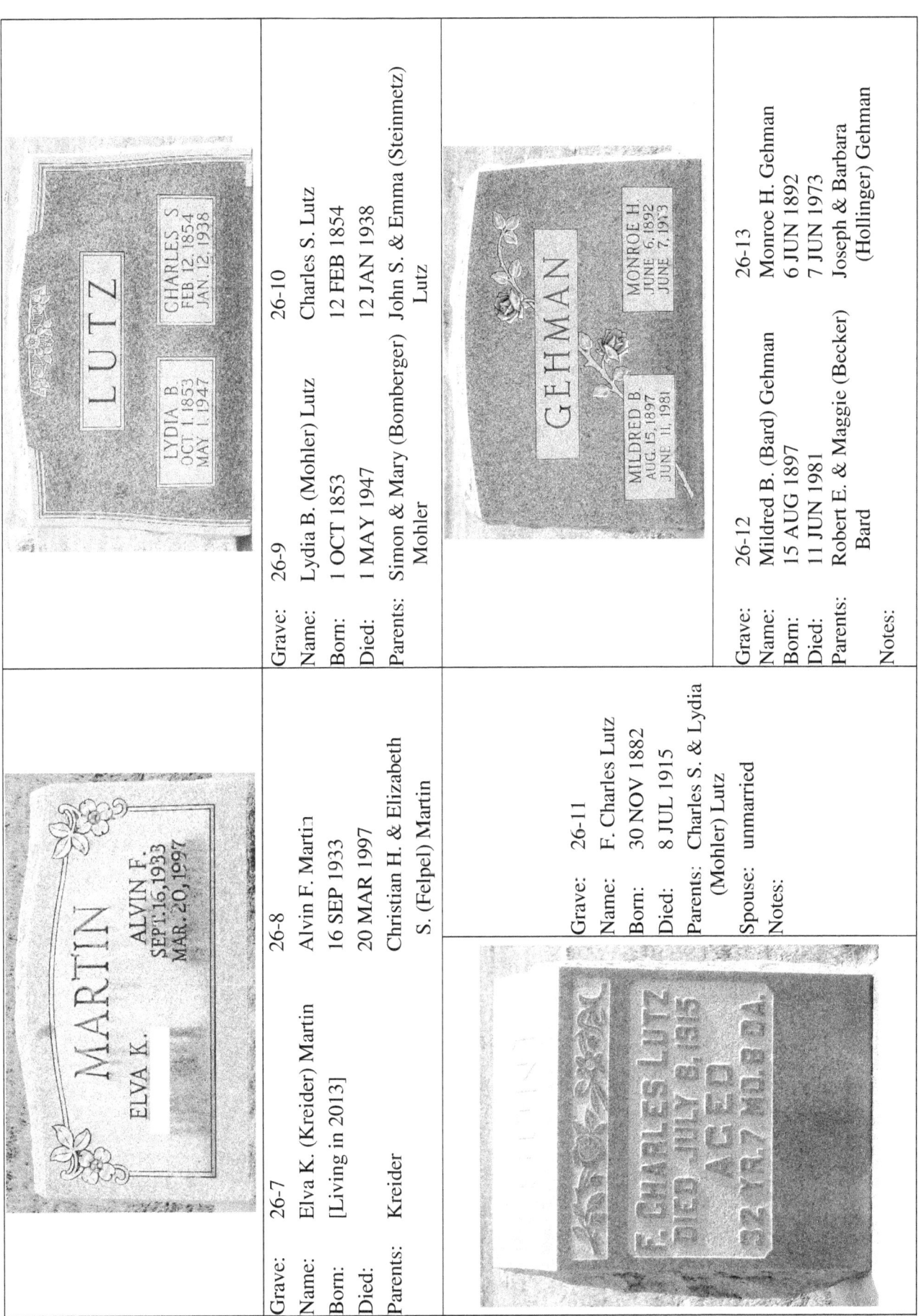

	LUTZ
	CHARLES S FEB. 12. 1854 JAN. 12. 1938
	LYDIA B. OCT. 1. 1853 MAY. 1. 1947

Grave:	26-9
Name:	Lydia B. (Mohler) Lutz
Born:	1 OCT 1853
Died:	1 MAY 1947
Parents:	Simon & Mary (Bomberger) Mohler

Grave:	26-10
Name:	Charles S. Lutz
Born:	12 FEB 1854
Died:	12 JAN 1938
Parents:	John S. & Emma (Steinmetz) Lutz

	GEHMAN
	MONROE H. JUNE 6, 1892 JUNE 7, 1913
	MILDRED B. AUG. 15, 1897 JUNE 11, 1981

Grave:	26-12
Name:	Mildred B. (Bard) Gehman
Born:	15 AUG 1897
Died:	11 JUN 1981
Parents:	Robert E. & Maggie (Becker) Bard
Notes:	

Grave:	26-13
Name:	Monroe H. Gehman
Born:	6 JUN 1892
Died:	7 JUN 1973
Parents:	Joseph & Barbara (Hollinger) Gehman

	MARTIN
	ELVA K.
	ALVIN F. SEPT. 16, 1933 MAR. 20, 1997

Grave:	26-7
Name:	Elva K. (Kreider) Martin
Born:	[Living in 2013]
Died:	
Parents:	Kreider

Grave:	26-8
Name:	Alvin F. Martin
Born:	16 SEP 1933
Died:	20 MAR 1997
Parents:	Christian H. & Elizabeth S. (Felpel) Martin

Grave:	26-11
Name:	F. Charles Lutz
Born:	30 NOV 1882
Died:	8 JUL 1915
Parents:	Charles S. & Lydia (Mohler) Lutz
Spouse:	unmarried
Notes:	

F. CHARLES LUTZ
DIED JULY 8, 1915
AGED
32 YR. 7 MO. 8 DA.

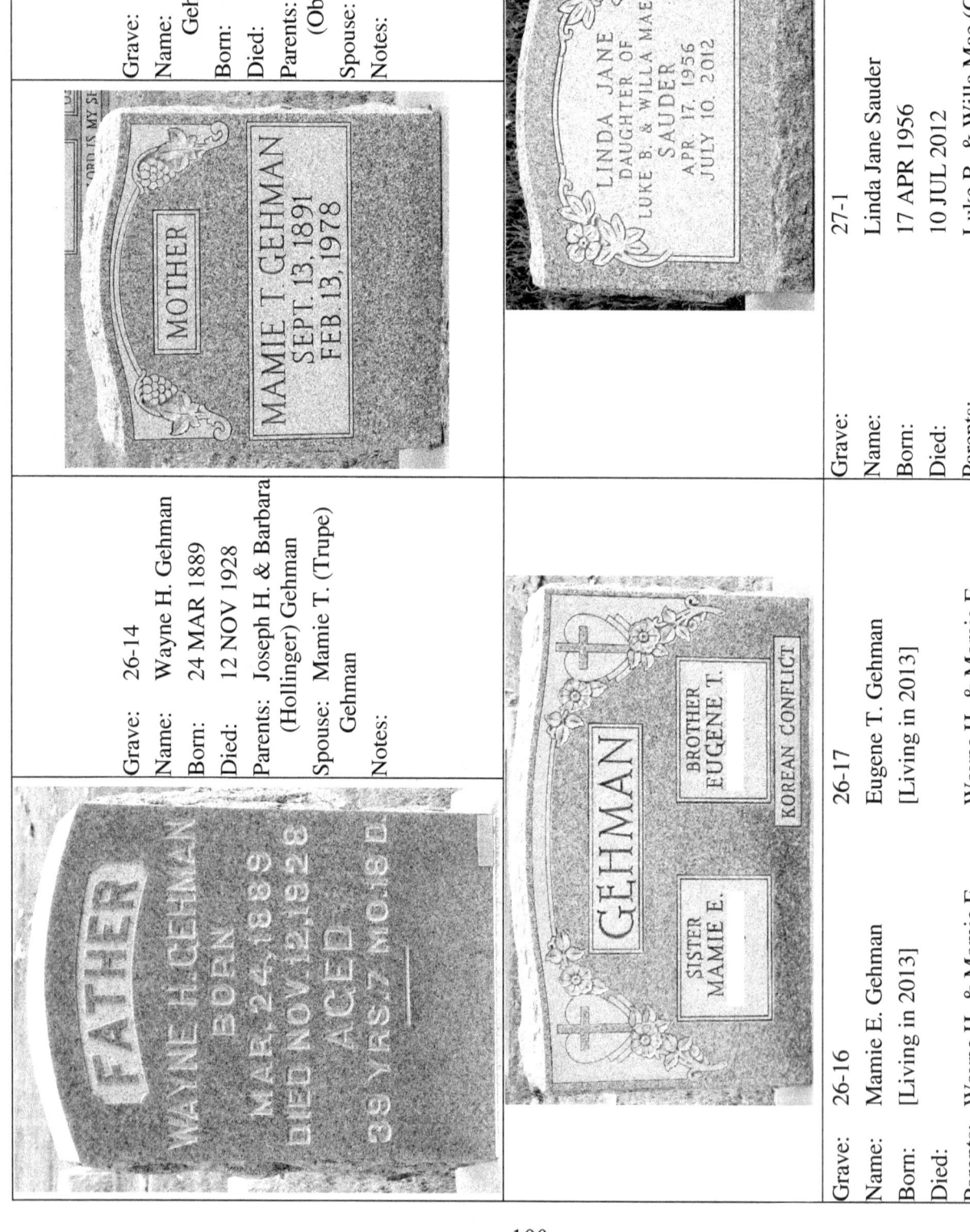

Grave: 26-15
Name: Mamie T. (Trupe) Gehman
Born: 13 SEP 1891
Died: 13 FEB 1978
Parents: Eli & Catharine (Oberholtzer) Trupe
Spouse: Wayne H. Gehman
Notes:

Grave: 27-1
Name: Linda Jane Sauder
Born: 17 APR 1956
Died: 10 JUL 2012
Parents: Luke B. & Willa Mae (Good) Sauder
Spouse:
Notes: unmarried

Grave: 26-14
Name: Wayne H. Gehman
Born: 24 MAR 1889
Died: 12 NOV 1928
Parents: Joseph H. & Barbara (Hollinger) Gehman
Spouse: Mamie T. (Trupe) Gehman
Notes:

Grave: 26-16
Name: Mamie E. Gehman
Born: [Living in 2013]
Died:
Parents: Wayne H. & Mamie E. (Trupe) Gehman
Notes:

Grave: 26-17
Name: Eugene T. Gehman
Born: [Living in 2013]
Died:
Parents: Wayne H. & Mamie E. (Trupe) Gehman
Notes: Eugene served in the military during the Korean War.

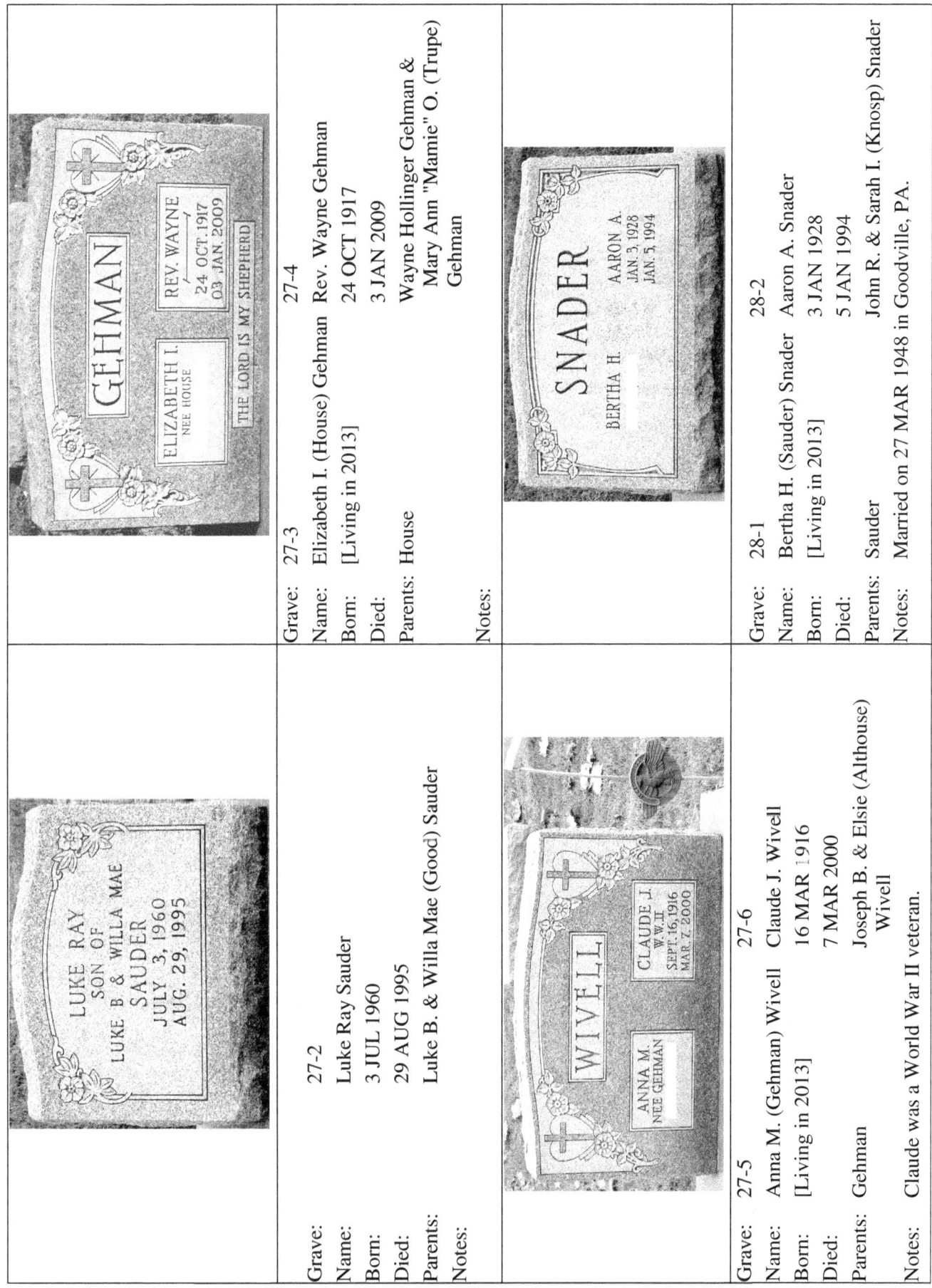

Grave: 27-3	**Grave:** 28-1
Name: Elizabeth I. (House) Gehman	**Name:** Bertha H. (Sauder) Snader
Born: [Living in 2013]	**Born:** [Living in 2013]
Died:	**Died:**
Parents: House	**Parents:** Sauder
Notes:	**Notes:** Married on 27 MAR 1948 in Goodville, PA.

Grave: 27-4	**Grave:** 28-2
Name: Rev. Wayne Gehman	**Name:** Aaron A. Snader
Born: 24 OCT 1917	**Born:** 3 JAN 1928
Died: 3 JAN 2009	**Died:** 5 JAN 1994
Parents: Wayne Hollinger Gehman & Mary Ann "Mamie" O. (Trupe) Gehman	**Parents:** John R. & Sarah I. (Knosp) Snader

Grave: 27-2	**Grave:** 27-5
Name: Luke Ray Sauder	**Name:** Anna M. (Gehman) Wivell
Born: 3 JUL 1960	**Born:** [Living in 2013]
Died: 29 AUG 1995	**Died:**
Parents: Luke B. & Willa Mae (Good) Sauder	**Parents:** Gehman
Notes:	

	Grave: 27-6
	Name: Claude J. Wivell
	Born: 16 MAR 1916
	Died: 7 MAR 2000
	Parents: Joseph B. & Elsie (Althouse) Wivell
	Notes: Claude was a World War II veteran.

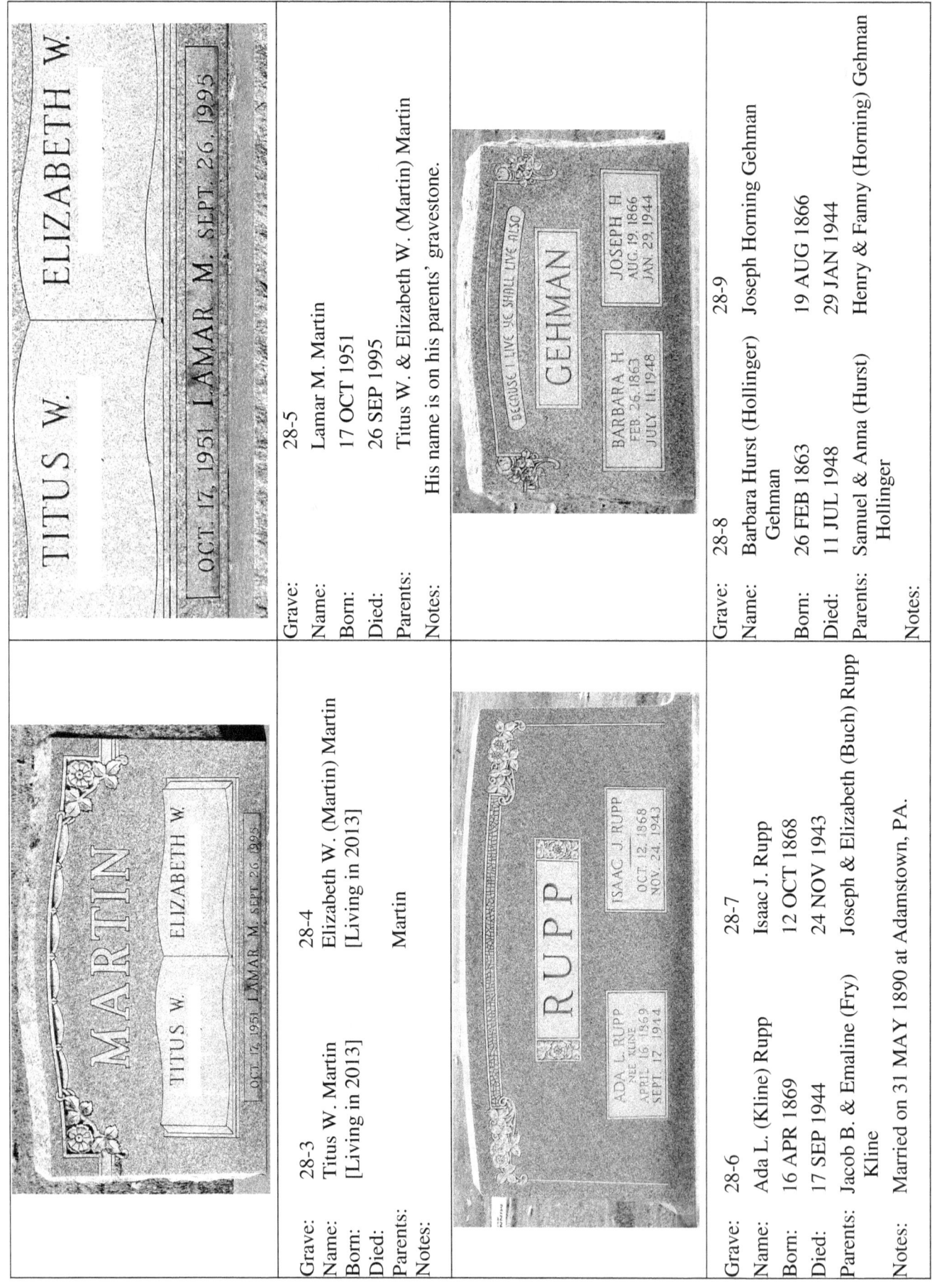

Grave:	28-5
Name:	Lamar M. Martin
Born:	17 OCT 1951
Died:	26 SEP 1995
Parents:	Titus W. & Elizabeth W. (Martin) Martin
Notes:	His name is on his parents' gravestone.

Grave:	28-3	28-4
Name:	Titus W. Martin	Elizabeth W. (Martin) Martin
Born:	[Living in 2013]	[Living in 2013]
Died:		
Parents:		Martin
Notes:		

Grave:	28-9
Name:	Joseph Horning Gehman
Born:	19 AUG 1866
Died:	29 JAN 1944
Parents:	Henry & Fanny (Horning) Gehman

Grave:	28-8
Name:	Barbara Hurst (Hollinger) Gehman
Born:	26 FEB 1863
Died:	11 JUL 1948
Parents:	Samuel & Anna (Hurst) Hollinger
Notes:	

Grave:	28-6	28-7
Name:	Ada L. (Kline) Rupp	Isaac J. Rupp
Born:	16 APR 1869	12 OCT 1868
Died:	17 SEP 1944	24 NOV 1943
Parents:	Jacob B. & Emaline (Fry) Kline	Joseph & Elizabeth (Buch) Rupp
Notes:	Married on 31 MAY 1890 at Adamstown, PA.	

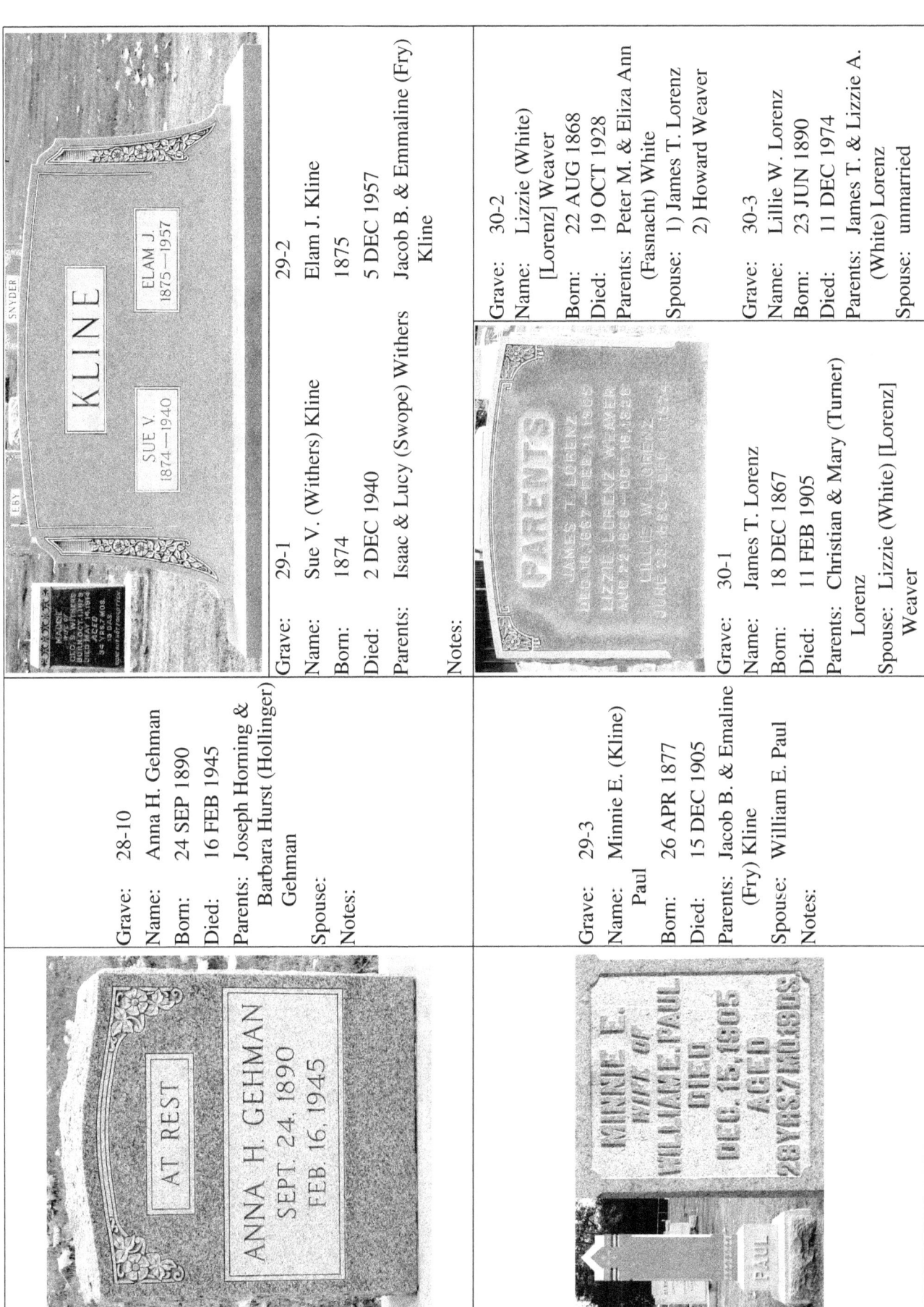

Grave: 28-10
Name: Anna H. Gehman
Born: 24 SEP 1890
Died: 16 FEB 1945
Parents: Joseph Horning & Barbara Hurst (Hollinger) Gehman
Spouse:
Notes:

Grave: 29-1
Name: Sue V. (Withers) Kline
Born: 1874
Died: 2 DEC 1940
Parents: Isaac & Lucy (Swope) Withers
Notes:

Grave: 29-2
Name: Elam J. Kline
Born: 1875
Died: 5 DEC 1957
Parents: Jacob B. & Emmaline (Fry) Kline

Grave: 29-3
Name: Minnie E. (Kline) Paul
Born: 26 APR 1877
Died: 15 DEC 1905
Parents: Jacob B. & Emaline (Fry) Kline
Spouse: William E. Paul
Notes:

Grave: 30-1
Name: James T. Lorenz
Born: 18 DEC 1867
Died: 11 FEB 1905
Parents: Christian & Mary (Turner) Lorenz
Spouse: Lizzie (White) [Lorenz] Weaver

Grave: 30-2
Name: Lizzie (White) [Lorenz] Weaver
Born: 22 AUG 1868
Died: 19 OCT 1928
Parents: Peter M. & Eliza Ann (Fasnacht) White
Spouse: 1) James T. Lorenz
2) Howard Weaver

Grave: 30-3
Name: Lillie W. Lorenz
Born: 23 JUN 1890
Died: 11 DEC 1974
Parents: James T. & Lizzie A. (White) Lorenz
Spouse: unmarried

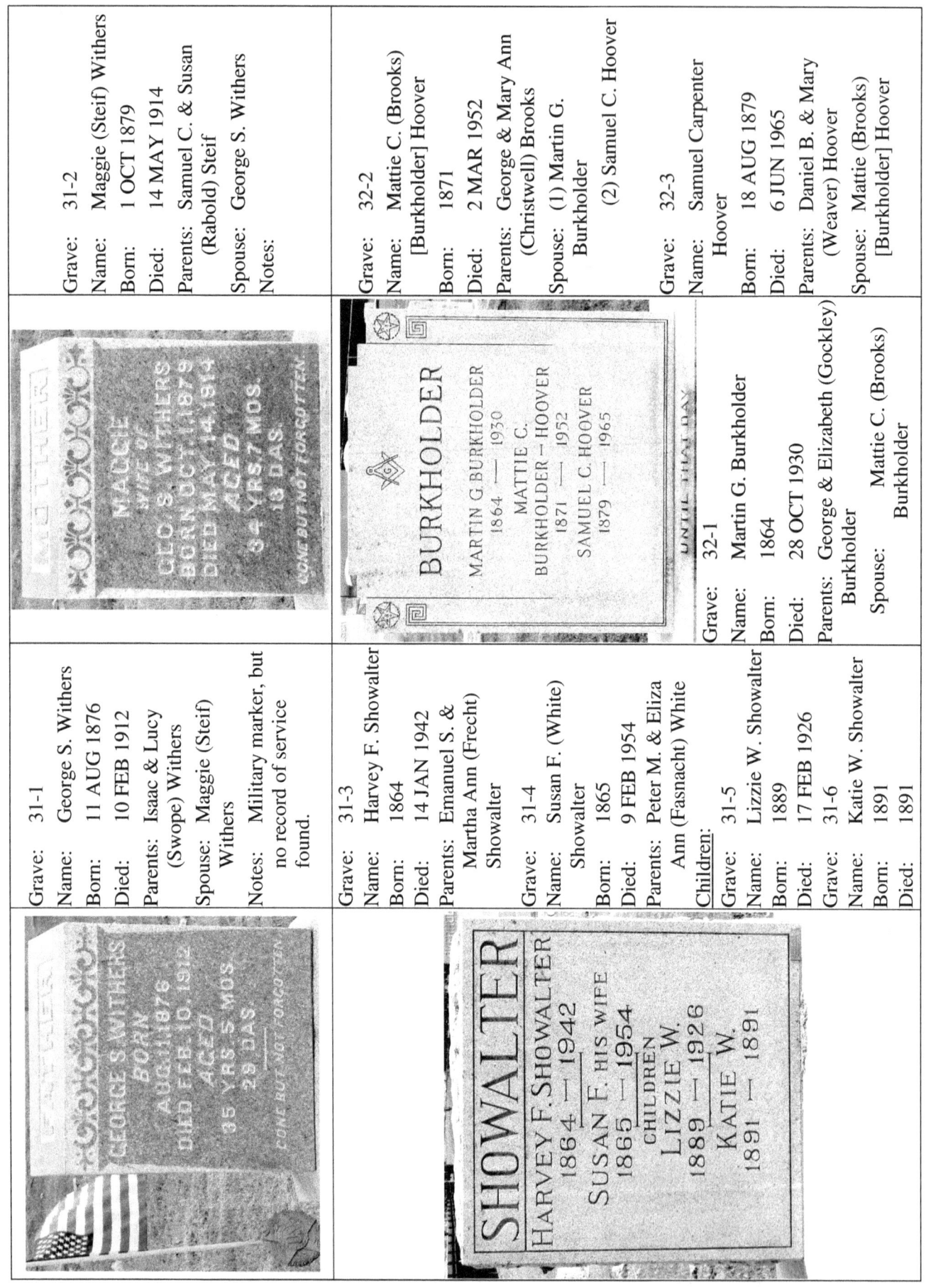

Grave: 31-2
Name: Maggie (Steif) Withers
Born: 1 OCT 1879
Died: 14 MAY 1914
Parents: Samuel C. & Susan (Rabold) Steif
Spouse: George S. Withers
Notes:

Grave: 32-2
Name: Mattie C. (Brooks) [Burkholder] Hoover
Born: 1871
Died: 2 MAR 1952
Parents: George & Mary Ann (Christwell) Brooks
Spouse: (1) Martin G. Burkholder
(2) Samuel C. Hoover

Grave: 32-3
Name: Samuel Carpenter Hoover
Born: 18 AUG 1879
Died: 6 JUN 1965
Parents: Daniel B. & Mary (Weaver) Hoover
Spouse: Mattie (Brooks) [Burkholder] Hoover

Grave: 32-1
Name: Martin G. Burkholder
Born: 1864
Died: 28 OCT 1930
Parents: George & Elizabeth (Gockley) Burkholder
Spouse: Mattie C. (Brooks) Burkholder

Grave: 31-1
Name: George S. Withers
Born: 11 AUG 1876
Died: 10 FEB 1912
Parents: Isaac & Lucy (Swope) Withers
Spouse: Maggie (Steif) Withers
Notes: Military marker, but no record of service found.

Grave: 31-3
Name: Harvey F. Showalter
Born: 1864
Died: 14 JAN 1942
Parents: Emanuel S. & Martha Ann (Frecht) Showalter

Grave: 31-4
Name: Susan F. (White) Showalter
Born: 1865
Died: 9 FEB 1954
Parents: Peter M. & Eliza Ann (Fasnacht) White
Children:

Grave: 31-5
Name: Lizzie W. Showalter
Born: 1889
Died: 17 FEB 1926

Grave: 31-6
Name: Katie W. Showalter
Born: 1891
Died: 1891

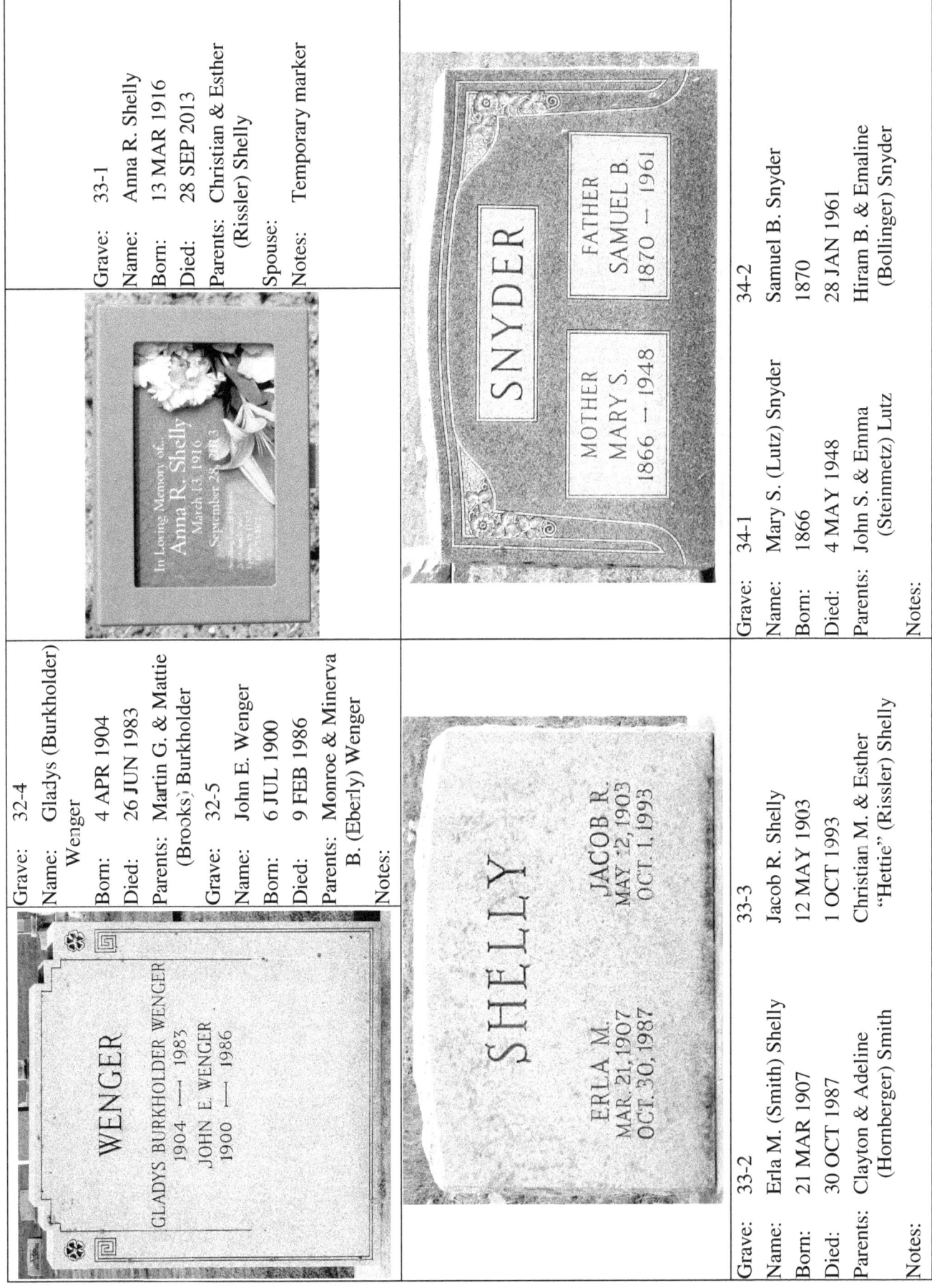

Grave: 32-4	**Grave:** 33-1
Name: Gladys (Burkholder) Wenger	**Name:** Anna R. Shelly
Born: 4 APR 1904	**Born:** 13 MAR 1916
Died: 26 JUN 1983	**Died:** 28 SEP 2013
Parents: Martin G. & Mattie (Brooks) Burkholder	**Parents:** Christian & Esther (Rissler) Shelly
	Spouse:
Grave: 32-5	**Notes:** Temporary marker
Name: John E. Wenger	
Born: 6 JUL 1900	
Died: 9 FEB 1986	
Parents: Monroe & Minerva B. (Eberly) Wenger	
Notes:	

Grave: 34-1	
Name: Mary S. (Lutz) Snyder	
Born: 1866	
Died: 4 MAY 1948	
Parents: John S. & Emma (Steinmetz) Lutz	
Notes:	

Grave: 34-2	
Name: Samuel B. Snyder	
Born: 1870	
Died: 28 JAN 1961	
Parents: Hiram B. & Emaline (Bollinger) Snyder	

Grave: 33-2	**Grave:** 33-3
Name: Erla M. (Smith) Shelly	**Name:** Jacob R. Shelly
Born: 21 MAR 1907	**Born:** 12 MAY 1903
Died: 30 OCT 1987	**Died:** 1 OCT 1993
Parents: Clayton & Adeline (Hornberger) Smith	**Parents:** Christian M. & Esther "Hettie" (Rissler) Shelly
Notes:	

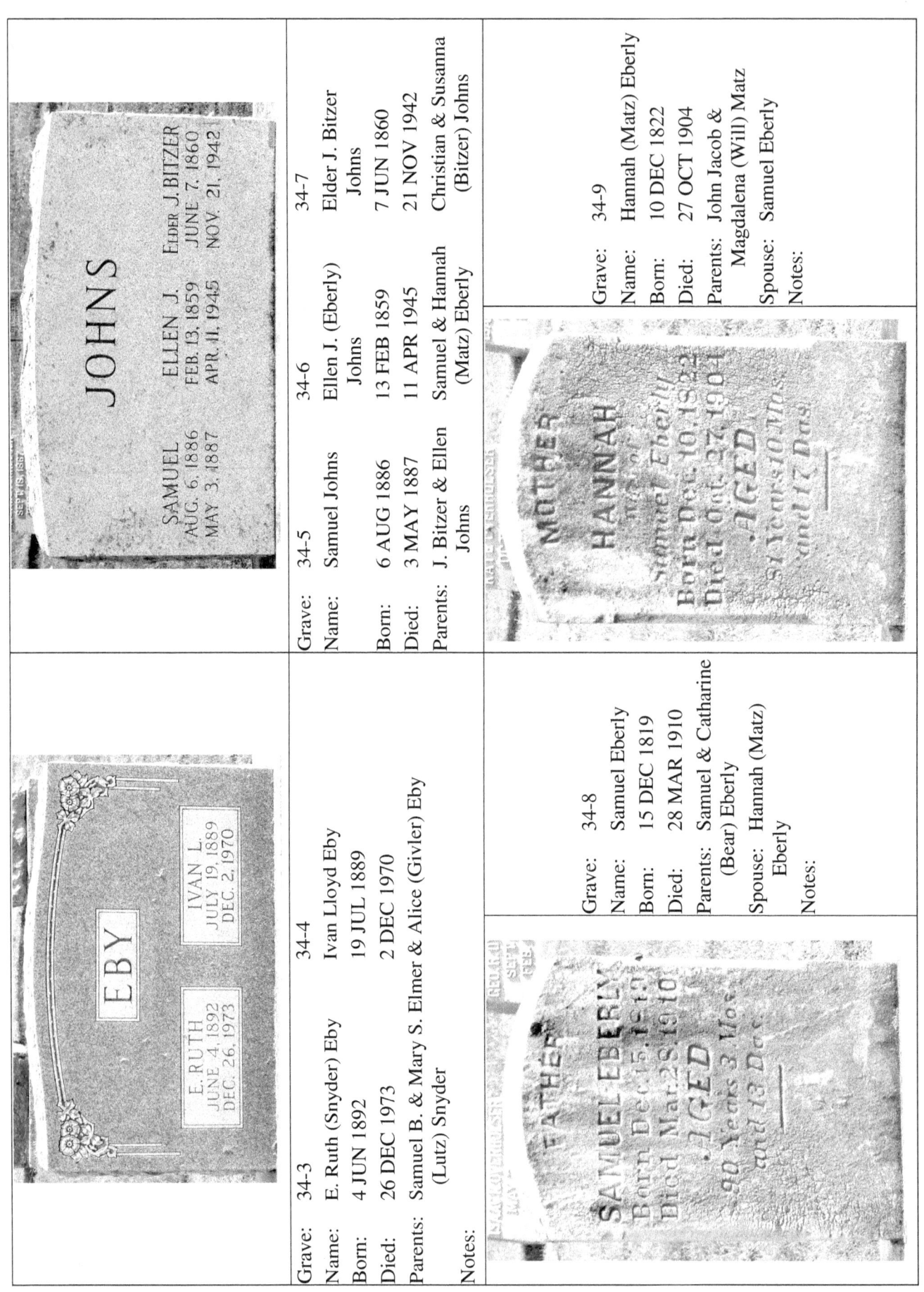

JOHNS

SAMUEL
AUG. 6, 1886
MAY 3, 1887

ELLEN J.
FEB. 13, 1859
APR. 11, 1945

ELDER J. BITZER
JUNE 7, 1860
NOV. 21, 1942

EBY

E. RUTH
JUNE 4, 1892
DEC. 26, 1973

IVAN L.
JULY 19, 1889
DEC. 2, 1970

Grave:	34-3	
Name:	E. Ruth (Snyder) Eby	
Born:	4 JUN 1892	
Died:	26 DEC 1973	
Parents:	Samuel B. & Mary S. Elmer & Alice (Givler) Eby (Lutz) Snyder	
Notes:		

	34-4
	Ivan Lloyd Eby
	19 JUL 1889
	2 DEC 1970

Grave:	34-5
Name:	Samuel Johns
Born:	6 AUG 1886
Died:	3 MAY 1887
Parents:	J. Bitzer & Ellen Johns

	34-6
	Ellen J. (Eberly) Johns
	13 FEB 1859
	11 APR 1945
	Samuel & Hannah (Matz) Eberly

	34-7
	Elder J. Bitzer Johns
	7 JUN 1860
	21 NOV 1942
	Christian & Susanna (Bitzer) Johns

Grave:	34-8
Name:	Samuel Eberly
Born:	15 DEC 1819
Died:	28 MAR 1910
Parents:	Samuel & Catharine (Bear) Eberly
Spouse:	Hannah (Matz) Eberly
Notes:	

Grave:	34-9
Name:	Hannah (Matz) Eberly
Born:	10 DEC 1822
Died:	27 OCT 1904
Parents:	John Jacob & Magdalena (Will) Matz
Spouse:	Samuel Eberly
Notes:	

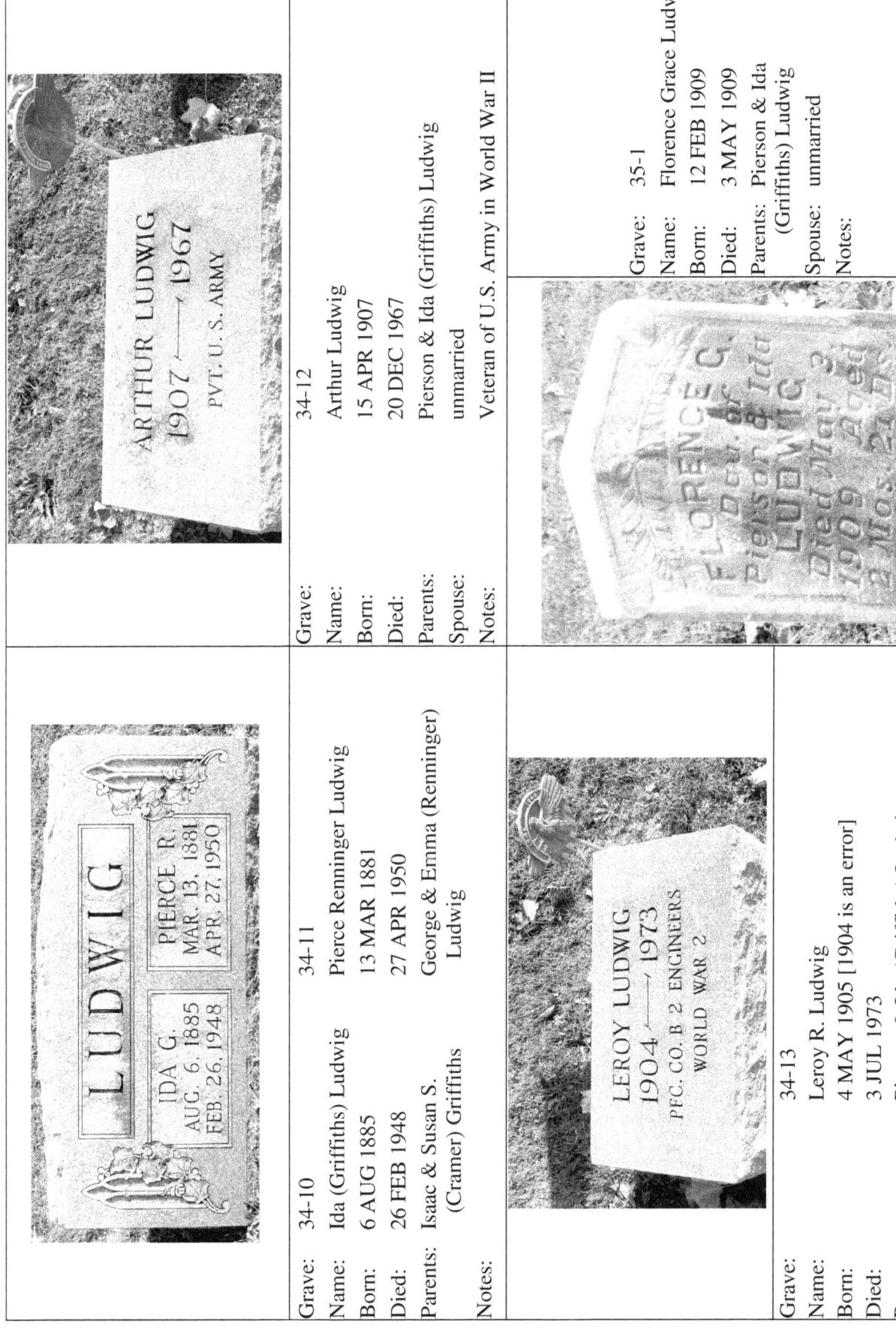

	Grave: 35-1
	Name: Florence Grace Ludwig
	Born: 12 FEB 1909
	Died: 3 MAY 1909
	Parents: Pierson & Ida (Griffiths) Ludwig
	Spouse: unmarried
	Notes:

Grave: 34-12
Name: Arthur Ludwig
Born: 15 APR 1907
Died: 20 DEC 1967
Parents: Pierson & Ida (Griffiths) Ludwig
Spouse: unmarried
Notes: Veteran of U.S. Army in World War II

Grave: 34-10
Name: Ida (Griffiths) Ludwig
Born: 6 AUG 1885
Died: 26 FEB 1948
Parents: Isaac & Susan S. (Cramer) Griffiths
Notes:

34-11
Pierce Renninger Ludwig
13 MAR 1881
27 APR 1950
George & Emma (Renninger) Ludwig

Grave: 34-13
Name: Leroy R. Ludwig
Born: 4 MAY 1905 [1904 is an error]
Died: 3 JUL 1973
Parents: Pierson & Ida (Griffiths) Ludwig
Spouse: unmarried
Notes: Veteran of U.S. Army in World War II

Grave:	36-1
Name:	Edwin Shimp
Born:	26 JAN 1871
Died:	18 JUN 1951
Parents:	Henry & Fianna (Hagy) Shimp
Spouse:	Amelia (Miller) Shimp
Notes:	

Grave:	36-3
Name:	John H. Overholser
Born:	30 DEC 1864
Died:	11 JUL 1865
Parents:	Isaac K. & Catharine (Regar) Overholser
Spouse:	unmarried
Notes:	

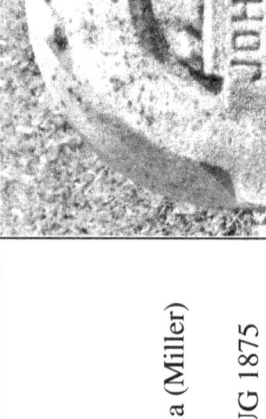

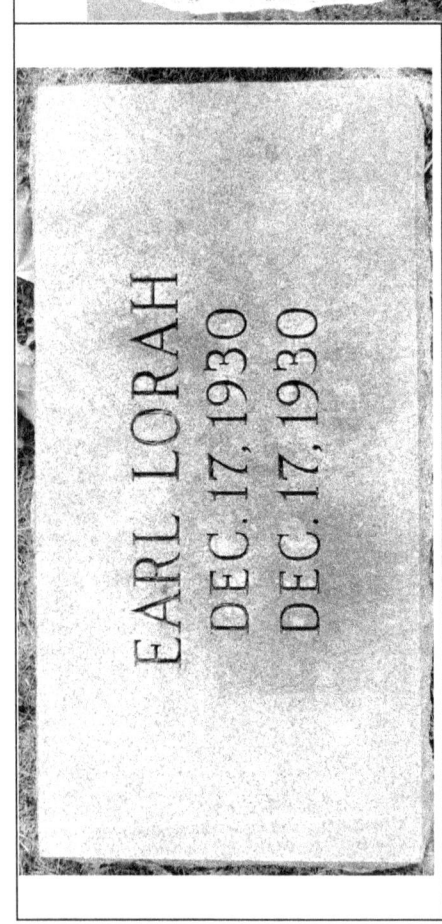

Grave:	35-2
Name:	Earl Lorah
Born:	17 DEC 1930
Died:	17 DEC 1930
Parents:	Horace E. & Dorothy (Ludwig) Lorah
Spouse:	unmarried
Notes:	

Grave:	36-2
Name:	Amelia (Miller) Shimp
Born:	28 AUG 1875
Died:	24 MAY 1914
Parents:	Peter L. & Clementine (Ott) Miller
Spouse:	Edwin Shimp
Notes:	

Grave:	36-4
Name:	George R. Overholser
Born:	18 SEP 1867
Died:	8 FEB 1913
Parents:	Isaac K. & Catharine (Regar) Overholser
Spouse:	

Grave:	36-6
Name:	Kate (Regar) Overholser
Born:	17 OCT 1830
Died:	8 DEC 1907
Parents:	Henry & Eve (Keplinger) Regar
Spouse:	Isaac K. Overholser
Notes:	

Overholser
Family
Monument

Grave:	36-5
Name:	Isaac K. Overholser
Born:	21 MAY 1836
Died:	11 DEC 1922
Parents:	John & Margaret (Kurtz) Overholser
Spouse:	Catharine "Kate" (Regar) Overholser
Notes:	

Grave: 36-8
Name: Lizzie Overholser
Born: 24 APR 1869
Died: 15 NOV 1948
Parents: Isaac K. & Catharine (Regar) Overholser
Spouse:
Notes: unmarried

Grave: 37-1
Name: Peter Fry
Born: 17 JUN 1850
Died: 13 AUG 1923
Parents: Jacob & Elizabeth (Frankhouser) Fry
Spouse:
Notes: unmarried

Grave: 36-7
Name: Maggie Overholser
Born: 6 JUL 1873
Died: 23 NOV 1932
Parents: Isaac K. & Catharine (Regar) Overholser
Spouse:
Notes: unmarried

Grave: 36-9
Name: Mary Overholser
Born: 17 MAR 1866
Died: 18 APR 1949
Parents: Isaac K. & Catharine (Regar) Overholser
Spouse:
Notes: unmarried

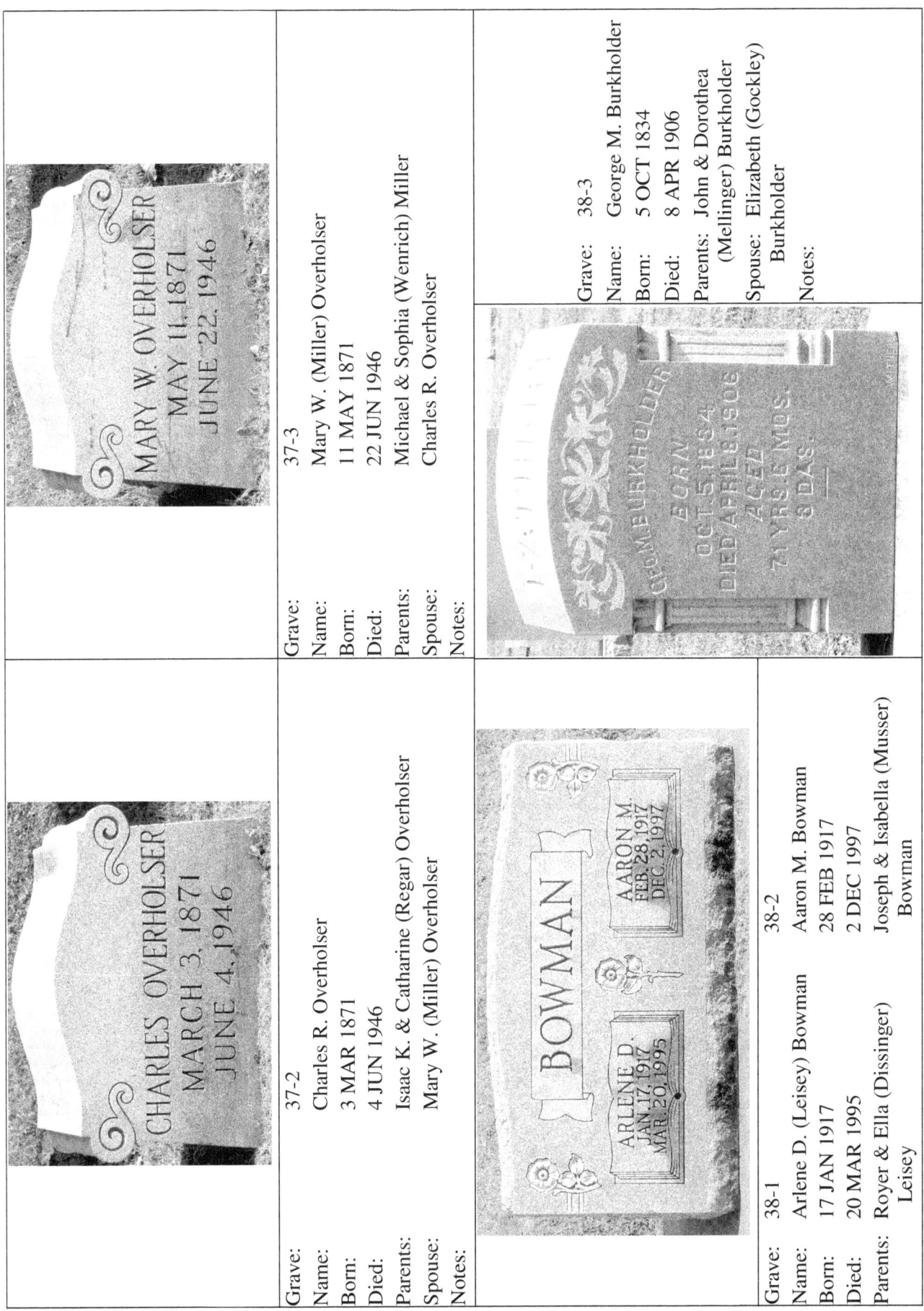

Grave:	Grave: 38-3
Name:	Name: George M. Burkholder
Born:	Born: 5 OCT 1834
Died:	Died: 8 APR 1906
Parents:	Parents: John & Dorothea (Mellinger) Burkholder
Spouse:	Spouse: Elizabeth (Gockley) Burkholder
Notes:	Notes:

37-3
Mary W. (Miller) Overholser
11 MAY 1871
22 JUN 1946
Michael & Sophia (Wenrich) Miller
Charles R. Overholser

Grave:
Name:
Born:
Died:
Parents:
Spouse:
Notes:

37-2
Charles R. Overholser
3 MAR 1871
4 JUN 1946
Isaac K. & Catharine (Regar) Overholser
Mary W. (Miller) Overholser

Grave:
Name:
Born:
Died:
Parents:
Spouse:
Notes:

38-2
Aaron M. Bowman
28 FEB 1917
2 DEC 1997
Joseph & Isabella (Musser) Bowman

38-1
Arlene D. (Leisey) Bowman
17 JAN 1917
20 MAR 1995
Royer & Ella (Dissinger) Leisey

Grave:
Name:
Born:
Died:
Parents:

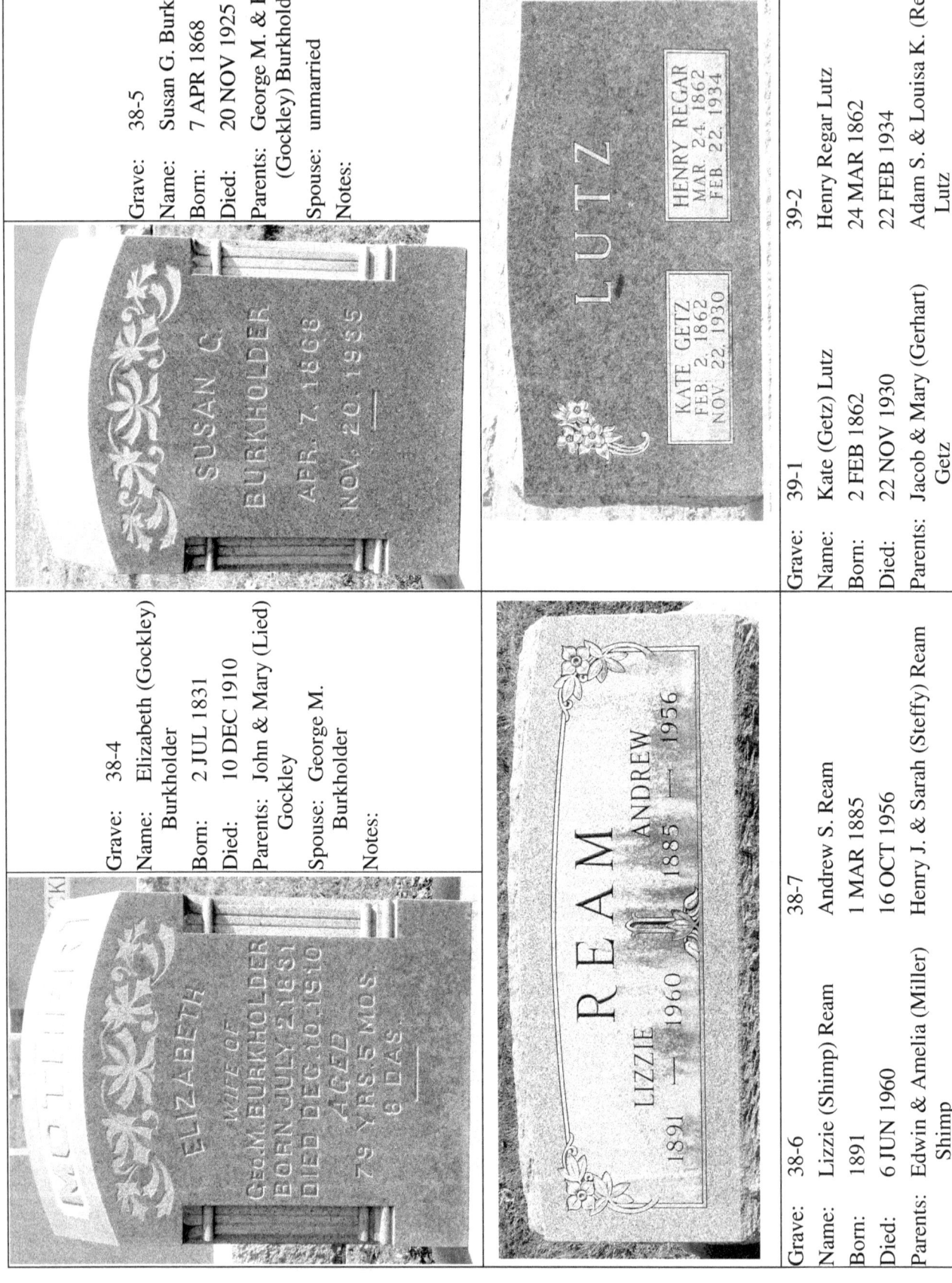

Grave:	38-5
Name:	Susan G. Burkholder
Born:	7 APR 1868
Died:	20 NOV 1925
Parents:	George M. & Elizabeth (Gockley) Burkholder
Spouse:	unmarried
Notes:	

Grave:	39-2
Name:	Henry Regar Lutz
Born:	24 MAR 1862
Died:	22 FEB 1934
Parents:	Adam S. & Louisa K. (Regar) Lutz

Grave:	38-4
Name:	Elizabeth (Gockley) Burkholder
Born:	2 JUL 1831
Died:	10 DEC 1910
Parents:	John & Mary (Lied) Gockley
Spouse:	George M. Burkholder
Notes:	

Grave:	39-1
Name:	Kate (Getz) Lutz
Born:	2 FEB 1862
Died:	22 NOV 1930
Parents:	Jacob & Mary (Gerhart) Getz

Grave:	38-7
Name:	Andrew S. Ream
Born:	1 MAR 1885
Died:	16 OCT 1956
Parents:	Henry J. & Sarah (Steffy) Ream

Grave:	38-6
Name:	Lizzie (Shimp) Ream
Born:	1891
Died:	6 JUN 1960
Parents:	Edwin & Amelia (Miller) Shimp

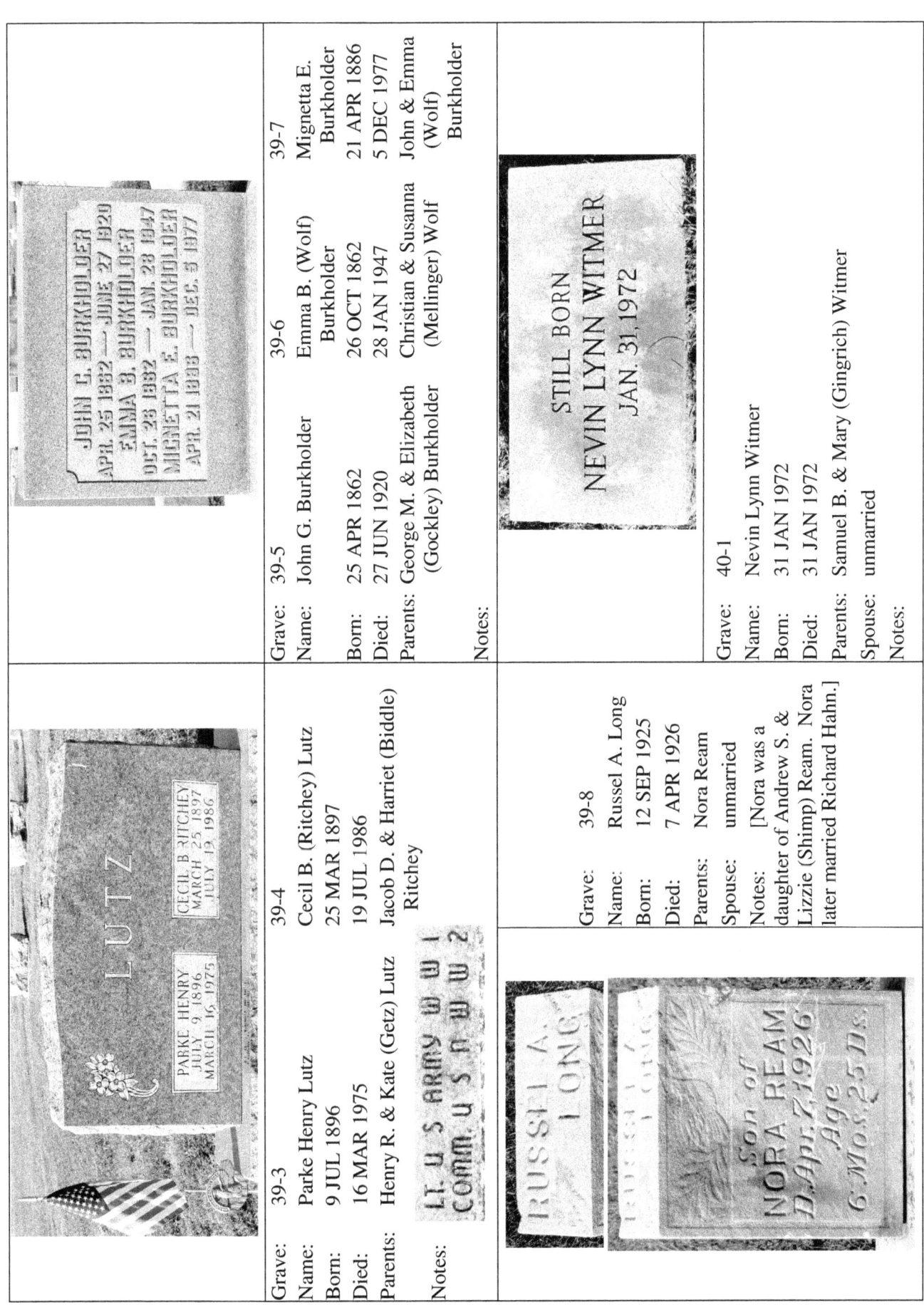

Grave: 39-7
Name: Mignetta E. Burkholder
Born: 21 APR 1886
Died: 5 DEC 1977
Parents: John & Emma (Wolf) Burkholder

Grave: 39-6
Name: Emma B. (Wolf) Burkholder
Born: 26 OCT 1862
Died: 28 JAN 1947
Parents: Christian & Susanna (Mellinger) Wolf

Grave: 39-5
Name: John G. Burkholder
Born: 25 APR 1862
Died: 27 JUN 1920
Parents: George M. & Elizabeth (Gockley) Burkholder
Notes:

Grave: 40-1
Name: Nevin Lynn Witmer
Born: 31 JAN 1972
Died: 31 JAN 1972
Parents: Samuel B. & Mary (Gingrich) Witmer
Spouse: unmarried
Notes:

Grave: 39-3
Name: Parke Henry Lutz
Born: 9 JUL 1896
Died: 16 MAR 1975
Parents: Henry R. & Kate (Getz) Lutz
Notes: LT. U.S ARMY WW 1 COMM. U S N WW 2

Grave: 39-4
Name: Cecil B. (Ritchey) Lutz
Born: 25 MAR 1897
Died: 19 JUL 1986
Parents: Jacob D. & Harriet (Biddle) Ritchey

Grave: 39-8
Name: Russel A. Long
Born: 12 SEP 1925
Died: 7 APR 1926
Parents: Nora Ream
Spouse: unmarried
Notes: [Nora was a daughter of Andrew S. & Lizzie (Shimp) Ream. Nora later married Richard Hahn.]

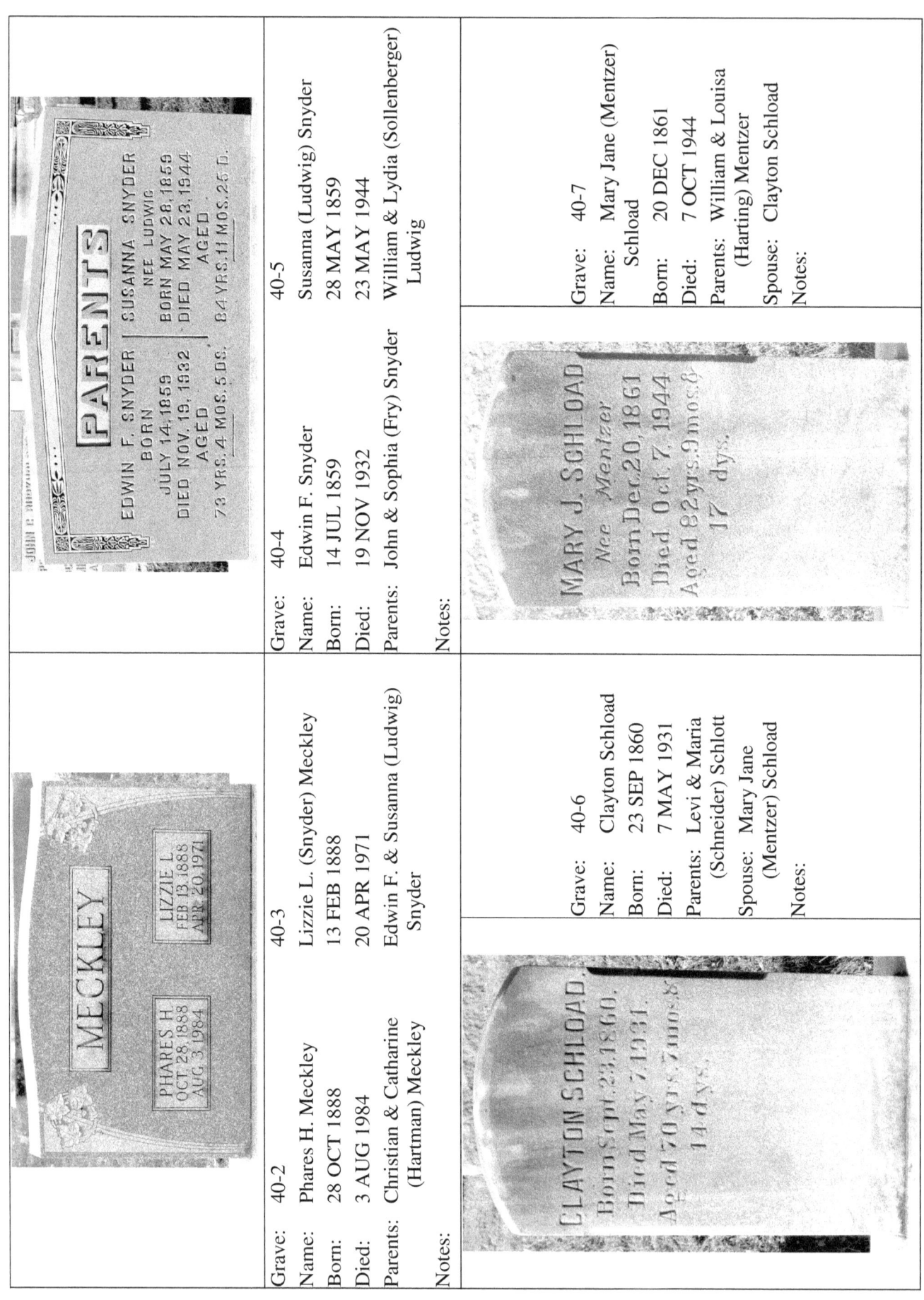

Grave:	40-4
Name:	Edwin F. Snyder
Born:	14 JUL 1859
Died:	19 NOV 1932
Parents:	John & Sophia (Fry) Snyder
Notes:	

Grave:	40-5
Name:	Susanna (Ludwig) Snyder
Born:	28 MAY 1859
Died:	23 MAY 1944
Parents:	William & Lydia (Sollenberger) Ludwig
Notes:	

Grave:	40-7
Name:	Mary Jane (Mentzer) Schload
Born:	20 DEC 1861
Died:	7 OCT 1944
Parents:	William & Louisa (Harting) Mentzer
Spouse:	Clayton Schload
Notes:	

MARY J. SCHLOAD
Nee Mentzer
Born Dec. 20, 1861
Died Oct. 7, 1944
Aged 82 yrs. 9 mos. &
17 dys.

Grave:	40-2
Name:	Phares H. Meckley
Born:	28 OCT 1888
Died:	3 AUG 1984
Parents:	Christian & Catharine (Hartman) Meckley
Notes:	

Grave:	40-3
Name:	Lizzie L. (Snyder) Meckley
Born:	13 FEB 1888
Died:	20 APR 1971
Parents:	Edwin F. & Susanna (Ludwig) Snyder
Notes:	

Grave:	40-6
Name:	Clayton Schload
Born:	23 SEP 1860
Died:	7 MAY 1931
Parents:	Levi & Maria (Schneider) Schlott
Spouse:	Mary Jane (Mentzer) Schload
Notes:	

CLAYTON SCHLOAD
Born Sept. 23, 1860.
Died May 7, 1931.
Aged 70 yrs. 7 mos. &
14 dys.

Grave: 41-1
Name: Infant Meckley
Born: 22 JUL 1915
Died: 22 JUL 1915
Parents: Phares & Lizzie (Snyder) Meckley
Spouse: unmarried
Notes:

Grave: 42-2
Name: Elam C. Messner
Born: 2 JAN 1871
Died: 4 AUG 1930
Parents: Christian G. & Mary P. (Coldren) Messner
Spouse: unmarried
Notes:

Grave: 40-8
Name: Mabel Schload
Born: 12 MAY 1906
Died: 13 JAN 2000
Parents: Clayton & Mary (Mentzer) Schload
Spouse: unmarried
Notes:

Grave: 42-1
Name: Ada L. (Leisey) Sweigart
Born: 21 Oct 1885
Died: 27 AUG 1931
Parents: Abraham G. & Matilda (Royer) Leisey
Spouse: Elam Sweigart
Notes:

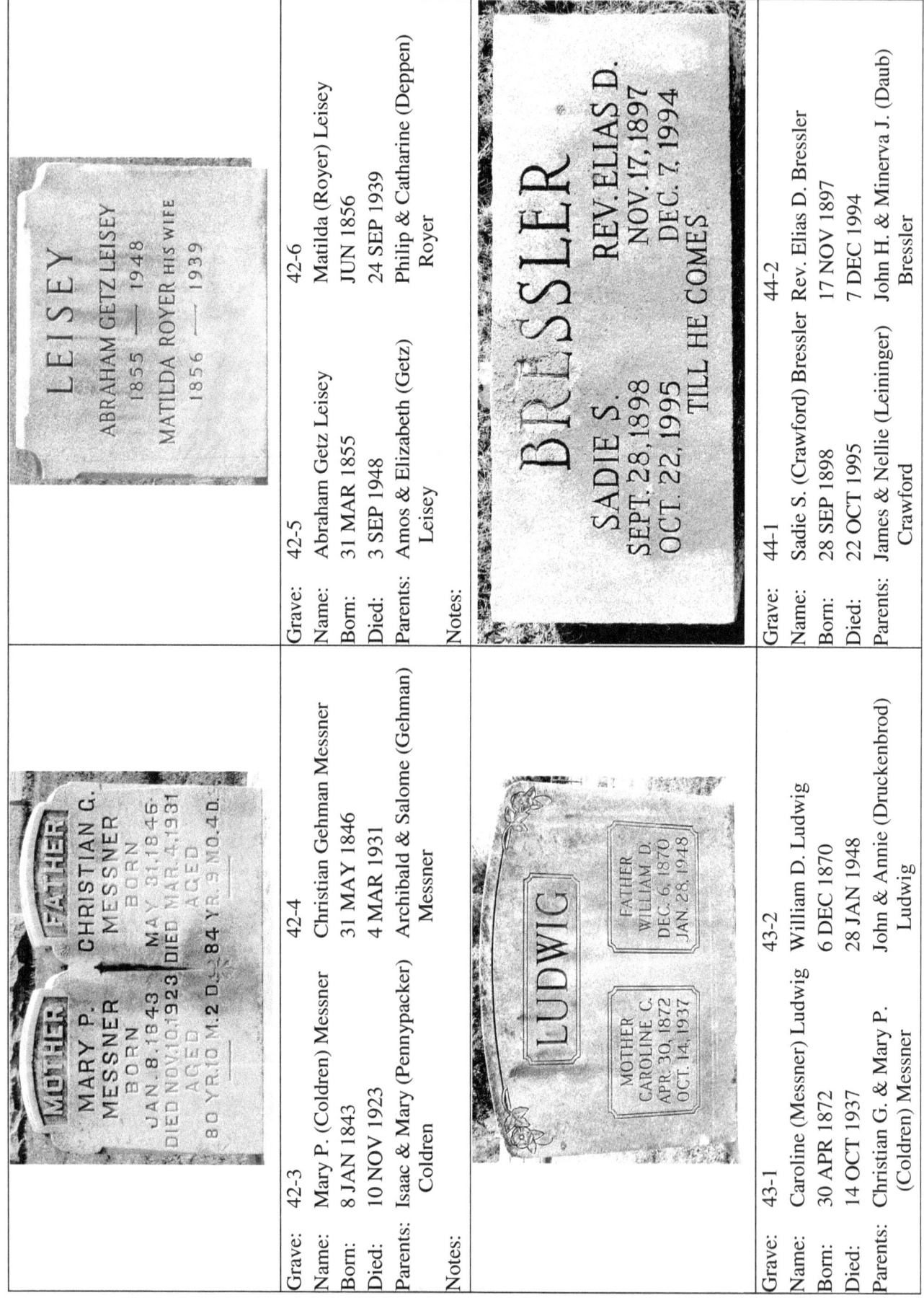

LEISEY
ABRAHAM GETZ LEISEY 1855 — 1948
MATILDA ROYER HIS WIFE 1856 — 1939

Grave:	42-3	42-4
Name:	Mary P. (Coldren) Messner	Christian Gehman Messner
Born:	8 JAN 1843	31 MAY 1846
Died:	10 NOV 1923	4 MAR 1931
Parents:	Isaac & Mary (Pennypacker) Coldren	Archibald & Salome (Gehman) Messner
Notes:		

Grave:	42-5	42-6
Name:	Abraham Getz Leisey	Matilda (Royer) Leisey
Born:	31 MAR 1855	JUN 1856
Died:	3 SEP 1948	24 SEP 1939
Parents:	Amos & Elizabeth (Getz) Leisey	Philip & Catharine (Deppen) Royer
Notes:		

FATHER CHRISTIAN G. MESSNER BORN MAY 31, 1846 DIED MAR. 4, 1931 AGED 84 YR. 9 MO. 4 D.
MOTHER MARY P. MESSNER BORN JAN. 8, 1843 DIED NOV. 10, 1923 AGED 80 YR. 10 M. 2 D.

LUDWIG
FATHER WILLIAM D. DEC. 6, 1870 JAN. 28, 1948
MOTHER CAROLINE C. APR. 30, 1872 OCT. 14, 1937

BRESSLER
REV. ELIAS D. NOV. 17, 1897 DEC. 7, 1994
SADIE S. SEPT. 28, 1898 OCT. 22, 1995
TILL HE COMES

Grave:	43-1	43-2
Name:	Caroline (Messner) Ludwig	William D. Ludwig
Born:	30 APR 1872	6 DEC 1870
Died:	14 OCT 1937	28 JAN 1948
Parents:	Christian G. & Mary P. (Coldren) Messner	John & Annie (Druckenbrod) Ludwig

Grave:	44-1	44-2
Name:	Sadie S. (Crawford) Bressler	Rev. Elias D. Bressler
Born:	28 SEP 1898	17 NOV 1897
Died:	22 OCT 1995	7 DEC 1994
Parents:	James & Nellie (Leininger) Crawford	John H. & Minerva J. (Daub) Bressler

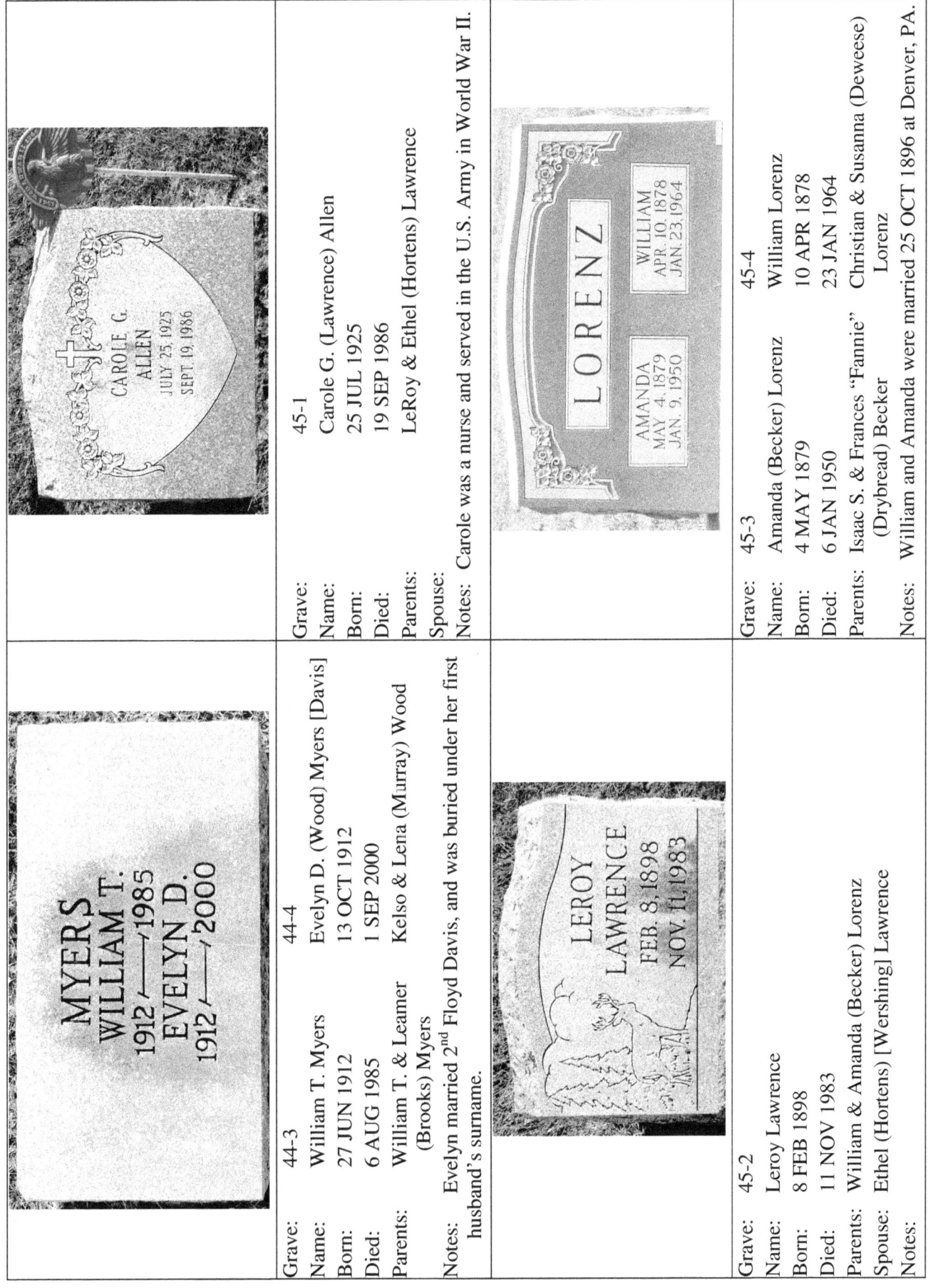

Grave:	44-3	Grave:	44-4
Name:	William T. Myers	Name:	Evelyn D. (Wood) Myers [Davis]
Born:	27 JUN 1912	Born:	13 OCT 1912
Died:	6 AUG 1985	Died:	1 SEP 2000
Parents:	William T. & Leamer (Brooks) Myers	Parents:	Kelso & Lena (Murray) Wood

Notes: Evelyn married 2nd Floyd Davis, and was buried under her first husband's surname.

Grave:	45-1
Name:	Carole G. (Lawrence) Allen
Born:	25 JUL 1925
Died:	19 SEP 1986
Parents:	LeRoy & Ethel (Hortens) Lawrence
Spouse:	

Notes: Carole was a nurse and served in the U.S. Army in World War II.

Grave:	45-2
Name:	Leroy Lawrence
Born:	8 FEB 1898
Died:	11 NOV 1983
Parents:	William & Amanda (Becker) Lorenz
Spouse:	Ethel (Hortens) [Wershing] Lawrence
Notes:	

Grave:	45-3	Grave:	45-4
Name:	Amanda (Becker) Lorenz	Name:	William Lorenz
Born:	4 MAY 1879	Born:	10 APR 1878
Died:	6 JAN 1950	Died:	23 JAN 1964
Parents:	Isaac S. & Frances "Fannie" (Drybread) Becker	Parents:	Christian & Susanna (Deweese) Lorenz

Notes: William and Amanda were married 25 OCT 1896 at Denver, PA.

Grave:	45-5	Grave:	45-6	Grave:	45-7
Name:	Lora Irene (Good) Lorenz	Name:	William Lorenz, Jr.	Name:	Kenneth Lorenz
Born:	1898	Born:	28 SEP 1900	Born:	20 JUL 1926
Died:	16 MAR 1955	Died:	6 MAY 1970	Died:	19 JUL 1934
Parents:	John & Annie (Prussman) Good	Parents:	William & Amanda (Becker) Lorenz	Parents:	William & Lora (Good) Lorenz
Spouse:	William Lorenz, Jr.	Spouse:	Lora Irene (Good) Lorenz	Spouse:	unmarried
Notes:		Notes:		Notes:	

Grave:	46-1	Grave:	46-2	Grave:	46-3	Grave:	46-4
Name:	Edwin M. Eberly	Name:	Mabel G. (High) Eberly	Name:	Elsie K. (High) Weaver	Name:	John Martin Weaver
Born:	13 MAR 1911	Born:	27 APR 1913	Born:	5 FEB 1912	Born:	13 APR 1909
Died:	25 MAR 1999	Died:	7 DEC 2007	Died:	7 MAR 1977	Died:	8 SEP 1999
Parents:	Henry Z. & Caroline (Musser) Eberly	Parents:	Christian & Mary (Good) High	Parents:	Clayton G. & Sallie G. (Keller) High	Parents:	Reuben B. & Lydia S. (Martin) Weaver
Spouse:							
Notes:				Notes:		Notes:	

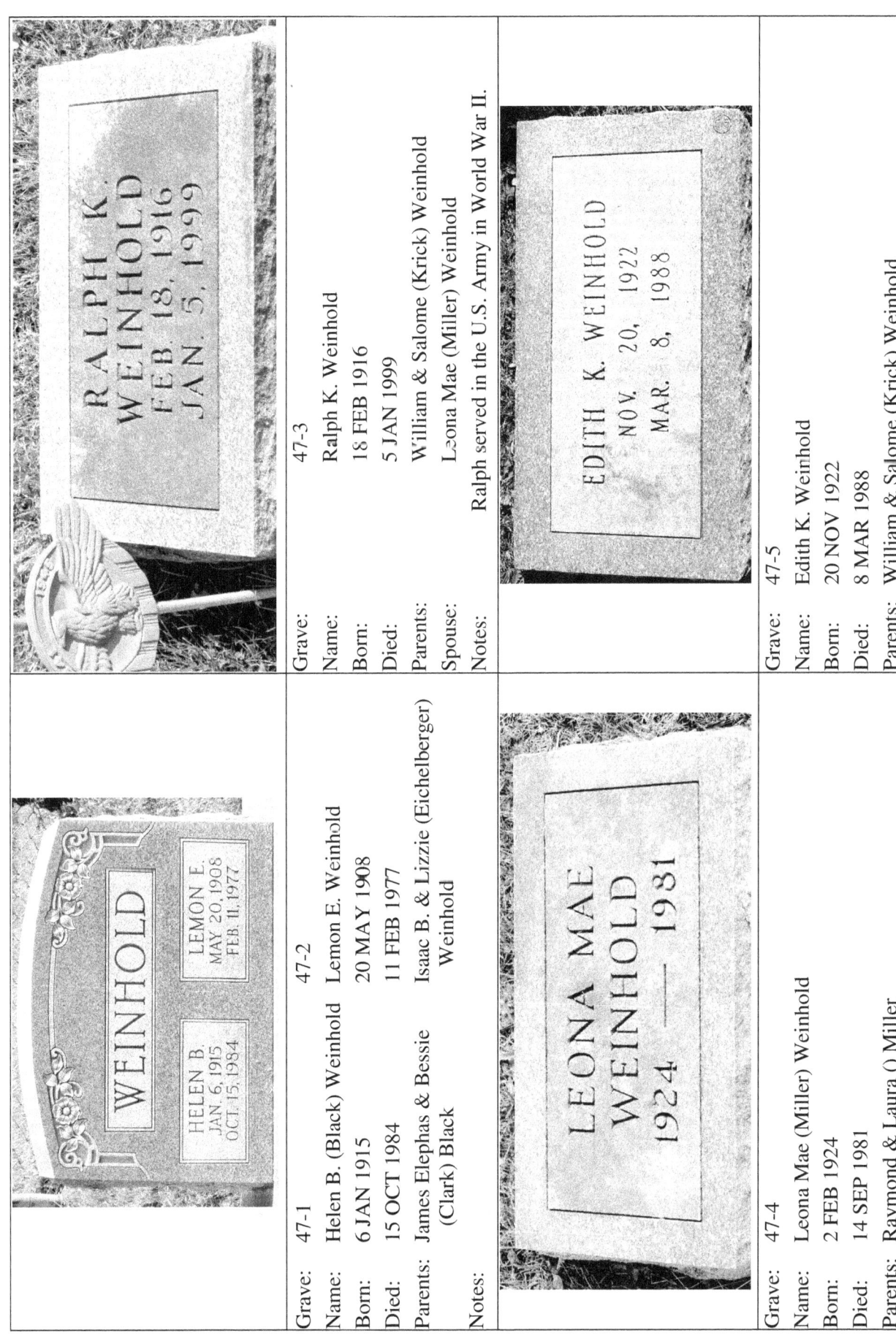

Grave:	47-1
Name:	Helen B. (Black) Weinhold
Born:	6 JAN 1915
Died:	15 OCT 1984
Parents:	James Elephas & Bessie (Clark) Black
Notes:	

Grave:	47-2
Name:	Lemon E. Weinhold
Born:	20 MAY 1908
Died:	11 FEB 1977
Parents:	Isaac B. & Lizzie (Eichelberger) Weinhold

Grave:	47-3
Name:	Ralph K. Weinhold
Born:	18 FEB 1916
Died:	5 JAN 1999
Parents:	William & Salome (Krick) Weinhold
Spouse:	Leona Mae (Miller) Weinhold
Notes:	Ralph served in the U.S. Army in World War II.

Grave:	47-4
Name:	Leona Mae (Miller) Weinhold
Born:	2 FEB 1924
Died:	14 SEP 1981
Parents:	Raymond & Laura () Miller
Spouse:	Ralph K. Weinhold

Grave:	47-5
Name:	Edith K. Weinhold
Born:	20 NOV 1922
Died:	8 MAR 1988
Parents:	William & Salome (Krick) Weinhold
Spouse:	unmarried

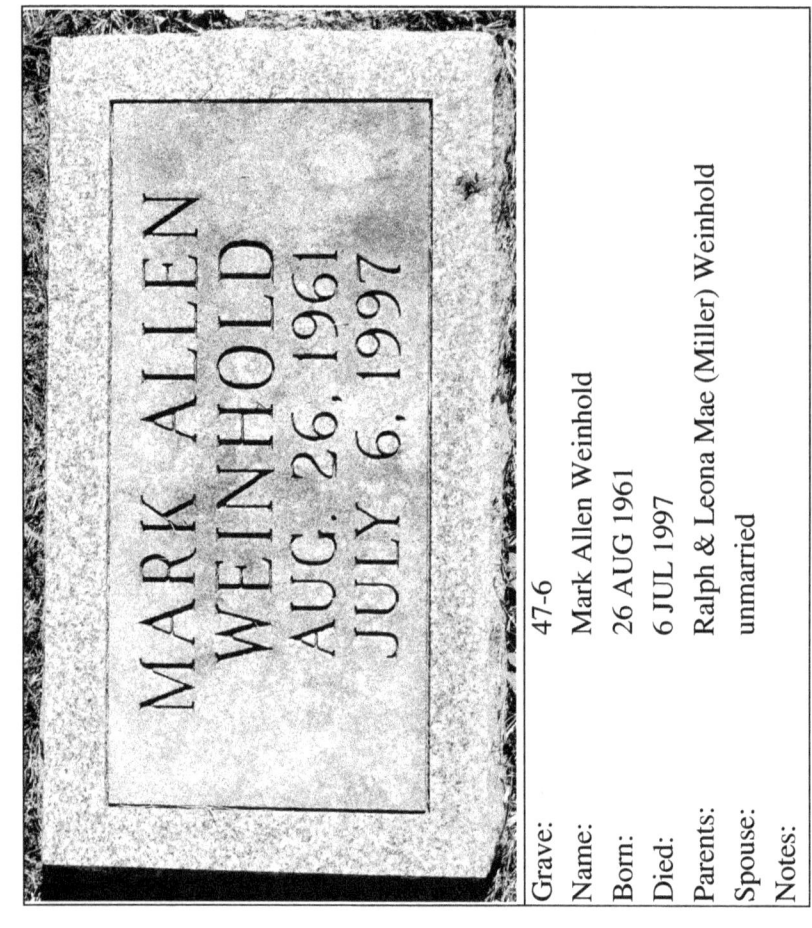

Grave:	47-6
Name:	Mark Allen Weinhold
Born:	26 AUG 1961
Died:	6 JUL 1997
Parents:	Ralph & Leona Mae (Miller) Weinhold
Spouse:	unmarried
Notes:	

120

Denver Union Cemetery – Selected References and Notes.

1-1 Johns, Christian R., b. 1836
Find A Grave Memorials# 69042299, 69042413
1850 census, Earl Twp., Lancaster Co., PA, page 207B

1-2 Johns, Susanna, b. 1836
Ephrata Review, 14 DEC 1894, page 2:
> Mrs. J. R. Johns and children have gone to Chadd's Ford, Delaware county, Mrs.
> John's (sic) former home, on a visit to remain until after Christmas.

1-3 Johns, Lizzie, b. 1864

1-4 Hermes, Eastman, b. 1880
Obituary of Abraham E. Kline, Ephrata Review, 10 MAR 1899, page 1

1-5 Ludwig, George S., b. 1852

1-6 Ludwig, Emmaline, b. 1856
Obituary of Emmaline Ludwig, Reading Eagle, 18 JUL 1928, page 23

1-7 Ludwig, Milton, b. 1884

2-1 Givler, Daniel Z., b. 1866
Marriage license of Daniel Givler and Anna Brubaker, Lancaster Co., PA marriage license,
#8115

2-2 Givler, Anna G., b. 1864
Obituary of Mary M. Brubaker, Ephrata Review, 24 JAN 1913, page 3
Obituary of Anna G. Givler, Ephrata Review, 25 JAN 1918, page 7
Obituary of Annie G. Givler, Reading Eagle, 23 JAN 1918, page 4

2-3 Givler, Infant Son, b. 1895

2-4 Givler, Katie B., b. 1893
Lancaster Co., PA Birth Records

2-5 Givler, Benjamin B., b. 1897
Lancaster Co., PA Birth Records

2-6 Gockley, Annie B., b. 1848
Obituary of Annie B. Gockley, Ephrata Review, 13 APR 1928, page 2
Pennsylvania death certificate of Annie B. Gockley, 1928, File # 40708
1900 census, Jackson Twp., Lebanon Co., PA, ED 120, page 12B

2-7 Gockley, Jonas, b. 1807
History of Lehigh County, Pennsylvania, by Charles R. Roberts, et al., 1914, Volume 3, page
1356

2-8 Royer, Susanna, b. 1833

2-9 Gockley, Susanna, b. 1808

2-10 Gockley, David, b. 1804

2-11 Kline, Jacob B., b. 1843
1880 census, East Cocalico Twp., Lancaster Co., PA, ED 105, page 21A

2-12 Kline, Emaline, b. 1843
1850 census, Ephrata Twp., Lancaster Co., PA, page 166B
Obituary of Emaline Kline, Ephrata Review, 4 APR 1930, page 1
Genealogical files of Brenda Creasy

2-13 Kline, Harvey Daniel, b. 1868

2-14 Kline, Levina, b. 1847

2-15 Kline, Daniel, b. 1855

2-16 Kline, Daniel, b. 1818
Lancaster County, PA Orphans' Court Records ("Miscellaneous Books"), 1828-1831,

page 436, estate of Jacob Kline, 20 DEC 1830
Obituary of Sophia Kline (wife of Abraham E. Kline), Lititz Record, 7 OCT 1907, page 5
Lancaster County, PA Deed K-12:102, Daniel Kline heirs to Daniel Kline Administrators, 1885
Lancaster Daily Intelligencer, 16 JAN 1883, page 2

Suicide

Daniel Kline, a wealthy retired farmer of Denver, this county, committed suicide Monday morning by drawing his pantaloons tightly over his head until suffocation ensued. He had been insane for some time.
Lancaster Daily Intelligencer, 17 JAN 1883, page 3

Daniel Kline's death

We mentioned yesterday the fact of Daniel Kline's death at Denver, on Monday. Later information shows that he was found between 6 and 7 o'clock in the morning sitting up and dead with his pantaloons drawn tightly over his head. Deputy Coroner G. S. Frey summoned a jury composed of Samuel M. Brubaker, Isaac Becker, John Lutz, Cyrus Regar, Levi Ranck and Jacob S. Brubaker, and held an inquest. They found that the man died from suffocation or suffocated while putting on his pantaloons. The supposition is that the man, who has been insane for some time past, mistook his pantaloons for his shirt and endeavored to put them over his head. While doing this he was taken in a fit and his head became entangled in the clothing, which were bitten into holes in several places and had to be cut from his neck.

2-17	Kline, Maria, b. 1816
2-18	K., M.
2-19	K., D.
2-20	Bear, Nancy, b. 1811
2-21	Bear, Abraham, b. 1781
2-22	Bare, Nancy, b. 1785
2-23	Bare, Samuel, b. 1814
3-1	Sensenig, Myrtle, b. 1915
	PA Death Certificate index, 1915
3-2	Sensenig, Carrie, b. 1930
3-3	Gensemer, William, b. 1846

1870 Census, East Cocalico Twp., Lancaster Co., PA, page 323B
Genealogical files of Milton Haldemam
Genealogical files of Brenda Creasy
Lancaster Daily Intelligencer, Monday, October 17, 1881

The Deadly Pistol
Its Fatal Work Saturday Night
Tragedy at Union Station
Samuel H. Miller Shoots and Kills William Gensemer, Both Well Known Citizens
Miller Arrested and Lodged in Jail

Union Station, a village in East Cocalico township, this county, on the line of the Reading & Columbia railroad, was the scene of a terrible tragedy at a late hour on Saturday night, resulting in the shooting and killing of a man named Wm. Gensemer at the hands of Samuel H. Miller, merchant and hotel keeper, at the village.

It appears that a short time before midnight a party consisting of Wm. Gensemer, A. L. Ludwig, Clayton Regar, Chas. Regar, Clinton Loush and others, who had been spending the evening at Eberly's tavern, started toward their homes, and on coming to

122

Miller's tavern, which has closed, halted upon his pavement, and some of them said, "Let us go in." Ludwig replied: "No, we will not go in; it will cost money to do so and I have no money." Some one of the party insisted on going in, and Miller, who was standing at a side gate adjoining the store-room, overheard the remark. He retorted that they should not go in even if they had money. One of the Regars said with an oath that they would go in - that it was a public house and they had a right to enter it. Miller warned them to go away; that they were under his roof, and if they did not leave he would make them do so. Drawing a pistol, he fired a shot upon the pavement, as he alleges, for the purpose of scaring the party off. Immediately they rushed towards him, Gensemer calling to one of the party, "Give me that," whereupon the one addressed handed him a revolver. Miller at once fired three more shots, all of which took effect in Gensemer's body - one of them entering near the groin, another penetrating the windpipe, and another entering the cheek, and perhaps penetrating the brain. Gensemer reeled backward, cried "I am shot," and after staggering backward a few steps fell on the pavement. Drs. Bleiler and Weist were hastily sent for and did all they could for the wounded man, but he died yesterday about noon.

Miller Arrested.

Almost immediately after the shooting Miller's bartender, Henry Musselman, hastened to the residence of J. G. Garman, justice of the peace, requesting him to hasten to Miller's tavern, as Gensemer was shot, that Miler was hurt and wanted him to come at once. Squire Garman visited the scene; there was a great crowd present; Gensemer had been carried across the street some distance from the tavern, and was taken thence to his home. During the row stones were thrown and Miller was struck upon the hand and badly bruised by one of them, but no bones were broken. Whether this was before or after he fired the pistol is not stated. He claims to have acted strictly in self-defense.

A complaint was made against Miller by A. L. Ludwig and he was arrested by Constable Wolfskill on a warrant issued by Squire Garman. After Gensemer's death, Squire Garman committed Miller to the Lancaster county jail for a hearing before him on Saturday next, and the accused was taken to prison last night by Constable Wolfskill and Wm. B. Graul.

The Coroner's Inquest.

Deputy Coroner Charles Carpenter empancled a jury yesterday to hold an inquest on the remains. They viewed the body, and adjourned until this afternoon, when a post mortem examination will be made by the surgeons.

Who the Men Are.

Both Miller and Gensemer have borne fair reputations up to the time of the present sad affair. Miller owns a large store and tavern in the village, is in good pecuniary circumstances, is almost fifty years of age, has a respectable family and has been as one of the most progressive men of the neighborhood. He was especially careful, it is said, in complying with all of the provisions of the liquor law, and was somewhat imperious, ill tempered and even insulting to those who wished him to violate them.

Gensemer was a tanner, a good and steady workman, though he sometimes drank more than was good for him. He was about 33 years of age and leaves a wife and child. He did not own the tannery in which he worked, but he owned the house in which he lived. He was not rich but his near relatives are among the most solid people in the northern end of county.

The tragedy has created great excitement in the community in which both men were so well known.

Miller has retained S. H. Reynolds and J. Hay Brown as counsel to defend him, and the friends of Mr. Gensemer have retained J. L. Steinmetz to assist the district attorney in the prosecution.

3-4 Dissinger, Isaac S., b. 1839

1850 Census, Heidelberg Twp., Lebanon Co., PA, page 10B

Civil War pension index card, Isaac S. Dissinger, FamilySearch.org

Family tree of Samuel Dissinger, Ancestry.com:

http://records.ancestry.com/Samuel_Dissinger_records.ashx?pid=94830132&te=4

3-5 Dissinger, Eliza Ann, b. 1838

3-6 S., L. M.?

3-7 G., A.

3-8 C., C.

3-9 L., E.

3-10 Bixler, Margareta, b. 1770

Lancaster Co., PA Deed 23:220, 1821, Margaret Bixler (heir of Abraham Bixler) to Henry Mohler

Will of Abraham Bixler, Lancaster Co., PA Will M-1:240, 1819

3-11 Brubaker, Nancy B., b. 1838

Obituary of Katie Coldren [daughter of Benjamin and Nancy Brubaker], Reading Eagle, 18 SEP 1949, page 37

3-12 Brubaker, Benjamin M., b. 1831

1870 census, East Cocalico Twp., Lancaster Co., PA, page 331B

Obituary of Maggie Mellinger [daughter of Benjamin Brubaker], Reading Eagle, 5 JAN 1953, page 21

3-13 Brubaker, Mary M., b. 1844

Obituary of Mary M. Brubaker, Ephrata Review, 24 JAN 1913, page 3

PA Death Certificate of Mary Brubaker, 1913, File #1536

Obituary of Elizabeth Brubaker [daughter of Benjamin and Mary Brubaker], Reading Eagle, 29 JUL 1971, page 47

1850 census, West Cocalico Twp., Lancaster Co., PA, page 364B

3-14 Brubaker, Susan G., b. 1863

Obituary of Susan G. Brubaker, Reading Eagle, 8 MAR 1938, page 22

3-15 R., C

3-16 Shimp, Jacob, b. 1854

3-17 Shimp, George, b. 1801

3-18 Shimp, Susanna, b. 1813

Eberly Family History 1700-1974, by Paul C. Bennetch, 1974

Obituary of Susanna Shimp, Ephrata Review, 27 FEB 1891, page 3

3-19 Shober, Susanna, b. 1847

4-1 Smith, Ralph N., b. 1911

Obituary of Ralph N. Smith, Lancaster New Era, 3 JUL 1984, page 3

4-2 Smith, Frances P., b. 1928

Obituary of Frances P. Smith, Lancaster Intelligencer Journal, 30 APR 2003

4-3 Schwear, Richard Samuel, b. 1912

Obituary of Richard Schwear, Reading Eagle, 19 SEP 1961, page 22

Denver Union Cemetery – Selected References and Notes.

4-4   Schwear, Emma Miller, b. 1911
         Obituary of Emma Schwear, Reading Eagle, 21 APR 1981, page 31

4-5   White, Peter M., b. 1835
         Obituary of Peter M. White, New Holland Clarion, 31 DEC 1921, page 1
         Baptismal records of Muddy Creek Lutheran Church
         Marriage license of James T. Lawrence [Lorenz] and Lizzie A. White [daughter of Peter M.
            White], Lancaster Co., PA Marriages, 1888, #2919
         Genealogical files of Brenda Creasy

4-6   White, Eliza Ann, b. 1843
         Obituary of Eliza White [under "Denver Borough Affairs"], Ephrata Review, 26 MAY 1905,
            page 5

4-7   White, Uriah, b. 1873

4-8   White, Mary N., b. 1871

4-9   White, Harry, b. 1884

4-10   Harnish, David B., b. 1852
         Genealogical files of Brenda Creasy

4-11   Harnish, Howard H., b. 1882
         Obituary of Katie H. Harnish, Reading Eagle, 20 SEP 1999, page 9

4-12   T., I.

4-13   L., A.

4-14   S., J.

4-15   S., S.

4-16   S., M.

4-17   Mischler, Margaretha, b. 1766
         Rootsweb.com, WorldConnect database, Justin Kirk Houser's Ancestry - Central Pennsylvania
            and beyond

4-18   I., I.

4-19   Zug, Margaret, b. 1793

4-20   Mishler, John, b. 1788

4-21   Showalter, Sarah, b. 1833
         1910 census, Church of the Brethren Home, Rapho Twp., Lancaster Co., PA, ED 134, Page 8B
         PA Death Certificate of Sarah Showalter, 1912, File #113725
         Obituary of Sarah Showalter, Ephrata Review, 27 DEC 1912, page 1
         Obituary of Sarah Showalter, Lititz Record, 26 DEC 1912, page 4

4-22   Renninger, Amanda, b. 1856
         Obituary of Amanda Renninger, Ephrata Review, 21 JAN 1910, page 2
         Obituary of Amanda Renninger, Reading Eagle, 14 JAN 1910, page 5

4-23   Renninger, Maude Mable, b. 1892

4-24   Renninger, Charles, b. 1889

5-1   Petticoffer, David, b. 1838

5-2   Petticoffer, Sarah, b. 1837
         1850 census, Cumru Twp., Berks Co., PA, page 353B
         1860 census, West Cocalico Twp., Lancaster Co., PA, page 895
         Obituary of Adam Petticoffer [son of David and Sarah Petticoffer], Reading Eagle,
            15 DEC 1947, page 14

5-3   Petticoffer, Peter O., b. 1878

5-4   Petticoffer, Infant

5-5   Hershberger or Hoffman, Elsie, b. 1877
5-6   L., S.
5-7   L., H.
5-8   W., H.
5-9   Bare, Abraham, b. 1747
        The Descendants and Ancestors of Samuel Carpenter Gockley 1859 – 1940, by Beverly J.
            Cayford, 1994
5-10   Bar, Juliana, b. 1753
        Lancaster Co., PA Deed GG:365, Abraham and Juliana Bear to George Wolfart, 1774
        Lancaster Co., PA Deed Z:448, Henry and Charlotte Walter to George Metzger, 1748
5-11   Schlott, John, b. 1786
5-12   Schlott, Elizabeth, b. 1792
        1850 census, East Cocalico Twp., Lancaster Co., PA, page 345
          Elizabeth was age 58 (born about 1792) and apparently a widow in the 1850 census.
5-13   L., F.
5-14   S., S.
5-15   Eberly, Anna
5-16   Eberly, Peter
5-17   G., M.
5-19   Eberly, Catharine, b. 1783
        Eberly Family History 1700-1974, by Paul C. Bennetch, 1974

5-20   Showalter, Samuel, b. 1834
        Lancaster Co., PA Will of John Showalter,
        Rootsweb.com, WorldConnect database - Shipley, Forster, Hudson, Mayer and Vawter:
        http://wc.rootsweb.ancestry.com/cgi-bin/igm.cgi?op=GET&db=jackrab&id=I14274
5-22   Showalter, Maria, b. 1807
        1850 census, East Cocalico Twp., Lancaster Co., PA, page 341B
        Genealogical files of Brenda Creasy
        Ephrata Review, 3 MAR 1883, page 1
                                    Died.
            Maria Eberly, widow of Samuel Eberly, of Warnersville (sic), Berks county, died on
        the 21st ult., of apoplexy. She was taken from the former place to the Union meeting
        house, near Denver, for interment. She was 75 years, 8 months and 1 day old. Elder
        Samuel Harley, of Ephrata, officiated. The funeral was largely attended by relatives
        and friends of the deceased. [This is apparently Maria, the widow of Samuel Showalter.
        The death date differs from the one on her gravestone by one day. The birth date
        calculated from the age given in the obituary, 20 JUN 1807, also differs from the one on
        the gravestone by one day. Eberly was her maiden name.]
5-23   Wolfskill, Henry, b. 1827
        PA Death Certificate of Samuel S. Wolfskill (son of Henry), 1914, file #119280
5-24   Eberly, Peter, b. 1815
5-25   Eberly, Susanna, b. 1821
        Obituary of Susanna Eberly, Ephrata Review, 23 FEB 1894, page 3
        Death certificate of Thomas J. Eberly (son of Peter and Susanna Eberly, 1930, file #40513
        Funeral of Susanna Eberly, 1894, Funeral records of Rev. Stephen Schweitzer
        1850 census, East Cocalico Twp., Lancaster Co., PA, page 358

6-1   Turner, Abraham, b. 1849
6-2   Turner, Stella, b. 1895
6-3   Turner, Charles, b. 1879
6-4   Turner, Ida Mengel, b. 1876
6-5   Turner, Emma, b. 1855
6-6   Ludwig, Samuel B., b. 1852
        Obituary of Samuel Ludwig, Ephrata Review, 17 JUL 1925, page 3
        Genealogical files of Milton Haldeman
6-7   Ludwig, Lizzie, b. 1854
        Obituary of Lizzie Ludwig, New Holland Clarion, 19 APR 1935, page 1
6-8   Ludwig, Samuel, b. 1889
6-9   Ludwig, Amos, b. 1888
6-10   Ludwig, Daniel, b. 1891
6-11   Ludwig, Anna, b. 1875
6-12   Ludwig, Ida, b. 1876
6-13   S., G.
6-14   R., M. M.
6-16   Harnish, David, b. 1828
6-17   Harnish, Jacob, b. 1793
6-18   Harnish, Anna, b. 1794
6-19   Harnish, Sarah, b. 1827
6-20   Harnish, Jacob, b. 1825
6-21   Bear, Henry, b. 1785
6-22   Kerling, Catharine, b. 1799
        Marriage records of Rev. J. J. Strine
6-23   Kerling, William G., b. 1843
6-24   Kerling, Barton A., b. 1859
        PA death certificate of Margaret Kerling, 1920, file #60867
6-25   Kerling, Henry A., b. 1864
        Genealogical files of Brenda Creasy
        Death certificate of Henry Kerling, Philadelphia, PA, 1866, FamilySearch.org
        PA death certificate of Margaret Kerling, 1920, file #60867
6-26   Kerling, James, b. 1800
        Death certificate of Lewis C. Kerling, Philadelphia, PA, 1901, FamilySearch.org
6-27   Showalter, Christian, b. 1853
        Obituary of Christian Showalter, Ephrata Review, 19 APR 1934, page 7
6-28   Showalter, Addie, b. 1854
        Genealogical files of Milton Haldeman
6-29   Showalter, Laura Mamie, b. 1869
6-30   Showalter, Jennie Mabel, b. 1880
7-1   Lord, Oliver, b. 1888
        Obituary of Matilda [Lutz] Fessler, Ephrata Review, 24 JUL 1914, page 2
7-2   G., L.
7-3   B., F.
7-4   B., H.
7-5   G., J.
7-6   Stark, Josiah, b. 1841

7-7   Stark, Daniel, b. 1817
Obituary of Daniel Stark, Ephrata Review, 13 APR 1894, page 3
Obituary of Daniel Stark, Lititz Record, 13 APR 1894, page 3
Will of Adam Sherb, Lancaster Co., PA Wills, R-1:132, written 1835
Orphans' Court Records of Samuel Stark, Lancaster Co., PA, "Miscellaneous Books," Vol.
   1833-1836, June 1834, page 190
New Holland Clarion, 14 APR 1894, page 8:

> Daniel Stark, an old citizen of Ephrata township, who lived about a mile east of the borough of Ephrata, committed suicide by hanging himself to a tree at an early hour on Friday morning of last week. The son of the deceased left home to go to work, and some time later his wife had occasion to go to the pump, about two hundred yards from the house. There she found the body of her father in law hanging to a tree by a rope. He was already dead and the woman, who was terribly frightened, alarmed the neighbors. The man had been troubled with rheumatism and other complaints for some time past, and it is believed that he became despondent over his ailments. He was seventy five years of age and three sons and two daughters survive him.

7-8   Gockley, Dietrich, b. 1767
7-9   Gockley, Barbara, b. 1764
7-10   Gockley, John, b. 1792
7-11   Gockley, Mary, b. 1805
7-12   Gockley, David, b. 1828
7-13   Gockley, Abraham, b. 1796
Will of Abraham Gockley, Lancaster Co., PA Wills, S-1:204, written 1838
7-14   Gockley, Levi, b. 1851
Genealogical files of Brenda Creasy
7-15   Gockley, John, b. 1859
7-16   Gockley, Maria, b. 1836
1850 census, East Cocalico Twp., Lancaster Co., PA, page 352
7-17   Stark, Catharine, b. 1818
7-18   Zern, John, b. 1813
 Marriage records of Rev. J. J. Strine
7-19   Zern, Susanna, b. 1835
7-20   B., H.
7-21   Harnish, Levi, b. 1850
Genealogical files of Brenda Creasy
7-22   Borry, Susanna, b. 1853
7-23   K., C.
7-24   Zern, Catharina, b. 1845
7-25   Borry, Aaron
8-1   Bixler, Jacob D., b. 1854

PA Death Certificate of Jacob D. Bixler, 1934, File #18519
Obituary of Jacob D. Bixler, Ephrata Review, 9 FEB 1934, page 2
Obituary of Jacob D. Bixler, Reading Eagle, 7 FEB 1934, page 14
Obituary of Benjamin Bixler [brother of Jacob], Lititz Record, 25 MAR 1909, page 3
Obituary of Daniel L. Bixler, Reading Eagle, 6 OCT 1919, page 4
8-2   Bixler, Eliza, b. 1859

The correct spelling of Macwate is probably "McQuate."

8-3   Lutz, William M., b. 1856
8-4   Lutz, Tilly, b. 1856
        Obituary of Matilda [Lutz] Fessler, Ephrata Review, 24 JUL 1914, page 2
        Divorce of Tillie Lord and Jonathan P. Lord, Lancaster Co., PA Divorces, SEP 1892 term, #37
        Marriage of Tilly Lutz and William Fessler, Lancaster Co., PA Marriages, 1900, #17558
        Lancaster Co., PA Deed E-11:349, Matilda Lutz to heirs of Louisa Kochel, 1878
8-5   Lutz, Elmer, b. 1877
8-6   Lutz, Stella, b. 1880
8-7   Bixler, Daniel L., b. 1879
        Obituary of Daniel L. Bixler, Reading Eagle, 6 OCT 1919, page 4
8-8   Bixler, Franklin, b. 1878
8-9   Bixler, Harry, b. 1887
8-10   Lutz, Samuel, b. 1848
8-11   Lutz, Henry, b. 1843
8-12   Lutz, Henry, b. 1771
        Genealogical files of Brenda Creasy
8-13   Lutz, Susanna, b. 1773
        Genealogical files of Brenda Creasy
8-14   Lutz, Daniel, b. 1807
8-15   Lutz, Elizabeth, b. 1816
        Obituary of Elizabeth Lutz, Ephrata Review, 14 DEC 1894, page 3
        Lancaster Examiner and Herald, 9 MAY 1839, page 3
MARRIED
        On the 21 inst. by the same [the Rev. Mr. Bruner], Mr. Daniel Lutz to Miss Elizabeth
        Macwate, of East Cocalico.
        The correct spelling of Macwate is probably "McQuate."
8-16   Gockley, William, b. 1861
        1880 census, Salisbury Twp., Lancaster Co., PA, ED 140, page 18B
        Obituary of William Gockley, Ephrata Review, 7 JUL 1938, page 2
        Obituary of William Gockley, Reading Eagle, 5 JUL 1938, page 16
8-17   Gockley, Sebastian, b. 1781
8-18   Gockley, Susanna, b. 1802
8-19   Gockley, Jacob, b. 1850
8-20   Gockley, Susanna, b. 1848
8-21   Gockley, Aaron, b. 1823
        1880 census, Salisbury Twp., Lancaster Co., PA, ED 140, page 18B
        Deed Sebastian Gockley heirs to Christian Wiest, 1853, Lancaster Co., PA Deeds C-8:466
        Will of Sebastian Gockley, Lancaster Co., PA Wills R-1:249, written 1836
8-22   Gockley, Catharine, b. 1822
        Obituary of Catharine Gockley, Ephrata Review, 25 MAR 1898, page 3
        Funeral record of Catharine Gockley, 23 MAR 1898, records of Rev. Benjamin G. Welder
8-23   Gockley, Anna, b. 1850
8-24   Gockley, Sarah, b. 1830
        Lancaster Co., PA Deed M-5:93, John Schwarr heirs to Christian Weist, 1826
        Rootsweb.com, WorldConnect, database: lacor
8-25   Gockley, John B., b. 1825

1850 census, East Cocalico Twp., Lancaster Co., PA, page 346

9-1   Lutz, Frances S., b. 1876

9-2   Lutz, Bertha M., b. 1881

9-3   Lutz, Clara Louise, b. 1879

9-4   Lutz, Mary C., b. 1874

9-5   Lutz, Daniel M., b. 1852

      The correct spelling of Macwate is probably "McQuate."

9-6   Lutz, Annie Caroline, b. 1853

      Obituary of Annie C. Lutz, Lancaster New Era, 14 OCT 1937, page 3

9-7   Lutz, Evan E., b. 1848

      Obituary of Morris F. Lutz, Reading Eagle, 12 FEB 1953, page 19

9-8   Lutz, Adda

9-9   Lutz, Eduard, b. 1830

9-10   Lutz, Jacob, b. 1806

9-11   Lutz, Sarah, b. 1809

      Obituary of "Sallie" Lutz, Ephrata Review, 22 DEC 1893, page 3

      Lancaster Co., PA Deed M-5:93, John Schwarr heirs to Christian Weist, 1826

      Rootsweb.com, WorldConnect, database: lacor

      Genealogical files of Brenda Creasy

9-12   Lutz, Susannah, b. 1832

9-13   Lutz, Adam, b. 1800

      1850 census, East Cocalico Twp., Lancaster Co., PA, page 352

9-14   Lutz, Lydia, b. 1804

      Deed John Senseman heirs to John Gross et al., Lancaster Co., PA Deed, B-7:405, 1846

9-15   Lutz, Henry, b. 1803

9-16   Lutz, John, b. 1797

      1850 census, East Cocalico Twp., Lancaster Co., PA, page 346

      Will of John Lutz, Lancaster Co., PA, 1870, Will A-2:9

9-17   Lutz, Susanna, b. 1804

      PA Death Certificate of Susanna (Lutz) Eberly, 1908, File # 14065

      Deed John Schwarr heirs to Christian Weist, Lancaster Co., PA Deed M-5:93, 1826

9-18   Lutz, Adam, b. 1764

9-19   Lutz, Magdalene, b. 1765

9-20   Burkholder, Lizzie Ann, b. 1866

10-1   Leisey, Clinton D., b. 1923

      Obituary of Clinton D. Leisey, Reading Eagle, 11 JAN 1979, page 33

10-2   Leisey, Lloyd D., b. 1913

      Obituary of Lloyd D. Leisey, Reading Eagle, 9 JAN 1979, page 27

10-3   Leisey, Royer R., b. 1892

10-4   Leisey, Ella S, b. 1883

      Obituary of Priscilla Dissinger [mother of Ella Leisey], Reading Eagle, 27 MAY 1937, page 29

      1900 census, Ephrata, Lancaster Co., PA, ED 37, page 10A

      Obituary of Ella S. Leisey, Reading Eagle, 15 FEB 1937, page 26

10-5   Althouse, Esrom, b. 1827

10-6   Althouse, Rachel, b. 1819

      Genealogical files of Brenda Creasy

10-7   Lutz, Franklin, b. 1878

10-8   Lutz, John M., b. 1841
        Marriage license of Alice Lutz [daughter of John M. Lutz] and Harvey Eberly, Lancaster Co.,
            PA Marriage #4611
        1900 census, East Cocalico Twp., Lancaster Co., PA, ED 22, page 19B
10-9   Lutz, Kate, b. 1845
        Obituary of Alice Eberly [daughter of John and Kate Lutz], Reading Eagle, 26 JUL 1963,
            page 19
        Obituary of Emma (Lutz) Hacker [daughter of John and Kate Lutz], Reading Eagle, 15 AUG
            1951, page 26
10-10   Lutz, Adam H., b. 1875
        1870 census, Ephrata Twp., Lancaster Co., PA, page 71B
        1900 census, Warwick Twp., Lancaster Co., PA, ED 113, page 11A
        Obituary of Julian Lutz, Reading Eagle, 16 DEC 1925, page 2
10-11   Lutz, Emma, b. 1865
10-12   Lutz, John Frank, b. 1872
        Obituary of J. Frank Lutz, Reading Eagle, 19 OCT 1959, page 22
10-13   Lutz, Lizzie S., b. 1860
10-14   Lutz, John S., b. 1828
10-15   Lutz, Emma, b. 1831
        Obituary of Emma Lutz, Ephrata Review, 13 JAN 1911, page 1
        Find A Grave Memorials# 62692807, 62692850
        Will of Charles Steinmetz, Lancaster Co., PA Will Z-1:281
        Lancaster Co., PA Deed M-5:93, John Schwarr heirs to Christian Weist, 1826
        Rootsweb.com, WorldConnect, database: lacor
10-16   Sallade, Cassiah, b. 1820
10-17   Sallade, Jeremiah M., b. 1816
10-18   Grosh, Emma, b. 1849
10-19   Nolde, John S., b. 1844
10-20   Nolde, Alma S., b. 1882
10-21   Sallade, infant daughter, b. 1856
10-22   Nolde, infant son, b. 1880
10-25   O., J. H.
11-1   Frankhouser, Ada Emma, b. 1877
11-2   Frankhouser, Byram L., b. 1849
11-3   Frankhouser, Sarah J., b. 1842
11-4   Lutz, Henry E., b. 1840
11-5   Lutz, Fianna E., b. 1845
12-1   Miller, Ada, b. 1887
        Genealogical files of Brenda Creasy
12-2   Miller, William L., b. 1839
12-3   Miller, Harriet, b. 1846
        Obituary of Harriet Miller, Ephrata Review, 20 FEB 1920, page 1
        Obituary of Mary Ochs [daughter of William and Harriet Miller], Reading Eagle,
            30 NOV 1948, page 27
        Obituary of Alice M. Weller [daughter of William and Harriet Miller], Reading Eagle,
            16 OCT 1965, page 15
12-4   Rhoads, William H., b. 1856

1860 census, Earl Twp., Lancaster Co., PA, page 122

Marriage license of William H. Rhoads and Lavinia Gibble, Lancaster Co., PA Marriages, 1886, #821

12-5   Rhoads, Lavina, b. 1865

1880 census, Penn Twp., Lancaster Co., PA, ED 121, page 47C

1900 census, Ephrata, Lancaster Co., PA, ED 40, page 20B

12-6   Rhoads, Aaron, b. 1890

1930 census, 2nd Ward, Ephrata Borough, Lancaster Co., PA, ED 195, page 7B

12-7   Rhoads, William H., b. 1891

12-8   Rhoads, Bessie B., b. 1896

Obituary of Bessie b. Rhoads, Lancaster New Era, 1 SEP 1963, page 3

12-9   Shiffer, Mayme R., b. 1888

12-10 Miller, Edwin O., b. 1873

Obituary of Edwin O. Miller, Reading Eagle, 3 JUN 1918, page 4

Genealogical files of Milton Haldeman

Marriage license of Edwin O. Miller and Annie Haldeman, Lancaster Co., PA Marriages, 1895, #10495

12-11 Miller, Annie, b. 1877

Genealogical files of Milton Haldeman

12-12 Miller, Edwin, b. 1897

12-13 Miller, Peter L., b. 1849

Obituary of Peter Miller, Ephrata Review, 10 MAR 1916, page 2

Obituary of Peter Miller, Reading Eagle, 4 MAR 1916, page 4

Pennsylvania Death Certificate of Peter Miller, 1916, file #27698

12-14 Miller, Clementine, b. 1851

Obituary of Clementine Miller, Ephrata Review, 26 MAY 1933, page 1

Pennsylvania Death Certificate of Clementine Miller, 1933, file #47032

12-15 Miller, Michael L., b. 1841

12-16 Miller, Polly, b. 1843

Baptismal records of Muddy Creek Reformed Church

Obituary of Polly Miller, Ephrata Review, 21 JAN 1927, page 3

Obituary of Polly Miller, Reading Eagle, 17 JAN 1927, page 2

12-17 Miller, Peter K., b. 1810

1870 census, East Cocalico Twp., Lancaster Co., PA, page 328

Website of Rusty Smith, Program Manager, WOUB Radio, Ohio University, Athens, OH: http://www.ohio.edu/people/smithma/genealogy%20public%20folder/ps19/ps19_374.htm

Baptismal records of Muddy Creek Reformed Church

12-18 Miller, Mary, b. 1819

1850 census, West Cocalico Twp., Lancaster Co., PA, page 376B

Genealogical files of Milton Haldeman

13-1   Kilhafner, Franklin K., b. 1856

Obituary of Franklin K. Kilhafner, Ephrata Review, 17 SEP 1936, page 2

Obituary of Franklin K. Kilhafner, Reading Eagle, 15 SEP 1936, page 20

13-2   Kilhafner, Lucetta, b. 1856

PA Death Certificate of Lucetta Kilhafner, 1942, File # 82227

Obituary of Lucetta Kilhafner, Reading Eagle, 8 SEP 1942, page 20

Obituary of Susan E. Sloat [daughter of Franklin and Lucetta Kilhafner], Reading Eagle,

17 JAN 1974, page 46

13-3   Trupe, Isaac, b. 1827

       PA Death Certificate of Isaac Trupe, 1915, File #74214

       1850 census, Caernarvon Twp., Lancaster Co., PA page 398

       Obituary of Isaac Trupe, Ephrata Review, 13 AUG 1915, page 7

       Obituary of Isaac Trupe, Reading Eagle, 13 AUG 1915, page 19

13-4   Trupe, Catharine, b. 1829

       PA Death Certificate of Lucetta Kilhafner, 1942, File # 82227

       Obituary of Catharine Trupe/Troop, Ephrata Review, 14 MAY 1897, page 3

13-5   Gerhart, William, b. 1825

       1850 census, West Cocalico Twp., Lancaster Co., PA page 380

       Obituary of William Gerhart, Lititz Record, 14 FEB 1896, page 2

       Genealogical files of Brenda Creasy

13-6   Gerhart, Maria, b. 1833

13-7   Gerhart, Sarah Jane, b. 1873

13-8   Gerhart, Hannah Elizabeth, b. 1862

14-1   Lutz, Ella M, b. 1893

14-2   Lutz, Charles Sweigart, b. 1892

       Obituary of Charles S. Lutz, Reading Eagle, 18 APR 1960, page 21

14-3   Lutz, Henry D., b. 1862

       Obituary of Henry D. Lutz, Ephrata Review, 25 AUG 1922, page 8

       PA Death Certificate of "Harry" D. Lutz, 1922, file # 77449

       Obituary of Henry D. [should be B.] Lutz, New Holland Clarion, 17 JUL 1915, page 1

       1870 census, Earl Twp., Lancaster Co., PA, page 286

       Find A Grave Memorials# 72269204, 72269283

       Death notice of Sarah Lutz, New Holland Clarion, 12 MAR 1887, page 3

       Marriage of Henry D. Lutz and Ada L. (Lawrence) Diffenderfer, Lebanon Co., PA Marriages,
         #16077, 15 MAR 1919, FamilySearch.org

14-4   Lutz, Infant Son

14-5   Lutz, Kate S., b. 1866

14-6   Bloch, Edna M., b. 1899

       Obituary of Edna Bloch, Reading Eagle, 25 MAR 1959, page 44

14-7   Myers, Florence V., b. 1901

14-8   Skidmore, Alice L., b. 1888

       Obituary of Alice L. Skidmore, Reading Eagle, 30 NOV 1973, page 26

       Obituary of Edna Bloch, Reading Eagle, 25 MAR 1959, page 44

14-9   Lutz, Ralph R., b. 1895

       Obituary of Ralph R. Lutz, Reading Eagle, 16 OCT 1967, page 8

14-10 Moyer, Violet Jane, b. 1918

       Obituary of Edna Bloch, Reading Eagle, 25 MAR 1959, page 44

       Obituary of Violet Jane Moyer, Reading Eagle, 6 NOV 1984, page 29

14-11 Moyer, John Albert, b. 1908

       Obituary of John Albert Moyer, Reading Eagle, 27 FEB 1986, page 49

14-12 Lutz, John, b. 1845

       Obituary of John Lutz, New Holland Clarion, 16 APR 1904, page 2

14-13 Lutz, Emma E., b. 1853

14-14 Lutz, Elmer R., b. 1884

14-15   Lutz, Adam S., b. 1827
       Lancaster Co., PA Deed M-5:93, John Schwarr heirs to Christian Weist, 1826
       Rootsweb.com, WorldConnect, database: lacor

14-16   Lutz, Louisa K., b. 1828

14-17   Artz, William, b. 1830
       Baptismal records of Muddy Creek Reformed Church
       1870 census, Adamstown, Lancaster Co., PA, page 339B

14-18   Artz, Louisa, b. 1839
       Rev. Benjamin G. Welder Burial records

14-19   Ziegler, Christian, b. 1797
       1870 census, Berks County Alms House, Cumru Twp., Berks Co., PA, page 212
       1880 census, Berks County Poor House, Cumru Twp., Berks Co., PA, ED 11, page 62B

15-1   Hagy, Dorothy M., b. 1914
       Obituary of Dorothy M. Hagy, Lancaster New Era, 4 OCT 1989, page B-4
       Berks County, PA Marriage license of John Hagy and Dorothy Lutz, 111:367, 26 OCT 1935
       Marriage notice, John Hagy and Dorothy Lutz, Reading Eagle, 6 NOV 1935, page 12

15-2   Lutz, Alice, b. 1893
       1900 census, West Cocalico Twp., Lancaster Co., PA, ED 116, page 2B
       1910 census, Warwick Twp., Lancaster Co., PA, ED 146, page 5B
       Marriage license of Jacob Harting and Annie Bartsh, Lancaster Co., PA Marriages, 1886, #1055
       Obituary of Alice Lutz, Ephrata Review, 15 DEC 1916, page 1

15-3   Lutz, Paul Henry, b. 1913

15-4   Lutz, William R., b. 1916

15-5   Snyder, Miriam Jane, b. 1930
       Obituary of Miriam J. Snyder, Reading Eagle, 14 NOV 1982, page 116

15-6   Snyder, Robert Charles, b. 1927
       Obituary of Robert C. Snyder, Roseboro Stradling Funeral Home web site

15-7   Lutz, Infant son, b. 1920
       Genealogical files of Brenda Creasy

15-8   Lutz, Florence, b. 1896

15-9   Lutz, Adam Ray, b. 1890
       Genealogical files of Brenda Creasy

16-1   Givler, Samuel, b. 1825
       Marriage record of Samuel Givler and Catharine Zell, Lancaster Co., PA marriages, 14 DEC 1853

16-2   Givler, Catharine, b. 1832
       Obituary of Catharine Givler, Lititz Record, 14 JAN 1909, page 3
       PA Death certificate of Catharine Givler, 1909, file #1884

16-3   Schlegel, John M., b. 1851
       Marriage of Jacob Schlegel and Maria Matz, 1841, Trinity Lutheran Church, Reading, Berks Co., PA

16-4   Schlegel, Leah L, b. 1849

16-5   Schlegel, Jacob L., b. 1879

16-6   Schlegel, Menno L., b. 1880

17-1   Groff, Christine W., b. 1968

18-1   Zimmerman, Caleb S., b. 1938

Obituary of Caleb S. Zimmerman, Lancaster New Era, 7 JUL 2003

18-2   Zimmerman, Mabel S., b. 1943

18-3   Zimmerman, Ronald A., b. 1965

18-4   High, Clair Leslie, b. 1959

19-1   Good, Raymond R., b. 1921

Obituary of Raymond R. Good, Lancaster New Era/Intelligencer, 22 FEB 2011, B-3

19-2   Landis, Anna C., b. 1896

19-3   Yoder, Salina E., b. 1901

Gospel Herald, 1 FEB 1966, page 117/118 [on Allen County (IN) Public Library website, http://www.acpl.lib.in.us/]

19-4   Yoder, Naomi, b. 1893

19-5   Yoder, Ruth E., b. 1896

Obituary of Ruth E. Yoder, Reading Eagle, 16 AUG 1956, page 31

19-6   Heller, Arthur I., b. 1894

Obituary of Arthur I. Heller, Reading Eagle, 5 JAN 1965, page 22

19-7   Heller, Sara E., b. 1901

Obituary of Sarah E. Heller, Lancaster New Era, 30 MAY 1942, page 3

20-1   Kurtz, Edwin N., b. 1933

Obituary of Edwin N. Kurtz, Lancaster New Era, 29 AUG 1987, page 3

20-2   Kurtz, Lydia M., b. 1934

20-3   Groff, Aaron L., b. 1914

Obituary of Aaron L. Groff, Lancaster New Era, 22 JAN 1998, page B-3

20-4   Groff, Mabel, b. 1912

Obituary of Mabel G. Groff, Lancaster New Era, 26 DEC 2001, page B-4

20-5   Martin, Rev. Edwin W., b. 1925

Obituary of Rev. Edwin W. Martin, Lancaster Intelligencer Journal, 9 JUN 2003

20-6   Martin, Martha B., b. 1924

Obituary of Martha B. Martin, Lancaster Intelligencer Journal/New Era, 25 MAR 2006

20-7   Gehman, Paul Hursh, b. 1927

Obituary of Paul H. Gehman, Reading Eagle, 22 JAN 1990, page 16

20-8   Gehman, Barbara Kilmer, b. 1930

Obituary of Barbara K. Gehman, Lancaster Intelligencer Journal/New Era, 9 MAY 2005

20-9   Bard, Robert E., b. 1874

Obituary of Robert E. Bard, Reading Eagle, 7 FEB 1961, page 19

20-10   Bard, Maggie, b. 1877

Obituary of Maggie Bard, Reading Eagle, 9 JUN 1956, page 11

20-11   Lefever, Harry S., b. 1906

Obituary of Harry S. Lefever, Ephrata Review, 25 MAR 1954, page 5

Obituary of Lizzie G. Lefever, Reading Eagle, 27 FEB 1959, page 19

Obituary of Esther M. (Lefever) Sweigart [half sister of Harry S. Lefever], Reading Eagle, 10 APR 1977, page 86

20-12   Lefever, Mary M., b. 1909

After the death of Harry S. Lefever, Mary married Ellsworth L. Sweigert

Obituary of Mary M. (Althouse) [Lefever] Sweigart, Reading Eagle, 21 APR 1984, page 13

1910 census, Manheim Twp., Lancaster Co., PA, ED 110, page 5A

1920 census, 3rd Ward, Ephrata Borough, Lancaster Co., PA, ED 46, page 15B

1930 census, Brecknock Twp., Lancaster Co., PA, ED 4, page 9A

Denver Union Cemetery – Selected References and Notes.

21-1   Weaver, Rufus M., b. 1917
Obituary of Rufus M. Weaver, Reading Eagle, 24 DEC 1983, page 14

21-2   Weaver, Ella Mae, b. 1919
Obituary of Ella Mae Weaver, Reading Eagle, 15 JUN 1992, page C-4

21-3   Harnish, Jacob R., b. 1904
Obituary of Jacob R. Harnish, Reading Eagle, 12 APR 1991, page 15

21-4   Harnish, Katie H., b. 1906
Obituary of Katie H. Harnish, Reading Eagle, 20 SEP 1999, page 9

21-5   Brenneman, Harold H., b. 1918
Obituary of Harold H. Brenneman, Lancaster Intelligencer Journal/New Era, 4 SEP 2010

21-6   Brenneman, Olive M., b. 1921
Obituary of Olive M. Brenneman, Lancaster Intelligencer Journal/New Era, 11 FEB 2001,
   page B-3

21-7   Martin, John W., b. 1937
Personal communication from David Martin

21-8   Martin, Nancy Jane, b. 1936
1940 census, Jackson Twp., Lebanon Co., PA, ED 38-11, Sheet 14B
Obituary of Nancy J. Martin, Lancaster New Era, 7 SEP 1993, page B-3

21-9   Martin, Philip Ray, b. 1971
Obituary of Philip R. Martin, Reading Eagle, 23 MAY 1971, page 78

21-10 Fry, Sallie L., b. 1879
Obituary of Mary M. Brubaker, Ephrata Review, 24 JAN 1913, page 3
Obituary of Anna G. Givler, Ephrata Review, 25 JAN 1918, page 7
Obituary of Susan G. Brubaker, Reading Eagle, 8 MAR 1938, page 22

21-11 Fry, Wayne Z., b. 1878
Obituary of Wayne Z. Fry, Reading Eagle, 8 OCT 1946, page 14

21-12 Noll, Jacob B., b. 1862
Obituary of Jacob B. Noll, Ephrata Review, 22 SEP 1938, page 14
Obituary of Jacob B. Noll, Reading Eagle, 17 SEP 1938, page 12
Descendants of Henry Noll and Julian Deppen:
http://freepages.genealogy.rootsweb.ancestry.com/~lnoll/noll/b7.htm
1860 census, Heidelberg Twp., Lebanon Co., PA, page 181
1870 census, Heidelberg Twp., Lebanon Co., PA, page 93B

21-13 Noll, Catharine R., b. 1863
Obituary of Amanda (Painter) Gehman [sister of Catharine (Painter) Noll, Reading Eagle,
   12 JUN 1950, page 16
Obituary of Catharine Noll, Ephrata Review, 23 JAN 1936, page 2

21-14 Noll, Robert P., b. 1884

22-1   Martin, Weaver B., b. 1932
Obituary of Weaver B. Martin, Lancaster Intelligencer Journal, 4 JUL 2003

22-2   Martin, Esther A., b. 1931
Obituary of Esther A. Martin, Lancaster New Era, 12 MAR 2004

22-3   Weaver, Melvin M., b. 1930

22-4   Weaver, Laura W., b. 1931

22-5   Sensenig, Isaac K., b. 1922
Obituary of Isaac K. Sensenig, Lancaster Intelligencer Journal, 3 APR 2007, page B-3

22-6   Sensenig, Ruth R., b. 1923

Obituary of Ruth R. Sensenig, Lancaster Intelligencer Journal, 3 MAR 2009, page B-4

22-7　Eby, Jonathan Dale, b. 1973

Genealogical files of Milton Haldeman

22-8　Engle, Katie M., b. 1896

22-9　Engle, Adam J., b. 1898

Obituary of Adam J. Engle, Reading Eagle, 10 APR 1958, page 36

World War I draft registration of Adam John Engle, FamilySearch.org

23-1　Beiler, Nathan Lamar, b. 1977

23-2　Miller, Phares H., b. 1910

Obituary of Phares H. Miller, Reading Eagle, 20 MAY 1992, page 19

23-3　Miller, Amanda B., b. 1907

Obituary of Amanda B. Miller, Reading Eagle, 7 AUG 1989, page 12

23-4　Showalter, Carl R., b. 1929

Obituary of Charles R. Showalter, Lancaster New Era, 12 JUL 1948, page 3

Obituary of Charles F. Showalter [father of Carl Showalter], Reading Eagle, 26 JUN 1934, page 20

Obituary of Daisy M. Showalter [mother of Carl Showalter], Reading Eagle, 20 MAR 1979, page 41

1930 census, West Cocalico Twp., Lancaster Co., PA, ED 123, page 7B

23-5　Miller, Henry E., b. 1934

23-6　Givler, Minnie W., b. 1897

Obituary of Minnie Givler, Reading Eagle, 21 APR 1937, page 20

23-7　Givler, Raymond B., b. 1899

Obituary of Raymond B. Givler, Reading Eagle, 17 FEB 1974, page 86

23-8　Miller, Clarence E., b. 1932

23-9　Miller, Ruth E., b. 1911

Obituary of Ruth E. Miller, Reading Eagle, 15 DEC 1982, page 64

23-10　Miller, Charles H., b. 1908

Obituary of Charles H. Miller, Lancaster Intelligencer Journal, 8 APR 2003

24-1　Clark, Dianne Marie, b. 1952

Obituary of Dianne Clark, Lancaster Intelligencer Journal, 12 APR 2000, page B-3

24-2　Givler, Raymond, b. 1923

24-3　Givler, Annie F., b. 1895

Obituary of Annie Givler, Reading Eagle, 16 MAR 1974, page 10

24-4　Miller, Edna Mae, b. 1922

24-5　Miller, James G., b. 1869

Marriage license of James G. Miller and Mamie Hoaster, Lancaster Co., PA Marriages, 1901, #18573

Obituary of James G. Miller, Reading Eagle, 6 MAR 1937, page 16

24-6　Miller, Mamie S., b. 1880

25-1　Martin, Melonie Joan, b. 1959

26-1　Weaver, Moses M., b. 1915

Obituary of Moses M. Weaver, Lancaster Intelligencer Journal, 20 SEP 2004

26-2　Weaver, Verna M., b. 1916

Obituary of Verna M. Weaver, Lancaster Intelligencer Journal/New Era, 8 APR 2013, page B-3

26-3　Stauffer, John S., b. 1926

26-4　Stauffer, Percy W., b. 1961

26-5   Stauffer, Lena S., b. 1924

26-6   Stauffer, Samuel W., b. 1956

26-7   Martin, Elva K., b. 1934

26-8   Martin, Alvin F., b. 1933
    Obituary of Alvin F. Martin, Lancaster Intelligencer Journal, 22 MAR 1997, page B-2

26-9   Lutz, Lydia B., b. 1853

26-10 Lutz, Charles S., b. 1854
    Obituary of Charles S. Lutz, Reading Eagle, 14 JAN 1938, page 26

26-11 Lutz, F. Charles
    Obituary of F. Charles Lutz, Ephrata Review, 16 JUL 1915, page 1

26-12 Gehman, Mildred B., b. 1897
    Obituary of Maggie Bard, Reading Eagle, 9 JUN 1956, page 11

26-13 Gehman, Monroe H., b. 1892
    Obituary of Monroe H. Gehman, Reading Eagle, 8 JUN 1973, page 33

26-14 Gehman, Wayne H., b. 1889
    Obituary of Wayne H. Gehman, Lancaster Intelligencer Journal, 7 JAN 2009, page B-3

26-15 Gehman, Mamie T., b. 1891
    Obituary of Mamie T. Gehman, Reading Eagle, 14 FEB 1978, page 24

26-16 Gehman, Mamie E., b. 1923

26-17 Gehman, Eugene T., b. 1927

27-1   Sauder, Linda Jane, b. 1956
    Obituary of Linda Jane Sauder, Lancaster Intelligencer Journal/New Era, 13 JUL 2012,
      page B-3

27-2   Sauder, Luke Ray, b. 1960
    Obituary of Luke Ray Sauder, Lancaster Intelligencer Journal, 30 AUG 1995, page B-3

27-3   Gehman, Elizabeth I., b. 1922

27-4   Gehman, Rev. Wayne, b. 1917
    Obituary of Wayne H. Gehman, Ephrata Review, 16 NOV 1928, page 9

27-5   Wivell, Anna M., b. 1920

27-6   Wivell, Claude J., b. 1916
    Obituary of Claude J. Wivell, Lancaster New Era, 8 MAR 2000, page B-3

28-1   Snader, Bertha H., b. 1927

28-2   Snader, Aaron A., b. 1928
    Obituary of Aaron Snader, Reading Eagle, 7 JAN 1994, page 15

28-3   Martin, Titus W., b. 1930

28-4   Martin, Elizabeth W., b. 1928

28-5   Martin, Lamar M., b. 1951
    Obituary of Lamar M. Martin, Lancaster Intelligencer Journal, 28 SEP 1995, B-3

28-6   Rupp, Ada L., b. 1869

28-7   Rupp, Isaac J., b. 1868
    Obituary of Isaac J. Rupp, Reading Eagle, 25 NOV 1943, page 19
    Marriage license of Isaac Rupp and Ada Kline, Lancaster Co., PA Marriages, 1890, #5063

28-8   Gehman, Barbara Hurst, b. 1863

28-9   Gehman, Joseph Horning, b. 1866
    Gayman/Gehman/Gahman Family book, page 125, Richard L. Miller, 2003
    Obituary of Joseph H. Gehman, New Holland Clarion, 4 FEB 1944, page 4

28-10 Gehman, Anna H., b. 1890

Denver Union Cemetery – Selected References and Notes.

Obituary of Anna H. Gehman, New Holland Clarion, 23 FEB 1945, page 4

29-1   Kline, Sue V., b. 1874

Obituary of Sue Kline, Reading Eagle, 4 DEC 1940, page 20

29-2   Kline, Elam J., b. 1875

Marriage license of Elam Kline and Susan Withers, Lancaster Co., PA Marriages, 1895, # 11561

Obituary of Elam J. Kline, Reading Eagle, 6 DEC 1957, page 24

29-3   Paul, Minnie E., b. 1877

Marriage license of William E. Paul and Minnie E. Kline, Lancaster Co., PA marriages, 1896, # 12658

1900 census, Ephrata Twp., Lancaster Co., PA, ED 37, page 2A

After the death of Minnie, William moved to Baltimore, MD. He remarried about 1908 to Nora A. () Paul, and died in 1950. William and his second wife Nora are buried in Loudon Park Cemetery, Baltimore City, MD

1910 census, 10th ward, Baltimore City, Baltimore Co., MD, ED 145, page 11B

30-1   Lorenz, James T., b. 1867

1870 census, East Cocalico Twp., Lancaster Co., PA, Page 316B

Obituary of James T. Lorenz, Ephrata Review, 17 FEB 1905, Page 2

Genealogical files of Milton Haldeman

Marriage license of James T. Lawrence [Lorenz] and Lizzie A. White, Lancaster Co., PA Marriages, 1888, #2919

Lititz Record, 17 FEB 1905, page 2.

> James Lorenz, a Reamstown cigar maker, was found hanging from the roof of his pig pen. He had been sued for slander by Prison Inspector, J. V. Sollenberger.

Ephrata Review, 17 FEB 1905, page 2

Suicide at Reamstown

James Lorenz, in a Fit of Despondency, Hangs Himself in His Barn

Some time between one and three o'clock, Saturday afternoon, James Lorenz, a well known resident of Reamstown, this county, committed suicide by hanging himself in the barn on his premises. His wife had been in Ephrata between the hours mentioned above attending to some shopping, leaving her husband and two children at home. At about 2 o'clock he left the house, and as he was noticed going to the barn, nothing was thought of the matter. As he had not returned to the house by the time his wife came home shortly after three o'clock, his wife went to the barn, her children having told her their father was there. On opening the door she was horrified at seeing her husband hanging from one of the rafters; his tragic death proved a great shock to the family. An alarm was immediately given and the body was cut down by a neighbor. Life was extinct, death having been due to strangulation. The news of the suicide spread rapidly, and it was the chief topic for conversation for the remainder of the day among the people of that usually quiet village.

Mr. Lorenz was thirty-five years of age, and was a cigarmaker by occupation, being employed for the past fifteen years or more by M. C. Killian, a well known cigar manufacturer, of Reamstown. He was a sober, industrious man, and was possessed of a lively, cheerful disposition usually, but at times suffered from fits of despondency, and it is believed that he was lead to commit the rash deed which ended his life, while under one of these despondent spells. Some time ago, he was sued for slander, and it is thought this preyed on his mind. During Saturday morning he was, however, in his usual cheerful frame of mind, and the members of his family and the neighbors had no thought that he would commit so rash a deed.

Deputy Coroner George Root, of Reamstown, with Dr. W. M. High, of Reamstown, as his physician, held an inquest. His jury consisted of Lemon Adams, Martin J. Root, David Keener, Charles Heitz, Pierce Killian and B. Y. Jacoby. The verdict rendered was that the deceased came to his death by hanging in his own barn while in a fit of despondency.

Lorenz was a native of Reamstown, having been born there and always resided there. He was a son of Constable Christian Lorenz, of East Cocalico township, who also resides in East Cocalico township. He leaves his wife and two daughters, Emma and Lillie, both at home. He also leaves the following sisters and brothers: Mary, at home; Mrs. Clayton Sweigart, residing near Red Run, Brecknock township; William, of Reamstown, who is also a cigar maker being employed at J. G. Root's cigar factory at that place, and Abraham, an iron moulder, residing in Pottstown.

The funeral took place on Wednesday morning from the home of the deceased on Church street, Reamstown. Interment was made in the Denver cemetery. Rev. Q. A. Dech, of Reamstown, officiated.

30-2   Weaver, Lizzie [Lorenz], b. 1868
      Obituary of Lizzie (White) [Lorenz] Weaver, Reading Eagle, 20 OCT 1928, page 2
      Obituary of Lizzie (White) [Lorenz] Weaver, Ephrata Review, 26 OCT 1928, page 9
30-3   Lorenz, Lillie W., b. 1890
      Obituary of Lillie W. Lorenz, Reading Eagle, 12 DEC 1974, page 35
31-1   Withers, George S., b. 1876
      1880 census, East Cocalico Twp., Lancaster Co., PA, ED 105, Page 18B
31-2   Withers, Maggie, b. 1879
      1880 census, Clay Twp., Lancaster Co., PA, ED 108, Page 10B
      Find A Grave Memorials# 39795556, 39797992
      Marriage license of George Withers and Maggie Stief, 1899, Lancaster Co., PA Marriage #15189
      Genealogical files of Milton Haldeman
31-3   Showalter, Harvey F., b. 1864
31-4   Showalter, Susan F., b. 1865
      Obituary of Susan F, Showalter, Reading Eagle, 10 FEB 1954, page 55
31-5   Showalter, Lizzie W., b. 1889
      Obituary of Lizzie W. Showalter, Reading Eagle, 18 FEB 1926, page 2
31-6   Showalter, Katie W., b. 1891
32-1   Burkholder, Martin G., b. 1864
32-2   Hoover, Mattie C., b. 1871
      Obituary of Mattie Hoover, Reading Eagle, 3 MAR 1952, page 18
32-3   Hoover, Samuel C., b. 1879
      Obituary of Samuel C. Hoover, Reading Eagle, 7 JUN 1965, page 20
      World War I draft registration card of Samuel Carpenter Hoover, FamilySearch.org
32-4   Wenger, Gladys, b. 1904
      Obituary of Gladys B. Wenger, Reading Eagle, 27 JUN 1983, page 30
32-5   Wenger, John E., b. 1900
      Obituary of John E. Wenger, Reading Eagle, 10 FEB 1986, page 24
33-1   Shelly, Anna R., b. 1916

Obituary of Anna R. Shelly, Lancaster Intelligencer Journal/New Era, 30 SEP 2013, page B-3

33-2 Shelly, Erla M., b. 1907

Obituary of Erla M. Shelly, Lancaster New Era, 31 OCT 1987, page 3

33-3 Shelly, Jacob R., b. 1903

Obituary of Jacob R. Shelly, Lancaster New Era, 2 OCT 1993, page A-7

34-1 Snyder, Mary S., b. 1866

34-2 Snyder, Samuel B., b. 1870

Marriage license of Samuel B. Snyder and Mary S. Lutz, 1890, Lancaster Co., PA Marriage #5558

Obituary of Samuel B. Snyder, Reading Eagle, 29 JAN 1961, page 39

34-3 Eby, E. Ruth, b. 1892

Obituary of E. Ruth Eby, Lancaster New Era, 27 DEC 1973, page 3

34-4 Eby, Ivan Lloyd, b. 1889

Obituary of Ivan L. Eby, Lancaster New Era, 3 DEC 1970, page 3

34-5 Johns, Samuel, b. 1886

34-6 Johns, Ellen J., b. 1859

Obituary of Charles M. Eberly, Reading Eagle, 11 DEC 1943, page 28

Obituary of Samuel Eberly, Ephrata Review, 1 APR 1910, page 2

Obituary of Ellen Johns, Reading Eagle, 12 APR 1945, page 23

1850 census, East Cocalico Twp., Lancaster Co., PA, page 230

1870 census, East Cocalico Twp., Lancaster Co., PA, page 315

34-7 Johns, Elder J. Bitzer, b. 1860

Obituary of J. Bitzer Johns, Reading Eagle, 23 NOV 1942, page 13

34-8 Eberly, Samuel, b. 1819

Obituary of Samuel Eberly, Ephrata Review, 1 APR 1910, page 2

PA Death Certificate of Samuel Eberly, 1910, File #23837

Marriage license of C. M. Eberly [son of Samuel Eberly], Lancaster Co., PA marriage license, 1885, #7

Obituary of Charles M. Eberly, Reading Eagle, 11 DEC 1943, page 28

1850 census, East Cocalico Twp., Lancaster Co., PA, page 230

1870 census, East Cocalico Twp., Lancaster Co., PA, page 315

34-9 Eberly, Hannah, b. 1822

Obituary of Charles M. Eberly, Reading Eagle, 11 DEC 1943, page 28

Estate papers of Jacob Matz, Berks County, PA, 1839, FamilySearch.org

34-10 Ludwig, Ida G., b. 1885

Find A Grave Memorials# 100243406, 100243423

1900 census, Earl Twp., Lancaster Co., PA, ED 19, Page 11A

Marriage license of Ida "Griffey" and Pierce Ludwig, 1902, Lancaster Co., PA Marriage #19665

Death notice of Ida Ludwig, Reading Eagle, 26 FEB 1948, page 34

34-11 Ludwig, Pierce Renninger, b. 1881

Obituary of Pierce Ludwig, Reading Eagle, 28 APR 1950, page 30

34-12 Ludwig, Arthur, b. 1907

1910 Census, 12th Ward, Reading City, Berks Co., PA, ED 86, Page 3A

Obituary of Arthur Ludwig, Ephrata Review, 28 DEC 1967, page A-2

Obituary of Arthur Ludwig, Reading Eagle, 21 DEC 1967, page 51

34-13 Ludwig, Leroy, b. 1904

Denver Union Cemetery – Selected References and Notes.

1910 Census, 12th Ward, Reading City, Berks Co., PA, ED 86, Page 3A
Department of Veterans Affairs BIRLS Death File, Fold3.com
Obituary of Leroy Ludwig, Reading Eagle, 3 JUL 1973, page 26

35-1   Ludwig, Florence Grace, b. 1909
35-2   Lorah, Earl, b. 1930
      Genealogical files of Milton Haldemam

36-1   Shimp, Edwin, b. 1871
      Obituary of Edwin Shimp, Reading Eagle, 19 JUN 1951, page 22

36-2   Shimp, Amelia, b. 1875
      Obituary of Amelia Shimp, Ephrata Review, 29 MAY 1914, page 4

36-3   Overholser, John H., b. 1864

36-4   Overholser, George R., b. 1867
      Obituary of George R. Overholser, New Holland Clarion, 15 FEB 1913, page 1
      Reading Eagle, 8 MAY 1914, page 15:

> G. S. Withers & Sons, proprietors of the Reamstown Marble and Granite Works, erected a large monument for George R. Oberholser and Kate Oberholser on the Brick Meeting House cemetery, near Denver.

36-5   Overholser, Isaac K., b. 1836
      Obituary of Isaac K. Overholser, Ephrata Review, 15 DEC 1922, page 1
      Obituary of Isaac K. Overholser, Reading Eagle, 12 DEC 1922, page 50
      Obituary of Martin K Overholser [brother of Isaac K. Overholser], New Holland Clarion, 11 MAY 1912, page 1
      Lancaster Co., PA Deed E-14:398, John Oberholser heirs to Mary Oberholser, 1881
      Genealogical files of Brenda Creasy
      Obituary of Anna (Overholser) Galt, New Holland Clarion, 23 SEP 1916, page 1
      1850 census, Blue Ball, Lancaster Co., PA, page 179B
      1880 census, East Cocalico Twp., Lancaster Co., PA, ED 105, page 23C
      1900 census, East Cocalico Twp., Lancaster Co., PA, ED 22, page 7B
      Lititz Record, 23 SEP 1920, page 2:

Does Farm Work at 84

Notwithstanding the fact that Isaac Overholser, of Reamstown, Lancaster county, who owns a large and well conducted farm, is 84 years of age, he supervises the management of his farm, assisted by his son, Charles R. Overholser, who is also employed by Lloyd Rhoads, baker at Reamstown.

Mr. Overholser is never happier than when he is at work. About five years ago he lost his left hand at the wrist through an accident in a corn shredder, and for a time was very much discouraged, thinking that his days of usefulness were over. For several years past, however, he has been taking more and more interest in the work and during the past season he mowed grass, manipulating the scythe with dexterity, notwithstanding his handicap.

He cultivated the corn and potatoes with the use of a team; he helped put the hay away in the mow and enjoyed it; he pitched and also loaded wheat, and has also done some other feats in the farm work which are marvelous when one considers his handicap.

Mr. Overholser is a man of strong rebust (sic) frame and enjoys excellent health.

36-6   Overholser, Kate, b. 1830
      Obituary of Kate Overholser, New Holland Clarion, 14 DEC 1907, page 1

36-7   Overholser, Maggie, b. 1873

Obituary of Maggie Overholser, Ephrata Review, 25 NOV 1932, page 12

36-8   Overholser, Lizzie, b. 1869
Obituary of Lizzie Overholser, Reading Eagle, 16 NOV 1948, page 24
Obituary of Maggie Overholser, Ephrata Review, 25 NOV 1932, page 12

36-9   Overholser, Mary, b. 1866
Obituary of Maggie Overholser, Ephrata Review, 25 NOV 1932, page 12
Obituary of Mary N. Overholser, Reading Eagle, 19 APR 1949, page 20

37-1   Fry, Peter, b. 1850
Obituary of Peter Fry, Ephrata Review, 17 AUG 1923, page 8
PA Death Certificate of Peter Fry, 1923, File #85834
1880 census, East Cocalico Twp., Lancaster Co., PA, ED 105, page 23C
1900 census, East Cocalico Twp., Lancaster Co., PA, ED 22, page 7B

37-2   Overholser, Charles R., b. 1871
Obituary of Maggie Overholser, Ephrata Review, 25 NOV 1932, page 12
Obituary of Charles R. Overholser, Reading Eagle, 5 JUN 1946, page 20

37-3   Overholser, Mary W., b. 1871
Obituary of Mary Overholser, Reading Eagle, 22 JUN 1946, page 8

38-1   Bowman, Arlene D., b. 1917
Obituary of Arlene D. Bowman, Lancaster Intelligencer Journal, 21 MAR 1995, page B-2

38-2   Bowman, Aaron M., b. 1917
Obituary of Aaron M. Bowman, Lancaster Intelligencer Journal, 3 DEC 1997, page B-3

38-3   Burkholder, George M., b. 1834
38-4   Burkholder, Elizabeth, b. 1831
38-5   Burkholder, Susan G., b. 1868
38-6   Ream, Lizzie, b. 1891
Obituary of Lizzie Ream, Reading Eagle, 8 JUN 1960, page 53

38-7   Ream, Andrew S., b. 1885
Obituary of Andrew Ream, Ephrata Review, 18 OCT 1956, page 6
Obituary of Ida S. Hacker [sister of Andrew Ream], Reading Eagle, 20 OCT 1939, page 23
1900 census, West Cocalico Twp., Lancaster Co., PA, ED 111, page 4B

39-1   Lutz, Kate, b. 1862
39-2   Lutz, Henry Regar, b. 1862
39-3   Lutz, Parke Henry, b. 1896
39-4   Lutz, Cecil B, b. 1897
Obituary of Cecil B. Lutz, Reading Eagle, 22 JUL 1986, page 28

39-5   Burkholder, John G., b. 1862
39-6   Burkholder, Emma B., b. 1862
Obituary of Emma Burkholder, Reading Eagle, 29 JAN 1947, page 21

39-7   Burkholder, Mignetta E., b. 1886
Obituary of Mignetta Burkholder, Reading Eagle, 6 DEC 1977, page 34

39-8   Long, Russel A., b. 1925
Obituary of Nora C. (Ream) Hahn, Reading Eagle, 22 MAY 1986, page 77

40-1   Witmer, Nevin Lynn, b. 1972
Obituary of Nevin L. Witmer, Lancaster New Era, 31 JAN 1972, page 3

40-2   Meckley, Phares H., b. 1888
Obituary of Phares H. Meckley, Reading Eagle, 4 AUG 1984, page 5

40-3   Meckley, Lizzie L., b. 1888

40-4   Snyder, Edwin F., b. 1859
        Obituary of Edwin F. Snyder, Ephrata Review, 25 NOV 1932, page 12

40-5   Snyder, Susanna, b. 1859
        Gospel Herald, 23 JUN 1944, page 238/239 [on Allen County (IN) Public Library website,
           http://www.acpl.lib.in.us/]

40-6   Schload, Clayton, b. 1860
        Obituary of Clayton Schload, Ephrata Review, 15 MAY 1931, page 7
        Obituary of Levi Schload [father of Clayton Schload], New Holland Clarion, 11 FEB 1905,
           page 1

40-7   Schload, Mary Jane, b. 1861
        Obituary of Mary Schload, Reading Eagle, 9 OCT 1944, page 17

40-8   Schload, Mabel, b. 1906
        Obituary of Mabel Schload, Reading Eagle, 15 JAN 2000, page 9

41-1   Meckley, Infant, b. 1915

42-1   Sweigart, Ada L., b. 1885
        Obituary of Ada Sweigart, Ephrata Review, 4 SEP 1931, page 9

42-2   Messner, Elam C., b. 1871
        Obituary of Elam Messner, Ephrata Review, 8 AUG 1930, page 1

42-3   Messner, Mary P., b. 1843
        Baptismal records of Muddy Creek Reformed Church
        Genealogical files of Brenda Creasy

42-4   Messner, Christian Gehman, b. 1846
        Obituary of Christian G. Messner, Ephrata Review, 6 MAR 1931, page 8
        Ancestry for Christian Messner:
        http://rainer.bnt.com/dmessner/famtree/famtree?width=04&id=64

42-5   Leisey, Abraham Getz, b. 1855

42-6   Leisey, Matilda, b. 1856
        Obituary of Matilda Leisey, Reading Eagle, 25 SEP 1939, page 16

43-1   Ludwig, Caroline, b. 1872
        Obituary of Caroline "Callie" Ludwig, Reading Eagle, 14 OCT 1937, page 31
        Ancestry for Christian Messner:
        http://rainer.bnt.com/dmessner/famtree/famtree?width=04&id=64

43-2   Ludwig, William D., b. 1870
        Obituary of William D. Ludwig, Reading Eagle, 29 JAN 1948, page 30

44-1   Bressler, Sadie S., b. 1898
        Obituary of Sadie S. Bressler, Lancaster Intelligencer Journal, 22 OCT 1995

44-2   Bressler, Rev Elias D., b. 1897
        Lebanon Co., PA marriage of Elias D. Bressler & Sadie Crawford, 1926, #20728

44-3   Myers, William T., b. 1912
        Obituary of William T. Myers, Reading Eagle, 8 AUG 1985, page 54

44-4   Myers, Evelyn D., b. 1912
        Obituary of Evelyn D. Davis, 6 SEP 2000, Carroll County Times, (Westminster, MD)

45-1   Allen, Carole G., b. 1925
        Obituary of Carole Allen, Lancaster New Era, 20 SEP 1986, page 3
        Obituary of Carole Allen, Reading Eagle , 20 SEP 1986, page 15

45-2   Lawrence, Leroy, b. 1898
        Obituary of Leroy Lawrence, Reading Eagle, 12 NOV 1983, page 18

45-3   Lorenz, Amanda, b. 1879
      1880 census, East Cocalico Twp., Lancaster Co., PA, ED 105, page 35C
      Obituary of John D. Becker (brother of Amanda), Reading Eagle, 9 DEC 1922, page 2
      Obituary of Amanda (Painter) [Lorenz] Gehman, Reading Eagle, 12 JUN 1950, page 16

45-4   Lorenz, William, b. 1878
      Marriage of William Lorenz and Amanda Becker, Lancaster Co., PA Marriages, 1896, #12433
      Obituary of William Lorenz, Reading Eagle, 23 JAN 1964, page 28
      Obituary of Mary J. Wolf [sister of William Lorenz], Reading Eagle, 30 JAN 1964, page 25

45-5   Lorenz, William Jr., b. 1900
      Obituary of William Lorenz, Jr., Reading Eagle, 7 MAY 1970, page 52

45-6   Lorenz, Kenneth, b. 1926

45-7   Lorenz, Lora Irene, b. 1898
      Obituary of Lora Irene Lorenz, Reading Eagle, 17 MAR 1955, page 32

46-1   Eberly, Edwin M., b. 1911
      Obituary of Edwin M. Eberly, Reading Eagle, 26 MAR 1999, page 13

46-2   Eberly, Mabel G., b. 1913
      Obituary of Mabel G. Eberly, Lancaster Sunday News, 9 DEC 2007

46-3   Weaver, Elsie K., b. 1912
      Obituary of Elsie K. Weaver, Reading Eagle, 8 MAR 1977, page 32

46-4   Weaver, John Martin, b. 1909
      Obituary of Reuben B. Weaver [father of John M. Weaver], Reading Eagle, 2 AUG 1976,
         page 24

47-1   Weinhold, Helen B., b. 1915
      1920 Census, Christiana Borough, Lancaster Co., PA, ED 7, page 1B
      Lancaster Co., PA Deed O-35:196, 1942, Bessie C. Black to Lemon E. & Helen B. Weinhold
      Find A Grave Memorials# 25665439, 25665430

47-2   Weinhold, Lemon E., b. 1908
      Obituary of Lemon E. Weinhold, Reading Eagle, 12 FEB 1977, page 14

47-3   Weinhold, Ralph K., b. 1916
      Obituary of Ralph K. Weinhold, Reading Eagle, 6 JAN 1999, page B-5

47-4   Weinhold, Leona Mae, b. 1924
      Obituary of Leona M. Weinhold, Reading Eagle, 15 SEP 1981, page 29

47-5   Weinhold, Edith K., b. 1922
      Obituary of Edith K. Weinhold, Reading Eagle, 10 MAR 1988, page 45

47-6   Weinhold, Mark Allen, b. 1961
      Obituary of Mark A. Weinhold, Lancaster New Era, 8 JUL 1997, page B-3

---   Beckey, Mary Francis, b. 1855
      PA Death Certificate of Mary Beckey, 1937, file # 737

---   Sweigart, John, b. 1858

---   Sweigart, Franklin, b. 1876

---   Sweigart, Samuel, b. 1864

---   Sweigart, Samuel, b. 1826

Drybread, William	23-3	Engle, Amelia (Krall)	22-9
Eberly, ---	R&N-3-3	Engle, Frank	22-9
Eberly, Alice	R&N-10-9	Engle, Katie M. (Noll)	22-8
Eberly, Anna (Flickinger)	5-15, 5-16	Erb, Eliza	2-12
Eberly, Caroline (Musser)	46-1	Erb, John	2-22
Eberly, Catharine (Bear)	3-18, 5-19, 5-22, 5-24, 34-8	Erb, Judith (Hull)	2-22
		Erb, Nancy	2-9, 2-17, 2-20, 2-21, 2-22, 2-23
Eberly, Catharine (Newcomer)	5-16		
Eberly, Charles M.	R&N-34-6, R&N-34-8, R&N-34-9	Eshelman, Annie	21-3
		Fahnestock, ---	16
		Fasnacht, Christian	14, 15
Eberly, Edwin M.	46-1	Fasnacht, Eliza Ann	4-5
Eberly, Ellen	34-5, 34-6	Faust, Mollie	16-1
Eberly, Hannah (Matz)	34-6, 34-8, 34-9	Felpel, Elizabeth S.	26-8
Eberly, Harvey	R&N-10-8	Fessler, Matilda [Lutz]	R&N-7-1, R&N-8-4
Eberly, Henry	9-11		
Eberly, Henry Z.	46-1	Fessler, Susanna	7-22, 7-25
Eberly, Mabel G. (High)	46-2	Fessler, William	8-4, R&N-8-4
Eberly, Magdalena	2-16, 7-8, 8-17	Fetter, Leah	12-3
Eberly, Maria	5-20, 5-22	Flickinger, Anna	5-15, 5-16
Eberly, Mary (Hagy)	9-11	Flickinger, Elizabeth	9-7
Eberly, Minerva B.	32-5	Flickinger, Esther	5-15
Eberly, Peter	5-15, 5-16, 5-24, 5-25, R&N-5-25	Flickinger, Joseph	5-15
		Folk, Annie	23-7
Eberly, Salme [=Sarah]	9-9	Folk, Annie F.	24-3
Eberly, Samuel	3-18, 5-19, 5-22, 5-24, 34-6, 34-8, 34-9, R&N-34-6	Folk, Ellen (Schwoyer)	24-3
		Folk, William	24-3
		Frankhouser, Ada Emma	11-1
Eberly, Sarah	9-7, 9-10, 9-11, 10-9, 11-4, 11-5	Frankhouser, Barbara	13-3
		Frankhouser, Byram L.	11-1, 11-2, 11-3
Eberly, Susan	20-9	Frankhouser, Catharine (Lorah)	11-2
Eberly, Susanna	3-16, 3-17, 3-18, 3-19	Frankhouser, Christian	11-2
		Frankhouser, Elizabeth	37-1
Eberly, Susanna (Kling)	5-24, 5-25	Frankhouser, Sarah J. (Root)	11-1, 11-2, 11-3
Eberly, Thomas J.	R&N-5-25	Frecht, Anna C.	9-1, 9-1, 9-3, 9-4
Eby, Alice (Givler)	34-4		
Eby, E. Ruth (Snyder)	34-3	Frecht, Annie Caroline	9-6
Eby, Elmer	34-4	Frecht, John	9-6
Eby, Ivan Lloyd	34-4	Frecht, Martha Ann	31-3
Eby, John D.	22-7	Frecht, Mary (Rhoads)	9-6
Eby, Jonathan Dale	22-7	Frey, Anna Maria (Frey)	10-6
Eby, Rhoda M. (Sensenig)	22-7	Frey, G. S.	R&N-2-16
Eichelberger, Lizzie	47-2	Frey, John	10-6
Eitnier, L. Y.	17	Fry, Eliza (Erb)	2-12
Engle, Adam John	22-9	Fry, Elizabeth (Frankhouser)	37-1

150

Ludwig, Milton	1-7	Lutz, Edna M.	14-6
Ludwig, Mrs. Samuel	15, 17	Lutz, Eduard	9-9
Ludwig, Pierce	R&N-34-10	Lutz, Elizabeth	8-1, 8-7, 8-8, 8-9
Ludwig, Pierce Renninger	34-11	Lutz, Elizabeth (Flickinger)	9-7
Ludwig, Pierson	34-12, 35-1, 34-13	Lutz, Elizabeth (Macwate)	8-2, 8-3, 8-10, 8-11, 8-14, 8-15, 9-5, 10-8
Ludwig, Rachel M. (Wendel)	12-18		
Ludwig, Samuel	16, 6-8, 6-9, 6-10, 6-11, 6-12	Lutz, Elizabeth "Eliza"	8-2
Ludwig, Samuel B.	6-6, 6-7	Lutz, Ella M. (Lausch)	14-1
Ludwig, Samuel W.	6-6	Lutz, Elmer	8-5
Ludwig, Susanna	40-3, 40-5	Lutz, Elmer R.	14-14
Ludwig, William	1-5, 40-5	Lutz, Emma	10-11, R&N-10-9
Ludwig, William D.	43-2		
Lutz, ---	4	Lutz, Emma (Steinmetz)	10-11, 10-12, 10-13, 10-14, 10-15, 26-10, 34-1
Lutz, Adam	7-16, 9-10, 9-12, 9-13, 9-13, 9-14, 9-15, 9-16, 9-18, 9-19		
		Lutz, Emma E. (Regar)	14-12, 14-13, 14-14
Lutz, Adam H.	10-10		
Lutz, Adam Ray	15-9	Lutz, Evan E.	9-7
Lutz, Adam S.	10-10, 14-15, 14-16, 39-2	Lutz, F. Charles	26-11
		Lutz, Fianna E.	11-5
Lutz, Adda	9-8	Lutz, Florence	15-8
Lutz, Alice	R&N-10-8	Lutz, Florence V.	14-7
Lutz, Alice (Harding)	15-1, 15-2, 15-3, 15-4	Lutz, Frances S.	9-1
		Lutz, Franklin	10-7
Lutz, Alice L.	14-8	Lutz, H. R.	10, 11
Lutz, Anna C. (Frecht)	9-1, 9-1, 9-3, 9-4, 9-6	Lutz, Hannah	7-14
		Lutz, Henry	16, 8-11, 8-12, 8-13, 8-14, 9-15
Lutz, Barton	15-3, 15-4		
Lutz, Barton S.	15-1, 15-2	Lutz, Henry B.	14-3
Lutz, Bertha M.	9-2	Lutz, Henry D.	14-2, 14-3, 14-6, 14-7, 14-8, 14-9
Lutz, Cecil B. (Ritchey)	39-4		
Lutz, Charles S.	26-10, 26-11	Lutz, Henry E.	11-4
Lutz, Charles Sweigart	14-2	Lutz, Henry R.	4, 5, 6, 15-9, 39-3
Lutz, Clara Louise	9-3		
Lutz, Daniel	8-2, 8-3, 8-10, 8-11, 8-14, 8-15, 9-5, 10-8, R&N-8-15	Lutz, Henry Regar	39-2
		Lutz, Howard R.	15-7
		Lutz, Infant Son	14-4, 15-7
		Lutz, Irwin B.	6
Lutz, Daniel M.	9-1, 9-1, 9-3, 9-4, 9-5	Lutz, J. Frank	4, 5, 6, 10, 11
		Lutz, Jacob	9-7, 9-9, 9-10, 9-11, 11-4, 11-5
Lutz, Dorothy	R&N-15-1		
Lutz, Dorothy M.	15-1		
Lutz, Edna	14-10		

Lutz, John	12, 13, 8-24, 9-16, 9-17, 10-7, 10-14, 14-12, 14-12, 14-13, 14-14, 14-15, 26-10, R&N-2-16, R&N-10-9
Lutz, John Frank	10-12
Lutz, John M.	10-8, 10-9
Lutz, John S.	10-11, 10-12, 10-13, 10-14, 10-15, 34-1
Lutz, Julian	R&N-10-10
Lutz, Julian (Hackman)	10-10
Lutz, Kate	16
Lutz, Kate (Getz)	15-9, 39-1, 39-3
Lutz, Kate (Lorah)	10-7, 10-8, 10-9
Lutz, Kate (Sweigart)	14-3, 14-5, 14-6, 14-7, 14-8, 14-9
Lutz, Katharine (Lutz)	11-4
Lutz, Katie (Sweigart)	14-2
Lutz, Lizzie S.	10-13
Lutz, Louisa K. (Regar)	14-15, 14-16, 39-2
Lutz, Lucile	14-4, 14-9
Lutz, Lydia (Mohler)	26-11
Lutz, Lydia (Senseman)	7-16, 9-12, 9-13, 9-14
Lutz, Lydia B. (Mohler)	26-9
Lutz, Mable Mae (Beam)	15-7
Lutz, Magdalena (Ream)	9-10, 9-13, 9-15, 9-16, 9-18, 9-19
Lutz, Maria	7-15, 7-16
Lutz, Martin R.	15-8
Lutz, Mary C.	9-4
Lutz, Mary J. (Keener)	15-8
Lutz, Mary S.	34-1, 34-3, R&N-34-2
Lutz, Matilda	R&N-7-1, R&N-8-4
Lutz, Matilda "Tilly" (Kachel)	7-1
Lutz, Morris F.	R&N-9-7
Lutz, Mrs. Henry	15
Lutz, Parke Henry	39-3
Lutz, Paul Henry	15-3

Lutz, Ralph	14-4, 14-9
Lutz, Salme [=Sarah] (Eberly)	9-9
Lutz, Samuel	8-10
Lutz, Sarah	8-23, 8-24, 8-25, R&N-14-3
Lutz, Sarah (Eberly)	9-7, 9-10, 9-11, 11-4, 11-5
Lutz, Sariah (Deibler)	14-3
Lutz, Stella	8-6
Lutz, Susan (Royer)	8-14
Lutz, Susanna (Royer)	8-12, 8-13
Lutz, Susanna (Swarr)	8-24, 9-16, 9-17, 10-14, 14-12, 14-15
Lutz, Susannah	9-12
Lutz, Tilly (Kachel)	8-3, 8-4, 8-6, 8-5
Lutz, William	8-5, 8-6
Lutz, William M.	8-3, 8-4
Lutz, William R.	15-4
Macwate, Elizabeth	8-2, 8-3, 8-10, 8-11, 8-14, 8-15, 9-5, 10-8, R&N-8-15
Marquet, Cynthia	3
Martin, Alvin F.	25-1, 26-8
Martin, Amos H.	20-5
Martin, Christian H.	26-8
Martin, David	3
Martin, Edna (Burkholder)	22-1
Martin, Elizabeth S. (Felpel)	26-8
Martin, Elizabeth W. (Martin)	28-4, 28-5
Martin, Elva K. (Kreider)	26-7
Martin, Elva Kilhefner (Kreider)	25-1
Martin, Esther A. (Yoder)	22-2
Martin, Henry M.	21-7
Martin, John	15
Martin, John F.	22-1
Martin, John W.	21-7, 21-9
Martin, Katie O. (Weaver)	20-5
Martin, Lamar M.	28-5
Martin, Lizzie	21-1
Martin, Lydia M.	20-2
Martin, Lydia S.	46-4

Schwear, Samuel	4-3	Shimp, Susanna (Eberly)	3-16, 3-17, 3-18, 3-19
Schweitzer, S.	16		
Schweitzer, Stephen	R&N-5-25	Shirk, Elizabeth	20-10
Schwoyer, Ellen	24-3	Shirk, J. R.	11
Scull, Nicholas	7	Shirker, Henry	15
Seidel, F. F.	18	Shober, Reuben E.	3-19
Senseman, Johannes	9-14	Shober, Susanna (Shimp)	3-19
Senseman, John	R&N-9-14	Shoups, Mrs. Albert	15
Senseman, Juliana Justina (Kimmel)	9-14	Showalter, Addie (Harnish)	6-27, 6-28, 6-29, 6-30
Senseman, Lydia	7-16, 9-12, 9-13, 9-14	Showalter, Charles	23-4
		Showalter, Charles "Carl" R.	23-4
Sensenig, Carrie	3-2	Showalter, Charles F.	R&N-23-4
Sensenig, Emma	23-6	Showalter, Christian	6-27, 6-28, 6-29, 6-30
Sensenig, Isaac G.	22-5		
Sensenig, Isaac K.	22-5	Showalter, Daisy (Regar)	23-4
Sensenig, Katie (Kurtz)	22-5	Showalter, Daisy M.	R&N-23-4
Sensenig, Myrtle	3-1	Showalter, Emanuel S.	31-3
Sensenig, Rhoda M.	22-7	Showalter, Harvey F.	31-3
Sensenig, Ruth R. (Gehman)	22-6	Showalter, Henry	4-21
Shelly, Anna R.	33-1	Showalter, Jennie Mabel	6-30
Shelly, Christian	33-1	Showalter, John	6-27, R&N-5-20
Shelly, Christian M.	33-3	Showalter, Katie W.	31-6
Shelly, Erla M. (Smith)	33-2	Showalter, Laura Mamie	6-29
Shelly, Esther "Hettie" (Rissler)	33-3	Showalter, Lizzie W.	31-5
		Showalter, Lydia	5-23
Shelly, Esther (Rissler)	33-1	Showalter, Lydia (Hoffard)	6-27
Shelly, Jacob R.	33-3	Showalter, Maria (Eberly)	5-20, 5-22
Sherb, Susanna	7-7	Showalter, Martha Ann (Frecht)	31-3
Shiffer, Elmer R.	12-9		
Shiffer, Mayme R.	12-9	Showalter, Mary (Smith)	6-27
Shimp, Amelia (Miller)	36-1, 36-2, 38-6	Showalter, Samuel	5-20, 5-20, 5-22, R&N-5-22
Shimp, Andrew	3-17		
Shimp, Edwin	36-1, 36-2, 38-6	Showalter, Sarah	4-21
Shimp, Eliza Ann (Kilhefner) [Dissinger]	3-5	Showalter, Sarah (Lausch)	4-21
		Showalter, Susan F. (White)	31-4
Shimp, Elizabeth (Mueller)	3-17	Shrantz, John	16
Shimp, Fianna (Hagy)	36-1	Shupp, Mrs. Albert	17
Shimp, George	3-16, 3-17, 3-18, 3-19	Skidmore, Alice L. (Lutz)	14-8
		Skidmore, Walter	14-8
Shimp, Henry	36-1	Sloat, Priscilla	10-4
Shimp, Henry F.	3-5	Sloat, Susan E.	R&N-13-2
Shimp, Jacob	3-16	Smith, Adeline (Hornberger)	33-2
Shimp, Lizzie	38-6, 39-8	Smith, Catharine	13-5
Shimp, Susanna	3-19	Smith, Clayton	33-2

Weinhold, Isaac B.	47-2	Wiest, Christian	R&N-8-21
Weinhold, Lemon E.	47-2, R&N-47-1	Will, Magdalena	34-9
Weinhold, Leona Mae (Miller)	47-3, 47-4, 47-6	Winehold, Peter	10
Weinhold, Lizzie (Eichelberger)	47-2	Wise, Mary	5-1
		Withers, G. S.	R&N-36-4
Weinhold, Mark Allen	47-6	Withers, George	R&N-31-2
Weinhold, Ralph	47-6	Withers, George S.	31-1, 31-2
Weinhold, Ralph K.	47-3, 47-4	Withers, Isaac	29-2, 31-1
Weinhold, Salome (Krick)	47-3, 47-5	Withers, Lucy (Swope)	29-2, 31-1
Weinhold, William	47-3, 47-5	Withers, Maggie (Steif)	31-1, 31-2
Weist, Christian	R&N-8-24, R&N-9-11, R&N-9-17, R&N-10-15	Withers, Sue V.	29-2
		Withers, Susan	R&N-29-1
		Witmer, Mary (Gingrich)	40-1
		Witmer, Nevin Lynn	40-1
Weist, Dr.	R&N-3-3	Witmer, Samuel B.	40-1
Weit, John	4-5	Wivell, Anna M. (Gehman)	27-5
Weit, Rachel (Mosser)	4-5	Wivell, Claude J.	27-6
Welder, Benjamin G.	R&N-8-22, R&N-14-18	Wivell, Elsie (Althouse)	27-6
		Wivell, Joseph B.	27-6
Weller, Alice M.	R&N-12-3	Wolf, Christian	39-6
Wendel, Rachel M.	12-18	Wolf, E. B.	16
Wenger, Gladys (Burkholder)	32-4	Wolf, Emma	39-7
Wenger, Israel	16	Wolf, Emma B.	39-6
Wenger, John E.	32-5	Wolf, Mary J.	R&N-45-4
Wenger, Minerva B. (Eberly)	32-5	Wolf, Susanna (Mellinger)	39-6
Wenger, Monroe	32-5	Wolfart, George	R&N-5-10
Wenrich, Magdalena	6-17	Wolfskill, ---	R&N-3-3
Wenrich, Sophia	37-3	Wolfskill, Henry	5-23
Wenrich, Susan	20-12	Wolfskill, Lydia (Showalter)	5-23
Wershing, Ethel (Hortens)	45-2	Wolfskill, Mary (Killian)	5-23
Wetzel, D. J.	18	Wolfskill, Samuel S.	R&N-5-23
White, Eliza Ann (Fasnacht)	4-5, 4-6, 4-7, 4-8, 4-9, 30-2, 31-4	Wood, Evelyn D.	44-4
		Wood, Kelso	44-4
		Wood, Lena (Murray)	44-4
White, Harry	4-9	Workman, Elizabeth	24-6
White, John	4-5	Yoder, Anna C.	19-2
White, Lizzie	30-1, 30-2	Yoder, Esther A.	22-2
White, Lizzie A.	30-3, R&N-4-5, R&N-30-1	Yoder, Ezra	19-2, 19-3, 19-4, 19-5
White, Mary N.	4-8	Yoder, John B.	22-2
White, Peter M.	4-5, 4-6, 4-7, 4-8, 4-9, 30-2, 31-4	Yoder, Lena (Hoffman)	22-2
		Yoder, Naomi	19-4
		Yoder, Ruth E.	19-5
White, Rachel (Mosser)	4-5	Yoder, Salina E.	19-3
White, Susan F.	31-4		
White, Uriah	4-7		

www.ingramcontent.com/pod-product-compliance
Lightning Source LLC
Chambersburg PA
CBHW080412290526
45791CB00008BA/2246